LEARNING RESOURCES CTR/NEW ENGLAND TECH.
GEN           PS3554.I32 Z75 1988
Kirschten, R      James Dickey and the gentl

3 0147 0001 2668 3

PS3554 .

Kirschte

W9-DAE-385

James Dickey and the gentle
ecstacy of earth

## DATE DUE

| | | | |
|---|---|---|---|
| | | | |
| | | | |
| | | | |
| | | | |
| | | | |
| | | | |
| | | | |
| | | | |
| | | | |
| | | | |
| | | | |
| | | | |
| | | | |
| | | | |
| | | | |
| | | | |
| | | | |

DEMCO 38-297

Southern Literary Studies

LOUIS D. RUBIN, JR., EDITOR

**JAMES DICKEY and
the Gentle Ecstasy of Earth**

# JAMES DICKEY
# and the Gentle Ecstasy
# of Earth

## *A Reading of the Poems*

Robert Kirschten

Louisiana State University Press
Baton Rouge and London

Copyright © 1988 by Louisiana State University Press
All rights reserved
Manufactured in the United States of America

Designer: Albert Crochet
Typeface: Trump Mediaeval
Typesetter: G & S Typesetters, Inc.
Printer: Thomson-Shore, Inc.
Binder: John H. Dekker & Sons, Inc.

The following poems are reprinted by permission of Wesleyan University Press: "Listening to Foxhounds," "In the Tree House at Night" copyright © 1960, 1961 by James Dickey, reprinted from *Drowning with Others;* "The Dusk of Horses," "The Poisoned Man" copyright © 1962 by James Dickey, reprinted from *Helmets;* "Buckdancer's Choice," "Fox Blood" copyright © 1964, 1965 by James Dickey, reprinted from *Buckdancer's Choice;* "The Bee," "Mary Sheffield," "Falling" copyright © 1964, 1966, 1967 by James Dickey, reprinted from *Falling;* "The Vegetable King" copyright © 1960 by James Dickey, reprinted from *Poems 1957–1967;* "Root-light, or the Lawyer's Daughter," "The Rain Guitar," "False Youth: Autumn: Clothes of the Age," "Remnant Water," "Exchanges," "Pine" (section II), "Madness," "The Eye-Beaters" copyright © 1969, 1972, 1971, 1973, 1979, 1968, respectively, by James Dickey, reprinted from *The Central Motion;* lines from other James Dickey poems are reprinted from *Poems 1957–1967.* "Listening to Foxhounds," "In the Tree House at Night," "The Dusk of Horses," "The Poisoned Man," "Buckdancer's Choice," "Falling," "Root-light, or the Lawyer's Daughter," "The Rain Guitar," "Pine," and "Madness" first appeared in *The New Yorker.* "False Youth: Autumn: Clothes of the Age" first appeared in *The Atlantic.* "The Eye-Beaters" first appeared in *Harper's.*
Excerpts from "The Lode" by James Dickey copyright © 1981 by Kenyon Review, first appeared in *Kenyon Review;* from *Puella* by James Dickey, reprinted by permission of Doubleday & Company, Inc. "Root Cellar" copyright 1943 by Modern Poetry Association, Inc. and "Meditations of an Old Woman" copyright © 1955 by Theodore Roethke, "The Longing" copyright © 1962 by Beatrice Roethke as Administratrix of the Estate of Theodore Roethke; all poems by Theodore Roethke from *The Collected Poems of Theodore Roethke,* reprinted by permission of Doubleday & Company, Inc. Excerpts from *Self Interviews* by James Dickey, copyright © 1970 by James Dickey, reprinted by permission of Doubleday & Company, Inc. Excerpt from "The Strength of James Dickey" by Dave Smith in *Poetry* CXXXVII (March, 1981) copyright © 1981 by The Modern Poetry Association, reprinted by permission of the editor of *Poetry.*

10  9  8  7  6  5  4  3  2  1

LIBRARY OF CONGRESS CATALOGING-IN-PUBLICATION DATA
Kirschten, Robert, 1947–
    James Dickey and the gentle ecstasy of earth.

    (Southern literary studies)
    Includes index.
    1. Dickey, James—Criticism and interpretation.
I. Title. II. Series.
PS3554.I32Z75   1987        811'.54        87-3440
ISBN 0-8071-1405-7

*For my mother*

# Contents

# Abbreviations

| | |
|---|---|
| BB | *Babel to Byzantium* (New York, 1971) |
| P | *Poems 1957–1967* (Middletown, Conn., 1967) |
| PU | *Puella* (New York, 1982) |
| SI | *Self-Interviews* (New York, 1970) |
| S | *Sorties* (New York, 1971) |
| TCM | *The Central Motion* (Middletown, Conn., 1983) |
| TEM | *The Early Motion* (Middletown, Conn., 1981) |

**JAMES DICKEY and
the Gentle Ecstasy of Earth**

# Preface

Part of the title of this book is taken from a long, narrative lyric entitled "Lodovico Martelli" by the minor nineteenth-century American poet Joseph Trumbull Stickney. Stickney's Browningesque narrator is Martelli himself, a dying Renaissance poet, far from home, who recounts a tragic love affair involving a duel. At poem's end, he asks that he be remembered with these words:

> "Within the color-cupped anemonies
> Lieth his heart, and all the leaves are he,
> The gentle ecstasy of earth, the wind
> That lifts so happily thy hair is he,
> And he the Spring that holds thee all about."[1]

Evoking both the tranquillity and exhilaration of Dickey's own poetry, "The gentle ecstasy of earth" is a line in Dickey's long lyric "Exchanges" cast in the form of a "dead-living dialogue" with Stickney. Lines, phrases, and images from Stickney's verse alternate with Dickey's recollection of time spent in Los Angeles with a lover who has since died. Dickey recalls looking out over an ocean cliff at the smog and oil slicks of southern California while playing for his living girl a gentle folk tune on his guitar. Stickney's lines are in italics:

> I playing from childhood also
> Like the Georgia mountains    the wind out of Malibu whipped her
> Long hair into "Wildwood Flower"    her blue eye   *—whose eye*
> *Was somewhat strangely more than blue*
> Closed
> *—and if we lived*
> *We were the cresting of a tide wherein*
> *An endless motion rose exemplified.*
> In

> *—The gentle ecstasy of earth*

1. Amberys R. Whittle (ed.), *The Poems of Trumbull Stickney* (New York, 1972), 31.

1

> And ruination, we lay on the threatened grass
> Of cliffs, she tangled in my strings, her dark hair tuned
> To me, the mountains humming back
> Into resolution, in the great low-crying key
> Of A.   *(TCM,* 124)

Although Dickey finds Stickney's graceful language attractive enough to integrate into his own poem, he alters Stickney's phrase by adding "And ruination" to *"The gentle ecstasy of earth."* This syntactic reversal of a delicate correlative is one of Dickey's favorite tricks of lineation and reveals his habit of mixing opposite emotions in a vision that is as ecstatic in its gentleness as it is striking in its preoccupation with violence and ruination. Dickey seems fully aware of the oxymoronic feelings in his work when, in his book of practical criticism *Babel to Byzantium,* he says: "What I have always striven for is to find some way to incarnate my best moments—those which in memory are most persistent and obsessive. I find that most of these moments have an element of danger, an element of repose, and an element of joy" (*BB,* 292). Not only does this poet wish "to incarnate" his experiences of danger, repose, and joy in his poems, he wants to combine these feelings in one "strongly mixed" and "overwhelming" emotion: "I would be most pleased if readers came away from my poems not at all sure as to where the danger and the repose separate, where joy ends and longing begins. Strongly mixed emotions are what I usually have and what I usually remember from events of my life. Strongly mixed, but giving the impression of being one emotion, impure and overwhelming—that is the condition I am seeking to impose on my readers, whoever they may be" (*BB,* 292).

Like many of Dickey's lyrics, his method in "Exchanges" is that of alternating moments of the danger of human and ecological ruination, the joy of recollected love for his girl, and the repose or balancing of these emotional opposites through the music of poetic utterance. Even amid the "rubber smoke / and exhaust" of Los Angeles, Dickey's poetic song, like his guitar, can joyously "tune" his girl's "dark hair" to him while the surrounding mountains are romantically "humming back / into resolution" (or repose), so that it is difficult to tell "where joy ends and longing begins":

> —*So here did mix the land's breath and the sea's:*
> Among the beautiful murders

> Showering down ballad
> After ballad on the rainbows of forever lost
> Petroleum that blew its caps and turned on
> All living things, we sang and prayed for purity, scattered everywhere
> Among the stones
> Of other worlds.   *(TCM, 124)*

Although Dickey's word selection in the preceding passage is romantic, his vision is fully realistic. He knows that his song of exchange cannot recover the dead. Yet, for all its failure, his attempt is heroic, vulnerable, and wonderfully human in the poem's conclusion, which he ends with another line of Stickney's:

> Nothing for me
> Was solved.   I wandered the beach
> Mumbling to a dead poet
> In the key of A, looking for the rainbow
> Of oil, and the doomed
> Among the fish.
>                               —*Let us speak softly of living.* (*TCM*, 128)

From this brief look at "Exchanges," we see that a central critical problem is to explain how Dickey's disparate feelings are "strongly mixed" in a poetic method that simultaneously allows the poet to convey a "gentle ecstasy" in the presence of natural things and yet also reflects the psychological realities of personal anxiety and loss.

Indeed, his subject matter is as mixed as his emotional effects. Dickey is equally at home writing with great sensitivity about his mother dying of angina in "Buckdancer's Choice" as he is dramatizing the compulsive voyeurism of a sex maniac in "The Fiend." He writes of the real suicide of a grammar school classmate in "The Leap" and then turns to an exuberant, joyous fantasy of a man becoming a graceful sea bird in midair in "Reincarnation II." With equal facility, he depicts the bizarre sight of a folksinger nailed Christlike to a boxcar in "A Folksinger of the Thirties" and constructs ritual poems of protection for his family in "The Vegetable King" and "To His Children in Darkness."

To describe Dickey's methods of organization in these obsessive mixtures is challenging. He has been called a "mystic, a vitalist, a pantheist, and anti-rationalist," an "American Romantic," a comic poet, and more. Each of these categories seems partially true. Like a mystic or pantheist, Dickey can "move at the heart of the world," in "In the Tree House at Night" (*P*, 67). Like the English romantics, his speakers gain redemptive vision through empathic communion with animals and nature, as in "The Owl King," in which a blind child describes his fantastic encounter with the feathered king of the wood:

> The owl's face runs with tears
> As I take him in my arms . . .
>              I go down
> In my weight lightly down
> The tree, and now
> Through the soul of the wood
> I walk in consuming glory
> Past the snake, the fox, and the mouse:
> I see as the owl king sees,
> By going in deeper than darkness.
> The wood comes back in a light . . .
> And I can tell
> By its breathing glow
> Each tree on which I laid
> My hands when I was blind.    (*P*, 76–77)

And, as Robert W. Hill points out, there is a darkly ironic, comic vein in Dickey's poetry.[2] For instance in "Falling," an airline stewardess plunging to her death from a plane is given this impossible, bizarre option, expressed in the imagery of a television commercial:

> . . . there is water   there is time to perfect all the fine
> Points of diving    feet together   toes pointed   hands shaped right
> To insert her into water like a needle   to come out healthily dripping
> And be handed a Coca-Cola.  (*P*, 295)

When we look more closely, however, these descriptions of Dickey's poetic methods appear incomplete. Often, the critics omit one of the crucial elements in his emotional mixtures. Hypotheses about Dickey's mysticism cannot explain the attractive power of danger in his work. Hypotheses about his romanticism cannot explain the peculiar primitive energy he gains from empathic entrance into nature. Neither the mystical, romantic, nor comic hypotheses separately can

2. Robert Hill, "James Dickey: Comic Poet," in Richard J. Calhoun (ed.), *James Dickey: The Expansive Imagination* (Deland, Fla., 1973), 147–48.

explain his distinctive balance of gentleness and savagery, his dazzling mixtures of realism and fantasy, or his fusions of common domestic experience with his pervasive sense of the sacred.

To see the limitations of much commentary on Dickey, we may turn briefly to Lawrence Lieberman's review of *Falling*, Dickey's fifth volume of verse. Lieberman sees the poet's primary intention as a mystical attempt to reconnect the two realms the critic calls "inner and outer" worlds, the "inner" being that of a "joyous expansive personality," the "outer" a "universe" that has chosen the poet "to act out a secret destiny." In this view, Dickey's "chief problem" is: "How does a man re-connect with common unchosen humanity when he has just returned from the abyss of nonhuman otherness?" When Dickey succeeds, he makes a poem that becomes "a medium, a perfect conductor" between the world and himself so that he may justifiably be called a "worldly mystic," while the central end of his oxymoronic reconnection is the infusion of all worlds with "personal intimacy" and "intensity."[3]

Although accurate on local details and on the right thematic track, this critical enterprise seems in principle based on a dualism so generally formulated that it could fit, to some degree, almost any poem by anyone. One does not doubt for a moment that there are wonderfully empathic moments occurring between Dickey's speaker and the things he beholds. Why these relations should be mystical is unclear, and why reconnection (presupposing antecedent states of connection with subsequent alienation not found in the poems Lieberman cites) between these two realms should distinguish this kind of mysticism is equally unclear.

There are few signs in Dickey's optimistic world of a natural or psychological "abyss" that necessitates compensatory satisfaction. In fact, Dickey often courts danger. Further, what does this hypothesis tell us about Dickey's poems in which the lyric action has an entirely different direction, such as the poet's very unmystical and unchosen sense of stunned helplessness when he reads of his classmate's suicide in "The Leap" or when he recalls his mother's breathless angina? Finally, the inner life of the spirit is not really a major issue for Dickey.

---

3. Lawrence Lieberman, "The Worldly Mystic," *ibid.*, 65–66.

From his very earliest poems, his agents have been so thoroughly involved in specific scenes with specific acts that their characters are
either totally situational with only a minimally developed "inner
life" or they manifest a given temperament underlying a particular perception or act rather than a fully moral or reflective nature. Dickey's
poetic action has continually been expansive, outward moving, with
little anxiety-inducing tension between the inner and outer. Consequently, one simply does not find in Dickey the pervasive compulsion
for this kind of reconnection, which may be a far more convincing description of Theodore Roethke's work, just as the "philosophy" that
Lieberman unjustifiably finds in "Power and Light" is more characteristic of Wallace Stevens. My argument is not with the selection of the
term *mysticism* but rather with its inadequacy in this and other criticism to account for the distinctive emotional and formal elements in
Dickey's poetry.

For a fuller understanding of Dickey, what is needed are hypotheses
that are accurate descriptions of Dickey's speaker and lyric universe
and that come as close as possible to the criteria Ronald Crane sets
out for "multiple working hypotheses." First, we need "a central principle of explanation that will enable us to see precisely the functional
relations between all the particular problems a writer has attempted
to solve and the form of his work as a whole." Second, we should aim
for "an explanation and judgment in terms adapted as closely as possible to the peculiar structure and power of the work before us."[4] Further, our hypotheses should be complex enough to account for as
many major poetic elements as possible, adequately coherent to reveal
principles of "internal unity," and economically expressed.

Because of the straightforward content and relatively simple linguistic surface of Dickey's lyrics, one wonders why formal analysis of
this poet's work has been so unsatisfactory. Part of the answer stems
from the terms used to undertake such analysis. When trying to describe and explain the value of Dickey's lyric methods—methods that
are some of the most powerful and innovative in American poetry—I
have often found myself, uncomfortably and ambiguously, using the

4. Ronald Crane, *The Languages of Criticism and the Structure of Poetry* (Toronto,
1953), 177–78.

same terms as the critics with whom I disagree. If his poems appear so simple on their surfaces and if they contain many things I usually don't care for—mysticism, violence, victimage—what moved me about Dickey's work and why were these poems so difficult to talk about?

The answer now seems embarrassingly simple: I lacked an adequate vocabulary for describing Dickey's central methods. Although the emotional effects of his work were very much present when I read him, I had missed a good many of his structural strategies and thus the rationale behind his techniques of representation. Even more important, I lacked a full understanding of many of the human values that are integral to the events he dramatizes. My problem was nothing less than the ancient one of invention—invention of a set of critical terms that permitted me to describe and account for the formal patterns I wished to make explicit. Even after scouring the literatures of mysticism, Romanticism, and the diverse schools of contemporary criticism, I still found myself at a loss to account for many of Dickey's principles, especially those through which gentleness and victimage were strongly mixed. To be sure, I found several helpful hypotheses but after a long search discovered that some of the most fruitful terms were to be found in anthropology. Thus in addition to labeling Dickey a "mystic, a vitalist, a pantheist, an anti-rationalist," I soon felt more at home using anthropological commonplaces such as the terms *magic, rites of passage,* and *ritual violence.*[5]

These three anthropological terms in no small way determine the structure of my present inquiry. I group them under the general head-

5. Long after completing this book, I came across an essay by Joyce Carol Oates entitled "Out of Stone, into Flesh: The Imagination of James Dickey," included in a recent collection of articles on Dickey. First published in 1974, Oates's essay mentions William James and Mircea Eliade as two writers whose work offers excellent entrance to understanding major thematic patterns in Dickey's poetry. Oates even uses the term *Monsters,* which, like the ideas of James and Eliade, I too have found extremely useful. Had my own scholarship been more thorough with regard to the critical literature on Dickey, Oates's seminal article would have started me in the right direction years sooner. Also especially useful for inventing terminological clues to solve the Dickey puzzle are N. Michael Niflis' comments on Dickey's romantic view of animals in "A Special Kind of Fantasy: James Dickey on the Razor's Edge" and Linda Mizejewski's criticism of "The Zodiac" in "Shamanism Toward Confessionalism: James Dickey, Poet." The above articles can be found in Bruce Weigel and T. R. Hummer (eds.), *The Imagination as Glory: The Poetry of James Dickey* (Urbana, Ill., 1984), 64–107, 56–63, 132–42.

ing of "primitivism" and place them last in a series of four terms—
Crane's "multiple working hypotheses"—that I use to explore, describe, analyze, and evaluate Dickey's lyric vision. My first three
terms—*mysticism, neoplatonism,* and *Romanticism*—serve primarily to align general traits in Dickey's poetry with esteemed literary
traditions. I then use *primitivism* as my differentiating term to show
what Dickey has added to these traditions. My goal is to clarify what
it means to call Dickey an American romantic primitive. By using all
four hypotheses in conjunction, I can best show why Dickey is a valuable poet while simultaneously satisfying Crane's requirements for
systematic formal criticism.

After inquiring into Dickey's general principles, I test the validity of
my terms by showing how they make explicit the aesthetic reasons
for the poet's lyric speakers, his central narrative devices, and his poetic diction. In the last chapter, I further test my principles by using
them to explain the formal structure in "The Shark's Parlor," one of
Dickey's best comic poems of redemption through victimage and ordeal. I hope to prove the value of my hypotheses in terms of compre-
hensiveness (explanation of the greatest number of major habits and
elements of construction) and particularity (accuracy of explanation
of particular poems).

As I suggested earlier, my intent is not to abandon terms used to
discuss Dickey but to refine them in application and to use them as
grounds for establishing both formal and human values in Dickey's
poetry. For instance, I read "Exchanges"—the title of this lyric is
surely a key to all of this poet's work—as an incantatory ritual designed to harmonize through music a number of disparate items, ranging from ecological and urban decay to the death of a lover and the
lines of a dead poet, by means of a series of empathic emotional exchanges whose animistic energy compensates for the poet's personal
loss. This reading accounts for mystical, musical, and romantic impulses in the poem in addition to the emotional texture of a world in
which "*all the air*" is both "*marvelous and sorrowful.*" The action in
"Exchanges" is not one solely of speculation or meditation. In many
ways, it is not even mental, for Dickey's forms are those of ritual and
participation, those of a poet for whom doing and thinking are inseparable, those in which the shaman-poet howls "note by note" to re-

cover the dead through the magical, trancelike "tangled dream of Los Angeles / And death and the moon."

Instead of poetic theory, raging social issues, or morbid, confessional introspection, Dickey's interests are stated in *Self-Interviews:* "The relationship of the human being to the great natural cycles of birth and death, the seasons, the growing up of plants and the dying of the leaves, the springing up of other plants out of the dead leaves, the generations of animals and of men, all on the heraldic wheel of existence" (*SI*, 68). This is a disturbing and dazzling world, emotionally charged with victimage and renewal, an unflagging faith in poetry and the expressive possibilities of language, and most of all, experiential intensity. For the reader willing to participate—one of Dickey's favorite words—in this graceful and compelling realm where "gentle ecstasy" and "ruination" are strongly mixed, even obsessive, the rewards are considerable. We will encounter in Dickey a poet deeply involved with new realities such as world war, suburban life, and technological annihilation, but nonetheless one with whom we may exuberantly chant like Whitman in "One's-Self I Sing":

> Of Life immense in passion, pulse, and power,
> Cheerful, for freest action form's under laws
> divine, The Modern Man I sing.[6]

Yet Dickey is simultaneously a poet of very old realities, a writer whose feelings for nature, survival, and the sacred are so strong that he constantly desires to draw us "back even farther than the poetry of the tribe and reach all the way back to the very root-beginnings, back to the state of mind of the first man himself, who stood on the shore and opened his arms to the world, that he and the world might possess each other" (*S*, 206).

6. Walt Whitman, *Leaves of Grass*, ed. Sculley Bradley and Harold W. Blodgett (New York, 1973), 1.

# I / Dickey's Lyric Universe:
# Four Hypotheses

## 1. MYSTICISM, or motion:

> . . . that blessed mood,
> In which the burthen of the mystery,
> In which the heavy and the weary weight
> Of all this unintelligible world,
> Is lightened:—that serene and blessed mood,
> In which the affections gently lead us on,—
> Until the breath of this corporeal frame
> And even the motion of our human blood
> Almost suspended, we are laid asleep
> In body, and become a living soul:
> While with an eye made quiet by the power
> Of harmony, and the deep power of joy,
> We see into the life of things.
>
> —WORDSWORTH

> The state called reverie, [when men] feel as if their nature were
> dissolved into the surrounding universe, or as if the surrounding
> universe were absorbed into their being. They are conscious of
> no distinction.
>
> —SHELLEY

> Most of us can remember the strangely moving power of passages
> in certain poems read when we were young, irrational doorways
> as they were through which the mystery of fact, the wildness and
> the pang of life, stole into our hearts and thrilled them. . . . Lyric
> poetry and music are alive and significant only in proportion as
> they fetch these vague vistas of a life continuous with our own.
> . . . We are alive or dead to the eternal inner message of the arts
> according as we have kept or lost this mystical susceptibility.
>
> —WILLIAM JAMES

In "The Marriage of Heaven and Hell," William Blake dines with the
prophets Isaiah and Ezekiel and asks them, "How they dared so roundly
to assert that God spoke to them." Isaiah replies, "I saw no God, nor
heard any, in a finite organical perception; but my senses discover'd
the infinite in everything." Only then was he "perswaded" to write.
When Blake counters by asking if "a firm perswasion that a thing is

so, make it so?" Isaiah replies that "all poets believe that it does, & in ages of imagination this firm perswasion removed mountains."[1] If James Dickey were at that particular dinner, he and Isaiah would have agreed immediately, for the mystical and visionary impulse to transcend "finite perception" is everywhere in Dickey's poetry.

As noted in the preface, mysticism is a popular hypothesis for describing Dickey's work. Unfortunately, as a principle in formal analysis, it easily slips into unserviceable ambiguity. This difficulty is caused by the problematic nature of the word itself and to an even greater extent by inadequate specification of its meaning when applied to the materials it presumes to illuminate. To use *mysticism* fruitfully in our examination of Dickey's poetry, we may best begin by following William James's method of inquiry which initiates his famous chapter "Mysticism" in *The Varieties of Religious Experience*. Because he finds *mysticism* so often used as a term of reproach for something "vague and vast and sentimental . . . without a base in either facts or logic," James employs several marks or qualities of mystical consciousness to demarcate his subject matter.[2] Let us borrow a number of these marks and use them both as hermeneutic devices and as constituent elements in definition to specify what it means to call James Dickey a poetic "mystic."

Two relevant traits of mystical experience are optimism and monism, about which James says: "We pass into mystical states from out of ordinary consciousness as from a less into a more, as from a smallness into a vastness, and at the same time as from an unrest to a rest. We feel them as reconciling, unifying states. They appeal to the yes-function more than to the no-function in us. In them the unlimited absorbs the limits and peacefully closes the account."[3] James's observation accurately describes the central action of "In the Tree House at Night," Dickey's gentle lyric of mystical union with his dead brother:

> And now the green household is dark.
> The half-moon completely is shining
> On the earth-lighted tops of the trees.

1. Geoffrey Keynes (ed.), *The Complete Writings of William Blake* (Oxford, 1972), 153.
2. William James, *The Varieties of Religious Experience* (1903; rpr. London, 1969), 299.
3. *Ibid.*, 326.

To be dead, a house must be still.
The floor and the walls wave me slowly;
I am deep in them over my head.
The needles and pine cones about me

Are full of small birds at their roundest,
Their fists without mercy gripping
Hard down through the tree to the roots
To sing back at light when they feel it.
We lie here like angels in bodies,
My brothers and I, one dead,
The other asleep from much living,

In mid-air huddled beside me.
Dark climbed to us here as we climbed
Up the nails I have hammered all day
Through the sprained, comic rungs of the ladder
Of broom handles, crate slats, and laths
Foot by foot up the trunk to the branches
Where we came out at last over lakes

Of leaves, of fields disencumbered of earth
That move with the moves of the spirit.
Each nail that sustains us I set here;
Each nail in the house is now steadied
By my dead brother's huge, freckled hand.
Through the years, he has pointed his hammer
Up into these limbs, and told us

That we must ascend, and all lie here.
Step after step he has brought me,
Embracing the trunk as his body,
Shaking its limbs with my heartbeat,
Till the pine cones danced without wind
And fell from the branches like apples.
In the arm-slender forks of our dwelling

I breathe my live brother's light hair.
The blanket around us becomes
As solid as stone, and it sways.
With all my heart, I close
The blue, timeless eye of my mind.
Wind springs, as my dead brother smiles
And touches the tree at the root;

A shudder of joy runs up
The trunk; the needles tingle;

> One bird uncontrollably cries.
> The wind changes round, and I stir
> Within another's life. Whose life?
> Who is dead? Whose presence is living?
> When may I fall strangely to earth,
>
> Who am nailed to this branch by a spirit?
> Can two bodies make up a third?
> To sing, must I feel the world's light?
> My green, graceful bones fill the air
> With sleeping birds. Alone, alone
> And with them I move gently.
> I move at the heart of the world.   (P, 66–67)

As the poet climbs into his tree house, he sees not only the moonlit tops of trees but "lakes of leaves" and "fields disencumbered of earth / that move with the moves of the spirit." To "the moves of the spirit" is soon added another kind of spiritual movement, namely the spirit of the dead brother who ascends "step by step" with his two siblings. As the dead brother embraces the tree trunk, he shakes its limbs empathically in time with the poet's heartbeat. And when the dead brother smiles, the wind "springs" and "touches the tree at the root" sending another kind of movement—"a shudder of joy"—up the trunk to the speaker, who stirs "Within another's life." At this point, commonplace earthly distinctions between living and dead and between man and animals are no longer felt. In the final stanza, the poet has become treelike as his "green, graceful bones fill the air / With sleeping birds," and he gently moves at nothing less than "the heart of the world." Expansive unifying movement is so pervasive in this poem that paradoxes are easily overcome: the speaker is simultaneously "alone," yet is "with" the birds; he seems to be in a dreamlike state, yet is fully conscious; he is motionless ("nailed" to a branch), yet is an active participant in the joyous monism which underlies, animates, and alters natural appearance (P, 66–67).

Because Dickey offers no philosophic evidence for an unlimited One to which he delicately binds his Many particulars, we may ask with good reason how his vast unity is effected. One answer is that we infer his mystical principle from his extensive metaphors of motion. His "fields" are "disencumbered of earth" because nothing is really nailed down in this poem. The entire lyric is in its structure nothing less than a systematic reversal of its fourth line, "To be dead, a house must be still." In Dickey's tree house nothing is still; therefore nothing is dead. All is in motion, with or without natural cause: "The floor and the walls wave me slowly"; "The pine cones danced without wind"; and "the needles tingle." If the dead brother's spirit is not only evoked but is also a motive force in this confluence of movement, then he too lives and becomes part of the progressive conversion of objects and agents into pure motion (or spirit). Living and dead meet harmoniously in this world because things are matter and spirit simultaneously. Ordinary opposites in this tree house no longer exclude one another: "The blanket around us becomes / As solid as stone and it sways."

Known primarily by its effects, the expansive flux of fantastic reconciliation is so extensive that there is no need for the poet to respond to the series of rhetorical questions posed in the last two stanzas:

> . . . I stir
> Within another's life. Whose life?
> Who is dead? Whose presence is living?
> When may I fall strangely to earth
>
> Who am nailed to this branch by a spirit?
> Can two bodies make up a third?   (*P*, 66–67)

Dickey's answers are implicit. Two bodies *can* make a third *if* this is a universe so full of the interchange of forces that tree limbs shake with the poet's heartbeat, *if* the poet's bones fill the air with birds, and *if* the poet can both move and be still in a tree house which is not a mere place but an event filled with magical communion.

Among American poets, Dickey is not alone in his exuberant monism. In "On the Beach at Night Alone," Walt Whitman makes his own monistic principle explicit:

> A vast similitude interlocks all,
> All spheres, grown, ungrown, small, large, suns, moons, planets,
>   comets, asteroids,
> All the substances of the same, and all that is spiritual upon
>   the same,
> All distances of place, however wide,
> All distances of time—all inanimate forms,
> All Souls—all living bodies, though they be ever so different,
>   or in different worlds,

> All gaseous, watery, vegetable, mineral processes—the fishes,
>    the brutes,
> All men and women—me also . . .
> This vast similitude spans them, and always has spann'd and shall
>    forever span them, and compactly hold them, and enclose them.

In *Democratic Vistas,* Whitman proclaims a pantheism that strongly resembles Dickey's ontology in the assumption of a comprehensive internal principle of pulsation running through all things:

> Lo! Nature (the only complete, actual poem), existing calmly in
> the divine scheme, containing all. . . . lo! the pulsations in all
> matter, all spirit, throbbing forever—the eternal beats, eternal
> systole and diastole of life in things—wherefrom I feel and know
> that death is not the ending, as was thought, but rather the real
> beginning—and that nothing ever is or can be lost, nor ever die, nor
> soul, nor matter.[4]

Unlike Whitman, Dickey tends to exhibit in more specific instances the extent to which his own "vast similitude" encloses his subjects. That is, instead of all spheres, Dickey narrows the effects of his monism to particular or personal occasions that he dramatizes the way a novelist describes a specific incident. Rather than encompassing all lives and deaths, Dickey ascends to his tree house where objects seem less realistic, less concrete than Whitman's, and more like dynamic centers of change than static substances. Dickey's is a world where matter always seems ready to dissolve into motion, thereby effecting to an extent even greater than Whitman the mystical assimilation of subject and object. Richard Howard, one of Dickey's most discerning and sympathetic readers, is one of the first critics to note these principles in his poetry. About Dickey's first book, *Into the Stone,* Howard observes: "Here nothing develops, grows or changes from its essence, yet everything can be transformed into anything else, the metal sun and stone moon, the winged tree and walking water woven into a net of correspondences thrown over life like a tarn-helm. And the energy that knots these elements together, that thrusts them against each other in harmony or thematic apposition, is a circular movement, a conjugation of rituals . . . there is no end to action,

---

4. Walt Whitman, *Leaves of Grass,* ed. Sculley Bradley and Harold W. Blodgett (New York, 1973), 261; Mark van Doren (ed.), *Walt Whitman* (New York, 1945), 462.

one is always in the process of it." Dickey's pervasive principle of perpetual movement is thus his own way of reintroducing to poetry the great Wordsworthian method whereby "the heavy and weary weight / of all this unintelligible world, / Is lightened" that brings us to a "blessed mood" in which we may truly discover that "The external World is fitted to the Mind."[5]

Dickey's synecdochic transcendentalism is like that of Emerson in "The Poet," where we find "that there is no fact in nature which does not carry the whole sense of nature." In many ways, Dickey's assimilative principle resembles Emerson's Oversoul, which is not part of nature and yet emerges through the objects of nature with effects that bear striking similarity to those of Dickey's Absolute Motion. Even Emerson's setting resembles Dickey's:

> Last night the moon rose behind four distinct pine-tree tops in the distant woods and the night at ten was so bright that I walked abroad. But the sublime light of night is unsatisfying, provoking; it astonishes but explains not. Its charm floats, dances, disappears, comes and goes, but palls in five minutes after you have left the house. Come out of your warm, angular house, resounding with few voices, into the chill, grand, instantaneous night, with such a Presence as a full moon in the clouds, and you are struck with poetic wonder. In the instant you leave far behind all human relations, wife, mother and child, and live only with savages—water, air, light, carbon, lime, and granite. . . . I become a moist, cold element. "Nature grows over me." Frogs pipe; waters far off tinkle; dry leaves hiss; grass bends and rustles, and I have died out of the human world and come to feel a strange, cold, aqueous, terraqueous, aerial, ethereal sympathy and existence. I sow the sun and moon for seeds.[6]

Dickey's implicit unstated principle of expansive unification points to two other traits associated with mystical consciousness that are also basic poetic elements in his vision. The first is an absence of a specific intellectual content or theology. The second is the feeling that a special knowledge or illumination has been achieved. On both topics, again we return to William James: "The mystical feeling of en-

    5. Richard Howard, *Alone With America* (New York, 1969), 76–77; "Tintern Abbey," in *The Poetical Works of Wordsworth*, ed. Paul D. Sheats (Rev. ed.; Boston, 1982), 92.
    6. Ralph Waldo Emerson, "The Poet," in *Essays by Ralph Waldo Emerson* (Boston, 1979), 17; Emerson, cited by Harold Bloom in "The New Transcendentalism," *Chicago Review*, XXIV (1975).

largement, union, and emancipation has no specific intellectual content of its own. It is capable of forming matrimonial alliances with material furnished by the most diverse philosophies and theologies, provided only they can find a place in their framework for its peculiar emotional mood." He continues: "Although so similar to states of feeling, mystical states seem to those who experience them to be also states of knowledge. They are states of insight into depths of truth unplumbed by the discursive intellect. They are illuminations, revelations, full of significance and importance, all inarticulate though they remain; and as a rule they carry with them a curious sense of authority for aftertime."[7]

Although not intellectual, Dickey's mysticism is a sophisticated poetic method that often gives penetrating bursts of serious observation, observation which, because of the poet's methods of enlargement, carries with it a distinctive feeling of authority. In "The Movement of Fish," the concluding perception comes with such speed and surprise that it feels like a revelation that no discursive inquiry could uncover as gracefully or powerfully:

> . . . suddenly his frame shakes,
>
> Convulses the whole ocean
> Under the trivial, quivering
> Surface, and he is
> Hundreds of feet away,
> Still picking up speed, still shooting
>
> Through half-gold,
> Going nowhere. Nothing sees him.
> One must think of this to understand
> The instinct of fear and trembling,
> And, of its one movement, the depth.   (P, 57–58)

Although realistic in setting and circumstance, this poem is mystical in its noetic method of penetrating depths of natural appearance to which the human speaker does not have normal access. Dickey begins with the rower's "mistaken," ineffective attempt to affect fish below the water's surface, then imagines, in spite of the intrusive human voice, that the fish sinks downward, almost below the reach of sun-

---

7. James, *The Varieties of Religious Experience,* 333, 300.

light, to a mysterious realm only half-intelligible where "gold" is "mixed / With absolute blackness" (*P*, 57). In the poet's mind, the fish suddenly darts away, and this initial movement convulses the whole ocean. Just as the ocean is shaken, the poet is quickly shaken from his narrative of "superficial agitation" into awareness of a truth that encompasses the worlds of man and animal: the instinct of fear and trembling. Mystical in its monistic assumption of movement as the principle of exchange between man and nature, this poem arrives at its conclusion through a correspondence of the movement of fish to the movement of the poet's thought. As the fish sinks slowly into a world of half-light and half-dark, and then darts off suddenly through "half-gold," so the poet glides easily on the surface of his perception until in the final three lines he darts noetically to deeper revelation, below which lies an ocean of even darker meaning. As Louis Martz says of Dickey, his "objects are only moving on the surface of some deeper reality."[8]

Unlike the ending of his tree house poem, Dickey's conclusion is less optimistic and abruptly severs his entrance into mindless nature with a startling reflexive awareness. As a man restricted in this watery world, he can follow the fish no further. Yet the poet returns to his human world with a serious perception unknown to animals. It is interesting that Dickey uses Kierkegaard's famous biblical phrase "fear and trembling" in his final lines. These words of course recall the title of the Danish thinker's famous lyrical inquiry into the passion and pain of human decision. Based on the story of Abraham and Isaac in the Old Testament, *Fear and Trembling* is an attempt to articulate the dreadful depths of tension between Abraham's love for Isaac and his own duty to God. While Dickey's conclusion is scarcely Kierkegaardian, both men clearly share a feeling for the inexpressible emotion that lies behind human fear, a fear that, for Abraham, is even more terrible because he cannot express it. Thus, behind Dickey's natural surfaces, we begin to *feel* truths that carry the significance, importance, and sense of authority James claims for mystical states.

Another aspect of Dickey's mystical method is a trancelike state, which predominates in "In the Tree House at Night" and is present to some extent in almost all of Dickey's poems. As methods of transport

8. Louis Martz, "Recent Poetry: The Elegiac Mode," *Yale Review*, II (1965), 289.

carrying a certain precariousness with them, trances have at least three marks that help us to understand Dickey: transiency, passivity, and ineffability. In a description that bears striking similarity to what occurs to Dickey's speakers, the mystic J. A. Symonds testifies to the obsessive and dangerous effects of trances in his own experience:

> The mood . . . took possession of my mind and will, lasted what seemed an eternity, and disappeared in a series of rapid sensations which resembled the awakening from anaesthetic influence. . . . I could not describe it to myself . . . It consisted in a gradual but swiftly progressive obliteration of space, time, sensation, and the multitudinous factors of experience which seem to qualify what we are pleased to call our Self.
>
> This trance . . . served to impress upon my growing nature the phantasmal unreality of all the circumstances which contribute to a merely phenomenal consciousness . . . are men the factors of some dream, the dream-like unsubstantiality of which they comprehend as such eventful moments? What would happen if the final stage of the trance were reached? [9]

In Symond's case, as James notes, the trance borders on the pathological because his dreamlike mood threatens to usurp the authority of waking consciousness. For Dickey, waking consciousness is usurped for higher ends. At times, his agents experience transient moments of ineffable experience in which they are passively absorbed into a phantasmal world of movement and change. Normal consciousness gives way to an "abstract" self that is one with the process of transport and through which these agents often undergo momentous personal transformation. In "Drinking From A Helmet," a young soldier climbs out of his foxhole, drinks water from the helmet of a dead soldier, and finds himself not on a bloody battleground in the Philippines in World War II but in a "vast military wedding," or in Symond's terms, in "a progressive obliteration of space, time, and sensation":

VI

I drank, with the timing of rust.
A vast military wedding
Somewhere advanced one step.

VII

All around, equipment drifting in light,
Men drinking like cattle and bushes,

9. J. A. Symonds quoted in James, *The Varieties of Religious Experience*, 303–304.

Cans, leather, canvas and rifles,
Grass pouring down from the sun
And up from the ground.
Grass: and the summer advances
Invisibly into the tropics.
Wind, and the summer shivers
Through many men standing or lying
In the GI gardener's hand
Spreading and turning green
All over the hill.

VIII

At the middle of water
Bright circles dawned inward and outward
Like oak rings surviving the tree
As its soul, or like
The concentric gold spirit of time.
I kept trembling forward through something
Just born of me.   (P, 174–75)

What is born of the living soldier is a "nearly dead power to pray,"
not to Heaven but to the spirits of the dead soldiers with whom he has
fought. As a result of this prayer, the young GI begins to grow emotionally. He feels the "difference between / Sweat and tears," magically inherits the last thought of the dead soldier, and vows to return
to California after the war to recount his experience of war and change
to the dead man's brother. The entire poem is nothing less than an
elaborate conversion of the living soldier into the spirit of the dead GI
whose place he takes and whose identity he assumes. Yet there is
more here, for the young soldier arrives at a greater awareness of both
war and peace, an awareness so dazzling and mysterious that he "could
have stepped up into air." As he trembles forward through his discovery, all seems joyous and ineffable. He could easily say, with another of
Dickey's speakers in "Approaching Prayer," that:

I don't know quite what has happened
Or that anything has,

Hoping only that
The irrelevancies one thinks of
When trying to pray
Are the prayer.   (P, 167)

Dramatized in glittering imagery, pervasive participles, and hypnotic, three-beat, anapestic lines, Dickey's war poem sets everything in motion around his speaker and reflects James's observation about similar mystical states: "The mystic feels as if his own will were in abeyance, and indeed sometimes as if he were grasped and held by a superior power."[10] For Dickey, this "superior power" is his poetic Absolute of Motion that lies behind appearance and mixes nature and human consciousness to such a degree that reality and fantasy, active and passive states, and self and other conjoin in a single mellifluous stream of poetic action. This effect is precisely what Dickey intends: "I worked most fruitfully in cases in which there was no clear-cut distinction between what was actually happening and what was happening in the mind of a character in the poem. I meant to try to get a fusion of inner and outer states, of dream, fantasy, and illusion where everything partakes of the protagonist's mental processes and creates a single impression" (*SI*, 287). This hypnotic fusion of mental states not only opens his speaker to communion with the universal but also allows the poet to flood his poem with a single sensation shared by man and nature alike. In "The Salt Marsh," the speaker enters a world of swaying "stalks of sawgrass" whose graceful movement assimilates grass and speaker to pure spirit:

> For when the embodying wind
> Rises, the grasses begin to weave
> A little, then all together,
> Not bending enough for you
> To see your way clear of the swaying,
> But moving just the same,
>
> And nothing prevents your bending
> With them, helping their wave
> Upon wave upon wave upon wave
> By not opposing,
> By willing your supple inclusion
> Among fields without promise of harvest,
> In their marvelous, spiritual walking
> Everywhere, anywhere. (*P*, 108)

At times, Dickey's mystical trances have realistic psychological ends, as we see in "The Lifeguard," where the hallucinatory method

10. James, *ibid.*, 300.

emotionally approximates the "delusion of grief and helplessness" of
a lifeguard who has failed to save a drowned child:

> . . . I am thinking of how I may be
> The savior of one
>
> Who has already died in my care.
> The dark trees fade from around me.
> The moon's dust hovers together.
> I call softly out, and the child's
> Voice answers through blinding water.
> Patiently, slowly . . .
>
> I wash the black mud from my hands.
> On a light given off by the grave
> I kneel in the quick of the moon
> At the heart of a distant forest
> And hold in my arms a child
> Of water, water, water.   (P, 51–52)

In many ways, the emotional effects of this lyric resemble those
from something by the Brothers Grimm. Behind the simple graceful
narrative lies a dark world of sinister forces that not only threaten
children but which strongly alter the enchanting nocturnal imagery
of the poem's surface. These subterranean forces of "immovable blackness" are minimally represented but nonetheless inject an unnerving
anxiety into the dreamy world of water swirling through the action.
This poem is really a fairy tale gone wrong. Present here in fluid form,
Dickey's principle of motion adds a frightening element to the poet's
optimistic mysticism. The child is dead; nature's selection is inexo-
rable and indifferent in its mindless darkness. Nonetheless, a kind of
redemption is present. The only way the poet can restore the child,
however, is to convert him into the very element that destroyed him.
Dickey's power of mystical assimilation has bridged once again the
distance between living and dead but this time with a conversion we
know to be a fiction, a fiction that, as part of the lifeguard's delirious
fantasy, makes even more poignant his failure to save the child.

We can now see that unlike many mystical monisms Dickey's version has its darker moments. Yet when he adds an element of danger—a lyric threat, if you will—to his pantheistic practices, he makes
some of his most interesting inventions in poetic method. His prin-

ciple of motion can be used to effect radical or violent change that involves emotional reversals, suspense, and the unexpected. Dickey's charming evocative surfaces thus give way to deeper and more complex transitions—at times, to more intense fear and trembling—while simultaneously participating in perpetual movement. As a result, the poet can strikingly convey the cyclic movement of life, death, and rebirth. Such a cycle animates "The Heaven of Animals":

> . . . those that are hunted
> Know this as their life,
> Their reward: to walk
>
> Under such trees in full knowledge
> Of what is in glory above them,
> And to feel no fear,
> But acceptance, compliance.
> Fulfilling themselves without pain
>
> At the cycle's center,
> They tremble, they walk
> Under the tree,
> They fall, they are torn,
> They rise, they walk again.   (P, 59–60)

Although it is the realm of hunter and hunted where "claws and teeth" have "grown perfect," Dickey's heaven contains no pain. Acts of victimage are assimilated in yet one more variation of his underlying principle. This heaven is a collocation of verbs and participles, propelling its subjects forward from stalking and crouching through a landscape of "instincts" that "wholly bloom" only in conjunction with the perfection of the perpetual cycle of which they are part. There is no gory detail here. The prey have "bright backs" as the hunters descend in "a sovereign floating of joy," and their victims feel no fear. Dickey's optimistic, yes-saying view is back in full swing. Yet the fact of violence, however joyous, charges this poem with a certain tension, a feeling of anxiety, an alertness to danger that stands in striking contrast to the purely benevolent mysticism we saw earlier in Dickey. Violence is not only an intrinsic part of the underlying movement in this poem, it is courted, affirmed, even rendered glamorous. Danger glows in this heaven and adds an active animating force not present in what we generally think of as mystical experience. This shift in Dickey's focus is a sign that we too are ready to shift our line of inquiry. However, the topic of danger better fits under our section on primitivism that falls later in this study. Before we leave mysticism, a few concluding observations are in order.

Dickey's mysticism is grounded in a monistic ontology in which an invisible, secular, implicit motion pervades all things. Known primarily by its effects, this force dominates man and nature in fantastic, even miraculous, ways. It is expansive, unifying, and in general, beneficent. It can transform matter into motion, death into life, and pain into joy. It can dissolve boundaries between subject and object, often by inducing a trancelike state in an agent who finds himself transported to a realm of hyperbolic probabilities to which he surrenders himself in an intoxicating yet gentle ecstasy of communion and exchange. In Dickey's mystical world, an event may be realistic, fantastic, or a peculiar mixture of both, although the emotional effects of his poems are fully accessible, usually involving a wonderful serenity that makes us feel hypnotized and yet more awake than ever.

For Dickey, mysticism is both a means and an end. In "In the Tree House at Night," his metaphors of assimilation carry us to a world of pure motion, whereas in "The Movement of Fish," his mystical movement serves as a method to produce an insight about instinct that is not mystical in character. Dickey's mystical impulse is only one of several important strategies open to him. Most of his exclusively mystical poems appear early in his career. "Walking on Water," "On the Hill Below the Lighthouse," "Inside the River," "The Common Grave," "The Being," and "Trees and Cattle," to name a few, all fit the pantheistic paradigm. To be sure, his assimilative principle is a major factor throughout all his work. But in his later poems, the assimilative process tends to be an instrument of exchange that is realistic or personal rather than cosmic. As we saw in "The Lifeguard," the central focus of Dickey's mystical movement is to render realistic the sensation of delirium and loss. As Dickey's subject matter grows more specific, his mysticism becomes only one of several strategies for mixing obsessive emotions. When a single person is his target of exchange or when violence is present, his poems often include sensations not usually associated with the gentle expansiveness of mystical reconciliation, and so we are forced to look elsewhere for operating principles.

Mysticism, as noted earlier, is a difficult subject. To some extent, Dickey's mystical methods must remain ineffable. As William James observed, ineffability is a negative quality of mystical consciousness that leads the mystic to claim that his experience defies expression, that it cannot be communicated, that it must be directly experienced. Dickey's experience of union with his monistic absolute demands participation, not understanding. Dickey does not intellectually prove his mysticism; he justifies its assumption through his poetic technique and through the value of the experiences he offers. Kenneth Burke says that "literary mysticism is a contradiction in terms" precisely because it must "express the ineffable." To resolve this problem, we must see that "not mere unity but unity of the individual with some *cosmic* or *universal purpose*" is mysticism's central mark.[11] Thus, we have been trying to make Dickey's mystical methods intelligible by postulating an implicit cosmic motion present in natural things that is ultimately mysterious.

The problem of describing mystical ineffability leads us back to the oxymoronic character of Dickey's vision noted in our introductory discussion of "Exchanges," especially with regard to the presence of music as a mediating force between man and the cosmos. James notes that "self-contradictory phrases" such as the "voice of silence" abound in mystical literature. He goes on to say that these phrases "prove that not conceptual speech, but music rather, is the element through which we are best spoken to by mystical truth." Further, "Music gives us ontological messages which non-musical criticism is unable to contradict."[12] As a vehicle of entrance to a larger vision or as a means of connection of some kind, music is everywhere in Dickey's poetry. It is an element for which we must account if we are to describe accurately the causal ontology in which this poet works. And while Dickey's music can often induce other-worldly trances, his music also works in a less mystical, more *this*-worldly way. In the following section, I will try to make clearer Dickey's sense of cosmic purpose—and our formal principles—by moving from the hypothesis of mysticism to that of Neoplatonism.

---

11. Kenneth Burke, *A Rhetoric of Motives* (New York, 1950), 324.
12. James, *The Varieties of Religious Experience*, 330.

## 2. NEOPLATONISM, or motion and music:

Harmony, which has motions akin to the revolutions of our
souls is not regarded by the intelligent votary of the Muses as
given by them with a view to irrational pleasure but as meant
to correct any discord which may have arisen in the courses of
the soul, and to be our ally in bringing her into harmony and
agreement with herself.
                              —PLATO

Nothing exists without music; for the universe itself is said
to have been framed by a kind of harmony of sounds, and the
heaven itself revolves under the tones of that harmony.
                              —ISIDORE OF SEVILLE

The mind of Man is fram'd even like the breath
And harmony of music. There is a dark
Invisible workmanship that reconciles
Discordant elements, and makes them move
In one society.
                              —WORDSWORTH

To label Neoplatonic a poet whose work by his own admission is "almost entirely physical rather than intellectual or mental" at first
seems preposterous. Yet Dickey's mystical method of mixing thematic and emotional opposites strongly resembles the Greek conception of "harmonia," the joining together of disparate elements in a
stable proportion by means of principles made manifest through music and thought to parallel those governing the stars. In fact, this
poet's empathic harmonizing of man and the cosmos occurs within a
causal ontology that at times seems Pythagorean. For the ancient
Greeks, the mathematical order in nature directly corresponded to the
proportion of intervals in the consonances of Greek music. Aristotle
claimed in his *Metaphysics* that the Pythagoreans believed that "the
properties and ratios of the musical consonances were expressible in
numbers, and that indeed all other things seemed to be wholly mod-
elled in their nature upon numbers, they took numbers to be the
whole of reality, the elements of numbers to be the elements of all
existing things, and the whole heaven to be a musical scale and a
number."[1]

1. Carolyn Kizer and James Boatwright, "A Conversation with James Dickey," in
Richard J. Calhoun (ed.), *James Dickey: The Expansive Imagination* (Deland, Fla.,

Although Dickey has little to say about number or scale in his poetry, his mystical world is so much a proportion of motion and music that his ontology bears close analogy to Greek and medieval conceptions of cosmic harmony even though he assumes no explicit astronomical theory. To see how this modern American poet is ancient, let us begin by looking at one of his most harmonious lyrics of love and recollection, "Mary Sheffield":

> Forever at war news    I am
> thinking there    nearly naked
> low green of water    hard overflowed forms
>
> water sits running    quietly carving
> red rocks forcing white from the current
>
> parts of midstream    join
> I sit with one hand    joining
> the other hand shyly    fine sand under
>
> still feet    and Mary Sheffield
> singing    passed-through
>
> sustained in the    poured forms of live oaks
> taking root    in the last tracks
> of left and right foot    river flowing
>
> into my mind    nearly naked
> the last day but one    before world war.
>
> When the slight wind dies
> each leaf still has    two places
> such music    touched alive
>
> guitar strings    sounds    join
> In the stone's shoal    of swimming
>
> the best twigs I have    the best
> sailing leaves    in memory
> pass    threading through
>
> all things spread sail    sounds gather
> on blunt stone    streaming white
>
> E minor    gently running
> I sit with one hand    in the strange life
> of the other    watching water throng

1973), 11; "Metaphysics," in *Introduction to Aristotle*, ed. Richard McKeon (Chicago, 1973), 289.

on one stone   loving Mary Sheffield
for her chord changes   river always

before war   I sit down and
anywhere   water flows   the breastplate of time
rusts off me   sounds   green forms   low voice

new music   long   long
past.   (*P,* 281–82)

We cannot begin to compare this poet with the Greeks and rivers
without introducing Heraclitus' famous aphorism: "You cannot step
twice into the same river, for other waters are continually flowing
on." In the *Cratylus,* Plato gives his equally famous interpretation of
this sentence: "Heraclitus is supposed to say that all things are in motion and nothing at rest; he compares them to a stream of a river, and
says that you cannot step into the same water twice."[2] In spite of
Plato's report, what Heraclitus really seems to be saying is that while
the *waters* are different, the *rivers* are the same; while things seem to
be in flux all around us, the configurations of such movement retain
some sort of intelligible shape.

In the natural flux of time and human emotion in "Mary Sheffield"
where "all things spread sail," there is one enduring element like that
of Heraclitus: the "river always" of memory through which "sounds
gather / on blunt stone." As it gathers the sounds of Mary's singing
and the poet's guitar playing, this river recovers "twigs" and "sailing
leaves" of the past so that the poet can claim a certain immunity to
perpetual change. For, if the flow of change takes away beautiful moments, it can, like a river, also bring them back, though they be in
different forms. Thus, the speaker concludes with both a new and old
music. This river is a fluid version of Dickey's unifying Absolute of
Motion that joins all things, past and present, in a perpetual process
of universal rhythm. What is different here is the explicit element of
music. In the tree house poem, Dickey's hypnotic anapests and three-
beat lines combined to produce a trancelike chant fully appropriate to
the fantastic spell the poet was trying to weave, but his chant was subordinate in power to natural movement. In "Mary Sheffield" music is
not merely an ornament of diction but a principle in itself.

2. Phillip Wheelright, *Heraclitus* (Princeton, 1959), 29; "Cratylus," in *Dialogues of
Plato,* ed. B. Jowett (New York, 1937), 442.

Motion and music combine to constitute a universe for Dickey which suggests a Neoplatonic "great circle"—M. H. Abrams' apposite term—of emanation and return. This circle has its historic roots in Plotinus' radical monism which assumes that All issues from the One through emanations that flow into things through a series of "hypostases" and then back to the One in a three-part process of unity, division, and reunion. Just as it was for Plato and Pythagoras, albeit in different cosmologies, the eternal movements of the universe, and thus its design and purpose, could be made intelligible by translation of its principles into music. Furthermore, these principles had a direct correspondence with those which governed the human soul. In the second book of Plato's *Laws*, order in movement is called "rhythm"; in the *Timaeus*, it is said that rhythm was given to man by the Gods to bring into souls a harmony which is an imitation of heavenly courses of intelligence, expressible in number. Again in the *Laws*, the Athenian argues that the true lawgiver will persuade if not compel poets to compose in rhythms which are imitations of the motions (or bearing) of men who are pure, valiant, and good.[3]

If we wed Plotinus' great circle to Plato's conception of rhythm, we come close to Dickey's poetic principle of music and motion. The intimacy-effecting bond between man and nature is Mary's past singing, which is recovered by the poet's memory yet is also "sustained in the poured forms of live oaks." That is, the poet's memory can retain and rejuvenate the past by using poetic rhythms to enter the eternal flow of nature that mixes permanence and change in One Motion emanating through the particular "hypostases" of live oaks. Nature is constituted here such that music serves as a mediating force between the poet and flux so that he can gain access to the forms not only of natural things but of human emotion. The principles of Dickey's poetic music, conveyed by the poet's lineal intervals and blocks of images, reflect the movement of rivers and the places where the twigs of memory gather for a moment and are recoverable. In short, Dickey can move with change and briefly arrest it. He thus moves from the present, through divisions produced by time, back to the nostalgic experience with Mary.

3. M. H. Abrams, *Natural Supernaturalism* (New York, 1971), 150; "Laws, II," in *Dialogues of Plato*, ed. B. Jowett, 442; "Timaeus," *ibid.*, 28; "Laws, II," *ibid.*, 438.

Although Dickey's One may not be precisely like that of Plotinus, the poet's method of recovery seems similar. Dickey's inferred Absolute is not metaphysical but poetic. Like the idea of the music of the spheres, his principle may not be a literal truth he believes, but it is one of the poetic truths he finds beautiful, an "emotional truth, a humanly dramatic and formally satisfying truth" (S, 161) that is his way of providing compensation "for the loss of a sense of intimacy with the natural process" (SI, 68) and for the loss of gentle moments with a girl for whom he once cared.

In his ritual poem of family protection "The Vegetable King," Dickey employs heavenly music he knows to be a fiction. After he sleeps out one spring night in a grove of pines behind his suburban house, the poet returns to his family rejuvenated with a new strength acquired through communion with gods and constellations. These gods are old-fashioned indeed, for they move through the heavens by music:

> This is the time foresaid, when I must enter
> The waking house, and return to a human love
> Cherished on faith through winter:
> That time when I in the night
>
> Of water lay, with sparkling animals of light
> And distance made, with gods
> Which move through Heaven only as spheres
> Are moved: by music, music. (P, 24–25)

Explicitly analogized to the Neoplatonic commonplace of the harmony of the spheres, Dickey's poetic motion is not only a cosmic principle but also a mediating magical link between man and nature. The poet thus acquires the restorative powers of the gods, because the objects in his universe are attuned to each other in an empathic harmony animated by an emanating movement shared by men and stars. At the end of poet's rite of rebirth, his emotional state directly corresponds to the rejuvenated order of nature in spring itself. Dickey's musical motion is nothing more than the transference of the ancient Pythagorean principle of cosmic harmony from the metaphysical to the fantastic. Dickey can harmonize natural opposites—life, death, and rebirth—through an emotional proportion we no longer believe to be scientific fact.

Just as Plotinus' descriptions of emanation are derived from the metaphor of a spring overflowing, so Dickey's musical motions are rendered intelligible through the imagery of water. In "The Vegetable King," the poet lay in a "night of water" that flows eventually to the heavens. In "The Rain Guitar," the poet's principle of eternal flow becomes tangible in music and water:

> The water-grass under had never waved
> But one way. It showed me that flow is forever
> Sealed from rain in a weir. For some reason having
> To do with Winchester, I was sitting on my guitar case
> Watching nothing but eelgrass trying to go downstream with all the right
> motions
> But one. I had on a sweater, and my threads were opening
> Like mouths with rain. It mattered to me not at all
> That a bridge was stumping
> With a man, or that he came near and cast a fish
> thread into the weir. I had no line and no feeling.
> I had nothing to do with fish
> But my eyes on the grass they hid in, waving with the one move of trying
> To be somewhere else. With what I had, what could I do?
> I got out my guitar, that somebody told me was supposed to improve
> With moisture—or was it when it dried out?—and hit the lowest
> And loudest chord. The drops that were falling just then
> Hammered like Georgia railroad track
> With E. The man went into a kind of fishing
> Turn. Play it, he said through his pipe. There
> I went, fast as I could with cold fingers. The strings shook
> With drops. A buck dance settled on the weir. Where was the city
> Cathedral in all this? Out of sight, but somewhere around.
> Play a little more
> Of that, he said, and cast. Music-wood shone,
> Getting worse or better faster than it liked:
> Improvement or disintegration
> Supposed to take years, fell on it
> By the gallon. It darkened and rang
> Like chimes. My sweater collapsed, and the rain reached
> My underwear. I picked, the guitar showered, and he cast to the mountain
> Music. His wood leg tapped
> On the cobbles. Memories of many men
> Hung, rain-faced, improving, sealed off
> In the weir. I found myself playing Australian
> Versions of British marching songs. Mouths opened all over me; I sang,
> His legs beat and marched

> Like companions. I was Air Force,
> I said. So was I; I picked
> This up in Burma, he said, tapping his gone leg
> With his fly rod, as Burma and the South
> west Pacific and North Georgia reeled,
> Rapped, cast, chimed, darkened and drew down
> Cathedral water, and improved. (*TCM*, 106–107)

In this poem, instead of aligning himself with the stars, Dickey follows the principle "flow is forever" and harmonizes a disparate assortment of cultures, songs, memories, and mouths in a rejuvenating shower of guitar playing that saturates his world with motion and music. Like so many of Dickey's poems of confluence and integration, "The Rain Guitar" begins realistically with a narrative that presents story elements later united in a fantastic order that comes as a surprise both to speaker and reader. Halfway through the poem, things begin simultaneously to fuse and expand: "Music-wood shone," and "Mouths opened all over me." As the speaker sings, his companionship with the fisherman, and with another culture, increases. Concluding with a cohesive "flow" of rain, watergrass, and fly fishing, the poem reels with a controlled frenzy, a trancelike ecstasy of unity, though muted on this dour rainy day by the restrained word "improved," which indicates the therapeutic telos or mystical purpose behind Dickey's mystical movement:

> . . . Burma and the South
> west Pacific and North Georgia reeled,
> Rapped, cast, chimed, darkened and drew down
> Cathedral water, and improved.

Dickey's entrancing guitar poem is but one musical step from his poetic principle of music as a magical method of harmonious transcendence. Even when his targets are not cosmic, his principles remain the same. When his aim is more personal, his music is gentler and more poignant. In "Buckdancer's Choice," the poet listens to his bedridden mother whistle an old minstrel tune and uses his "mother's prone music" to carry her to an enchanted state in which she is "nearly risen" from the dark "choices" of suffering and death:

> So I would hear out those lungs,
> The air split into nine levels,
> Some gift of tongues of the whistler

In the invalid's bed: my mother,
Warbling all day to herself
The thousand variations of one song;

It is called Buckdancer's Choice.
For years, they have all been dying
Out, the classic buck-and-wing men

Of traveling minstrel shows;
With them also an old woman
Was dying of breathless angina,

Yet still found breath enough
To whistle up in my head
A sight like a one-man band,

Freed black, with cymbals at heel,
An ex-slave who thrivingly danced
To the ring of his own clashing light

Through the thousand variations of one song
All day to my mother's prone music,
The invalid's warbler's note,

While I crept close to the wall
Sock-footed, to hear the sounds alter,
Her tongue like a mockingbird's break

Through stratum after stratum of a tone
Proclaiming what choices there are
For the last dancers of their kind,

For ill women and for all slaves
Of death, and children enchanted at walls
With a brass-beating glow underfoot,

Not dancing but nearly risen
Through barnlike, theatrelike houses
On the wings of the buck and wing.   (P, 189–90)

In this poem, Dickey domesticates the cosmic. Now at the familial level, the poet spins out a backwoods harmony from the "Thousand variations of one song" while, "Like a one-man band" and "like a mockingbird's tongue," his mother's music moves upward "Through stratum after stratum of a tone" until she proclaims

what choices there are
For the last dancers of their kind,

> For ill women and for all slaves
> Of death . . .

Dickey's irony is poignant, for his mother's choices are not choices at all. She must still face the existential realities of pain and death. Yet her situation is temporarily transcended by means of her son's principle of motion and music as she moves "Through barnlike, theatrelike houses / On the wings of the buck and wing." Once again, Dickey's neoplatonic assumptions are clearly fantastic. He fully realizes that his mother's transcendence is fictive, yet his imagination offers a certain emotional immunity to her fate. As in so many of his lyrics, he is consistent here in his view that an ancient world offers a more harmonious place for man than the modern. In a jotting from his notebooks in *Sorties*, he reveals his affinity for the illusion of a pre-Socratic world view: "The pre-Socratic philosophers have always fascinated me enormously. What must it have been like to be a thinker in those days, when men really *did* have the illusion that the whole composition of the universe could be reduced to one or two elements: when men really did think. . . . There were only a few basic laws of physics, which . . . applied to everything including the planets and the celestial bodies" (*S*, 32).

Although Dickey's Neoplatonism is an assumed fiction, his emotional effects of felt unity are not. Whether he binds us to the cosmos, nature, or a personal event, his ancient assumptions are so skillfully woven with realistic narratives that they seem nothing less than natural parts of his poetic landscape. At the halfway point in many of these "mystical" experiences, we begin to feel reality give way to those magical moments which transport us to the neoplatonic sublime. In this regard, Dickey's method is one with Whitman's in the first section of "Out of the Cradle Endlessly Rocking" as the poet's song and that of the mockingbird unite "here and hereafter" in mystical reminiscence.

> Out of the cradle endlessly rocking,
> Out of the mocking-bird's throat, the musical shuttle,
> Out of the Ninth-month midnight,
> Over the sterile sands, and the fields beyond, where the
>       child, leaving his bed, wander'd alone, bare-
>       headed, barefoot,
> Down from the shower'd halo,

> Up from the mystic play of shadows, twining and twist-
>     ing as if they were alive,
> Out from the patches of briers and blackberries,
> From the memories of the bird that chanted to me . . .
> I, chanter of pains and joys, uniter of here and here-
>     after,
> Taking all hints to use them—but swiftly leaping
>     beyond them,
> A reminiscence sing.[4]

In "Hunting Civil War Relics at Nimblewill Creek," Dickey partakes of Whitman's principles by using song to uncover the past and to
bind himself and his brother to their southern ancestors:

> As he moves the mine detector
> A few inches over the ground. . .
> I come into this war
> Slowly, with my one brother,
> Watching his face grow deep
> Between the earphones,
> For I can tell
> If we enter the buried battle
> Of Nimblewill
> Only by his expression.
>
> . . . A bird's cry breaks
> In two, and into three parts.
> We cross the creek; the cry
> Shifts into another,
> Nearer, bird, and is
> Like the shout of a shadow—
> Lived-with, appallingly close—
> Or the soul, pronouncing
> "Nimblewill":
> Three tones, your being changes . . .   (P, 98)

In this poem, as in "Buckdancer's Choice," our Neoplatonic hypothesis is useful yet begins to reveal its limitations. Although Dickey's flow-is-forever principle is evident once more in both the movement of the mine detector which the poet's brother makes "vitally
float / Among the ferns and weeds" and in the brother's own manner

4. Whitman, *Leaves of Grass*, 246–47.

when "Softly he wanders, parting / The grass with a dreaming hand,"
the poet really gains entrance to "the buried battle" by means of a romantic commonplace: sympathetic identification based on feeling
and on the plaintive songs of birds. Even before his brother receives a
signal from the mine detector as to the location of the relics, the poet
*feels* the presence of the dead soldiers and sympathetically begins to
join their ranks:

> But underfoot I feel
> The dead regroup,
> The burst metals all in place,
> The battle lines be drawn
> Anew to include us
> In Nimblewill,
> And I carry the shovel and pick
>
> More as if they were
> Bright weapons that I bore   (*P,* 98–99)

As soon as the poet enters the battle, "A bird's cry breaks . . . into
three parts," reflecting the three syllables in the word "Nimblewill,"
which are then amplified into a principle of transformation: "Three
tones; your being changes." While the poet hears the birds singing, his
brother hears the dead "all singing" through his earphones attached to
the mine detector, and soon the dead themselves are miraculously
"outsinging two birds." When Dickey reverently falls to his knees to
dig where his brother points, he silently sings himself underground to
uncover the spirits of the dead by uttering two words as magical and
evocative as the birds' cries: "Fathers! Fathers!"

The silent singing at Nimblewill is a far distance from the Pythagorean paradigm with which we began our inquiry. Yet the notion of an
emotional and pantheistic harmony based on a silent music shared by
man and nature is as true at Nimblewill Creek as it is in many a neoplatonic cosmography. Although Dickey's music in this war poem
does not issue from heavenly spheres and is considerably gentler in
force, it pervades man's world in a manner analogous to that of the
sound of Cicero's waterfall in *Somnium Scipionis*:

> The ears of mankind are filled with these sounds but have become deaf, for
> of all your senses it is the most blunted. Thus the people who live near the
> place where the Nile rushes down from very high mountains to the parts

which are called Catadupa are destitute of the sense of hearing, by reason of the greatness of the noise. Now the sound, which is effected by the rapid rotation of the whole system of nature, is so powerful that human hearing cannot comprehend it, just as you cannot look directly upon the sun, because your sight and sense are overcome by his beams.[5]

Even when music is not an explicit subject in Dickey's poems, his metric and rhythmic strategies play such important roles that it is tempting to view them as structural principles as well as aspects of diction. When coupled with the poet's circular ontology of perpetual transformation, his rhythmic music conveys the persistent power of his principles by constituting a recurrent ground rhythm that itself seems magically independent of the speaker. Dickey's preference for marchlike anapests—hypnotic, compulsive, primitive—is understandable because of his desire to wed his universe to a music that conveys the sensations of his ontological harmonies. In the preface to a recent reissue of his second and third volumes of verse, aptly entitled *The Early Motion*, Dickey speaks of his affinity for a "night-rhythm" that sustains the "self-generating on-go" he wants in his lyrics: "These poems emerged from what I call a night-rhythm, something felt in pulse not word. How this anapestic sound was engendered. . . . I have always liked heavy recurrence of stress. . . . What if images, insights, metaphors, evaluations, nightmarish narratives, all of originality and true insight, were put into—or *brought* into—the self-generating on-go that seems to have existed before any poem and to continue after any actual poem ends?"

If Dickey's use of motion and music is Neoplatonic, the "sound-before-meaning" principle in his "night-rhythms" is aesthetically plausible insofar as the sound of his poems is so crucial to making sense of his view of nature (*TEM*, vii–viii). Combined with his three-beat lines and thrumming anapests, his word selection is often so heavily gerundive that the sounds of nature and the sense of a poem's action are one.

Dickey's rhythms are fully consistent with his mystical strategies for inducing trancelike states. To read Dickey accurately, we must surrender ourselves to his music, even to the extent of partly suspending

5. "Scipio's Dream," in *Cicero's Three Books of Offices*, trans. Cyrus R. Edmonds (London, 1880), 296.

our analytic judgment. On this point, one thinks of Hazlitt's famous observation about the English Lake poets: "There is a *chaunt* in the recitation both of Coleridge and Wordsworth, which acts as a spell upon the hearer, and disarms the judgement."[6] To disarm the realistic judgment and make plausible his hyperbolic principles in "The Owl King," Dickey places a blind child in a tree with the Owl King and has the boy speak in the poet's three-beat "night-rhythms," thereby entering (and creating) the therapeutic realm of a fantastic forest where sound and touch, not sight, are the self-generating principles of the movements of nature:

> I learn from the master of sight
> What to do when the sun is dead,
> How to make the great darkness work
> As it wants of itself to work.
> I feel the tree where we sit
> Grow under me, and live . . .
>               I shut my eyes
>
> And my eyes are gold,
> As gold as an owl's,
> As gold as a king's . . .
>        I understand
> How beings and sounds go together . . .
>
> . . . I see
> The self of every substance
> As it crouches, hidden and free . . .
> I see as the owl king sees,
> By going in deeper than darkness.
> The wood comes back in a light
> It did not know it withheld,
> And I can tell
> By its breathing glow
> Each tree on which I laid
> My hands when I was blind.

In this gerundive chant of "flowing and streaming," Dickey's ancient intuition of "How beings and sounds go together" gives way to a world

6. William Hazlitt, "My First Acquaintance with Poets," in Russell Noyes (ed.), *English Romantic Poetry and Prose* (Oxford, 1956), 673.

where the poet's mysticism seems more romantic than Greek, closer to Wordsworth and Keats than Pythagoras and Plotinus. To be sure, Dickey's Absolute of Motion holds sway in the owl's kingdom, where the fluttering of wings dissolves into "Pure soundless dancing / Like leaves not leaves" (P, 76–77). But now the emotional harmony between man and nature is more modern, more melancholic, more mysterious.

Perhaps it is the introduction of the personal narrative that forces us to move away from mystical music as an exclusive hypothesis for reading this poem. For, as the child's father futilely searches the woods for his son, spatial coordinates are defined in terms of human feeling: "All distance is weeping and singing." We recall that Dickey said in his preface that as his poetry developed he wanted "to give more play to narrative movement, the story-value" of his lyrics, and consequently began to tone "down the heavy bombardment of stress." Although the narrative line is slight in "The Owl King," the story line does shift the focus of harmonious empathy to a more specific target. As the owl's vision is gained by the boy, Dickey's Absolute of Motion becomes as much a means to an end, a vehicle for sympathetic identification by the child with the imagined power of the bird, not unlike Keats's ecstatic rapport with his nightingale.

In our search for Dickey's poetic principles, "The Owl King" is a transitional poem. While it clearly incorporates many of the visionary elements we have chosen to call mystical or neoplatonic, its action points to a tradition of poetic topics in which the things of nature, in addition to music and motion, assume a primary place. Nature is certainly prominent in "In the Tree House at Night" and in "Mary Sheffield," but the movement of the speaker is *away* from material things *toward* the poet's principle of pure movement. In "The Owl King," the three speakers (really, one voice) move *through* specific objects of nature—the forest and its darkness—to a realm of motion that is emotionally qualified by the plight of the boy himself. Although "The Owl King" is a fantasy, its therapeutic end, like that of "Hunting Civil War Relics at Nimblewill Creek," returns us to the human subject, and thus brings us into the literary camp of those writers whom Dickey calls, when speaking of his favorite poet Theodore Roethke, "the great Empathizers, like Rilke and D. H. Lawrence." To these poets I would like to turn while also invoking the great nineteenth-century English poets who, like Wordsworth, constantly celebrate a miraculous musical harmony in the powers of nature:

> —Many are the notes
> Which, in his tuneful course, the wind draws forth
> From rocks, woods, caverns, heaths, and dashing shores;
> And well those lofty brethern bear their part
> In the wild concert . . .
>
> Theirs, too, is the song
> Of stream and headlong flood that seldom fails;
> And, in the grim and breathless hour of noon,
> Methinks that I have heard them echo back
> The thunder's greeting. Nor have nature's laws
> Left them ungifted with a power to yield
> Music of a finer tone; a harmony,
> So do I call it, though it be the hand
> Of silence, though there be no voice.[7]

7. "The Excursion," in *The Poetical Works of Wordsworth*, 432.

## 3. ROMANTICISM, or motion and nature:

From Nature doth emotion come, and moods
Of calmness equally are Nature's gift:
This is her glory; these two attributes
Are sister horns that constitute her strength.
Hence Genius, born to thrive by interchange
Of peace and excitation, finds in her
His best and purest friend; from her receives
That energy by which he seeks the truth,
From her that happy stillness of the mind
Which fits him to receive it when unsought.
—WORDSWORTH

. . . to speak in literature with
the perfect rectitude and insouciance of the movements
of animals and the unimpeachableness of the sentiment
of trees in the woods and grass by the roadside
is the flawless triumph of art.
—WALT WHITMAN

I would with the fish, the blackening salmon, and the mad lemmings,
The children dancing, the flowers widening.
Who sighs from far away?
I would unlearn the lingo of exasperation, all the distortions of malice and hatred;
I would believe my pain: and the eye quiet on the growing rose;
I would delight in my hands, the branch singing, altering the excessive bird;
I long for the imperishable quiet at the heart of form . . .
—THEODORE ROETHKE

We think of a romantic as someone who not only acquires knowledge of himself through nature but takes something from it. Whether Shelley sees poetry as a mode of discovery that "lifts the veil from the hidden beauty of the world" or whether Roethke's internal moods gladly sway with external nature, as when he says, "My heart lifted me up with the great grasses," the romantic poet depends on nature as a source of emotional renewal.[1] Abounding with animals, woods, rivers, and redemptions, Dickey's lyrics of perpetual exchange immediately invite us to use the word "romantic" as a term for de-

1. "Defense of Poetry," in *Shelley's Poetry and Prose*, ed. Donald H. Reiman and Sharon B. Powers (New York, 1977), 487; Theodore Roethke, *The Poet and His Craft* (Seattle, 1966), 25.

**41**

scribing his subject matter and for his attitude toward his materials. Not for a moment, however, would we be tempted to align his poetry with that of the post-romantic poets T. S. Eliot, Wallace Stevens, or Marianne Moore. They are indoor writers, and most of Dickey's poetry occurs outdoors, whether behind his house or in the vicinity of the stars.

If Dickey's matter and mentality are romantic, we would do well to develop the meaning of our third critical hypothesis by following to some extent the poet's own method of exchange: working through the things of nature to the effects of romantic interaction. We shall begin by examining Dickey's relation to animals, then examine his view of the surfaces of nature, and then combine both terms to see how movement between animals and surfaces constitutes his peculiar view of nature. Yet, for the serious romantic, mere material exchange with nature is only part of the truth. We must specify and judge the human value of the poet's experience in nature if his work is to have real significance. Consequently, the last two terms discussed in this chapter will center on the ends of interchange, namely, on different modes of renewal and on renewal and its relation to the macabre. This last term will, in addition, provide a topical bridge from Dickey's romanticism to his spectacular use of violence, a poetic strategy later to be treated under the heading of "primitivism."

My intention in this section is not simply to develop a series of facile analogies between Dickey and poets we have chosen to call "romantic." Even less do I wish to argue more simply that, because Dickey uses topics which his esteemed predecessors have used, therefore, Dickey is a good poet. On this point, however, I do acknowledge the implicit historical argument that if the romantics' topics are serious poetic issues, then so are Dickey's. Dickey is an exceptional poet not only because his themes are interesting but, more important, because he has rejuvenated romantic commonplaces by expanding the methods of his poetic fathers while simultaneously showing that these commonplaces have as strong an emotional currency as ever. If Dickey owes a great deal to the romantic tradition of which he is a part, that tradition owes at least as much to him. And, there is no way we can begin to specify the relation between the two until we note the differences and similarities between this poet and his methodological ancestors.

Animals

If Dickey's mystical impulse becomes "romantic" as his targets of exchange become more specific and concrete, his interest in the movements of animals will serve us well as a starting point for inquiry into his principles of nature and motion. That we are on the right course bears support from one of the poet's own remarks in *Self-Interviews:* "I have always believed—and I mean believed *blindly*—in what I choose to call 'instinct'. . . . This is one of the reasons why animals have always been so important to me. . . . It seems to me that most animals have this [an athlete's] superb economy of motion. The instinctual notion of how much energy to expend, the ability to do a thing thoughtlessly and do it right, is a quality that I esteem enormously. I want to get a feeling of this instinctualness into poetry" (*SI*, 60–61).

Dickey's desire to put the instinctual movement of animals into poetry coincides with Keats's view of the poet as "The man who with a bird, / Wren or Eagle, finds his way to / All its instincts."[2] Whereas Keats's degree of empathy with animals is limited—his poetic voice never fully fades "away into the forest dim" with his famous nightingale—Dickey enters more fully into the instinctual worlds of beasts. One of Dickey's greatest gifts is his capacity to retain a human voice while gaining an extraordinary degree of identification with the nonhuman. In "Reincarnation II," another of Dickey's bird poems, an office worker wakes to find that he is not at home in bed but instead is flying over an ocean of icebergs at the South Pole. As his journey continues, he discovers that he is slowly becoming a graceful seabird— probably an albatross—and that he possesses powers of navigation that are purely instinctual. Intermingling human perception with animal movement, the poet emotionally approximates the bird's sensations of flight by means of extensive catalogs of astronomical imagery embodied in a simple narrative of fantastic conversion.

> . . . he dreams
>
> He sees the Southern Cross
> Painfully over the horizon    drawing itself

2. "The Poet: A Fragment," in *The Poetical Works and Other Writings of John Keats*, ed. M. Buxton Forman (8 vols.; New York, 1970), IV, 64.

Together    inching
Higher each night of the world

   . . . he closes his eyes and feels himself
Turning whiter and whiter    upheld

At his whitest it is

Midnight    the equator    the center of the world
He sneaks across    afire
With himself    the stars change all their figures
Reach toward    closer
And now begin to flow
Into his cracked-open mouth    down his throat
A string of lights    emblems    patterns of fire    all
Directions    myths    Hydras
Centaurs    Wolves    Virgins
Eating them all    eating
The void possessing
Music    order    repose
Hovering    moving on his armbones    crawling
On warm air    covering the whole ocean    the sea deadens
He dulls    new constellations pale off
Him
                  . . . a good dream    it is all
Instinct    he thinks    I have been born
This way.    (*P*, 245–46)

The poet offers no justification for this hyperbolic change. Instead, the
possibility for Dickey's brand of metamorphosis lies once again in the
poet's miraculous world of motion and imaginative plenitude. Of
the office worker's magical transformation, Dickey simply asserts:

He thinks    the world is for everything born—
I always had
These wings    buried deep in my back:
There is a wing-growing motion
Half-alive in every creature.    (*P*, 248)

As the poem's initiating incident, the man's conversion is fantastic
yet his experience is presented in such realistic detail that we seem to
be with the man-bird as he soars. Gaining access to the movements of
nature through the miraculous is one of Dickey's most prominent paradoxical methods as we saw in "In the Tree House at Night" and "The

Owl King." Of all of Dickey's animal poems, "Reincarnation II" is the
most mystical, or cosmic, because of its celestial scenery and because
the bird's unearthly motion so closely resembles the "spiritual walking" of the poet's constantly reindividuated Absolute of Motion. Nonetheless, the emotional power of this poem stems from the concrete
sensations of the man-bird's experience, the ecstatic feeling of soaring
"In renewed light, utterly alone!" The poem dramatically conveys the
energizing instincts of animal movement in midair where even death
takes on the properties of flight in the concluding lines:

> bird-death

> Hovers for years on its wings
> With a time sense that cannot fail
> Waits to change
> Him again   circles   abides   no feather
> Falling   conceived by stars and the void
> Is born perpetually
> In midair   where it shall be
> Where it is.   (P, 251)

Dickey is hardly alone among romantic poets in his empathic en-
thusiasm for the flight of birds. In addition to the nightingales of
Keats and Coleridge, the skylarks of Shelley and Wordsworth, the
waterfowl of Bryant, and the swans of Yeats, one thinks immediately
of the resemblance of Dickey's seabird to Whitman's eagles:

> Skirting the river road, (my forenoon walk, my rest,)
> Skyward in air a sudden muffled sound, the dalliance of the eagles,
> The rushing amorous contact high in space together,
> The clinching interlocking claws, a living, fierce, gyrating wheel,
> Four beating wings, two beaks, a swirling mass tight grappling,
> In tumbling turning clustering loops, straight downward falling,
> Till o'er the river pois'd, the twain yet one, a moment's lull,
> A motionless still balance in the air, then parting, talons loosing,
> Upward again on slow-firm pinions slanting, their separate diverse
>     flight,
> She hers, he his, pursuing.[3]

Although Whitman's poem gracefully conveys the eagles' courting in
long sweeping lines and action-filled verbals, Dickey's poem carries

3. Whitman, *Leaves of Grass*, 273–74.

the empathic principle further by extending the process of flight over nine beautifully detailed pages instead of a mere ten lines. To be sure, Whitman wishes to express a moment of energy, a rush of instinctual mating in midair, yet Dickey's leisurely view more deeply involves the reader by making us feel closer to the central action rather than observing far below the event.

In "May Day Sermon to the Women of Gilmer County, Georgia, by a Woman Preacher Leaving the Baptist Church," Dickey's nature-as-motion principle is specified to sexual movement as nature reconstitutes itself in spring. Recounting the tale of a farm girl and her one-eyed lover, the preacher uses animal imagery to convey to her audience of women the compulsive "natural" instincts of male sexuality in language that is simultaneously ecstatic and gentle:

> Sisters, understand about men and sheaths:
>
> About nakedness: understand how butterflies, amazed, pass out
> Of their natal silks   how the tight snake takes a great breath   bursts
> Through himself and leaves himself behind   how a man casts finally
> Off everything that shields him from another   beholds his loins
> Shine with his children forever   burn with the very juice
> Of resurrection:   such shining is how the spring creek comes
> Forth from its sunken rocks   it is how the trout foams and turns on
> Himself   heads upstream, breathing mist like water, for the cold
> Mountain of his birth   flowing   sliding in and through the ego-
> maniacal sleep of gamecocks   shooting past a man with one new blind
> Side   who feels his skinned penis rise like a fish through the dark
> Woods, in a strange lifted-loving form   a snake about to burst
> Through itself on May Day (*P*, 7)

Dickey's motion here is clearly a motion of ejaculation and regeneration. Felt sympathetically and spontaneously by the girl's lover, these forces constitute an implicit, sacrosanct state of nature, one which is not only "spiritual" in the sense that its objects are to some extent the dematerialized moments of a subsumptive motion but a state which is intrinsically redemptive. For, the lover is spoken to "as beasts speak to themselves / Of holiness learned in the barn." And all things, natural and man-made, seem to radiate the light of spring's regeneration. At poem's end, not only are the creeks "resurrected" but even "the barn wanders over the earth" like the freed farm animals it once held who now walk in fog through "The white breast of the Lord" (*P*, 12–13).

In many ways, Dickey's redemptive sexuality produces a triumphant unity of movement which resembles Blake's orgiastic combination of senses in the concluding plate of *Jerusalem:*

South stood the Nerves of the Eye; East, in Rivers of bliss, the Nerves of the Expansive Nostrils: West flow'd the Parent Sense, the Tongue; North stood The labyrinthine Ear: Circumscribing & Circumcising the excrementitious Husk & Covering, into Vacuum evaporating, revealing the lineaments of Man, Driving outward the Body of Death in an Eternal Death & Resurrection, Awaking it to Life among the Flowers of Beulah, rejoicing in Unity In the
      Four Senses.

Edenic biblical imagery is paramount in both these writers and results in ecstatic entrance to a holy state in which deadly alienation from nature is overcome by a method of transport which continually integrates sensation and revelation. One of Blake's central goals (which may be Dickey's as well) is to invent a visionary state in which we find:

> All Human Forms identified, even Tree, Metal, Earth & Stone: all
> Human Forms identified, living, going forth & returning wearied
> Into the Planetary lives of Years, Months, Days & Hours; reposing,
> And then Awaking into his Bosom in the Life of Immortality.[4]

One reason for Dickey's sublime integration lies in his extraordinary capacity to fuse emotional opposites in the obsessive mode we noted earlier in our reading of "Exchanges." In Wordsworth's phrase, this "interchange / Of peace and excitation" produced by the preacher's frenetic cadences and the poet's extensive gentle nature imagery in "May Day Sermon" creates an alternating movement of passivity and activity that makes emotional exchange with nature thorough and complete.[5] By means of delicate pictures like that of the trout "breathing mist like water," we are lured peacefully into Dickey's world through entrancing images of butterflies and clouds that are simultaneously excited by the hypnotic rhythms of Baptist oratory, all of which results in an in-and-out effect, making empathic entrance

---

4. Keynes (ed.), *The Complete Writings of William Blake,* 745, 747.
5. "The Prelude," in *The Poetical Works of Wordsworth,* 212.

into this world of "beasts and sinners" intoxicating and obsessive. At this point, to schematize Dickey's romantic strategy, we would do well to recall Coleridge's famous conception of the power of the "secondary imagination," a faculty which itself is divinely synthetic. Here is M. H. Abrams' formulation: "Unlike the fancy, which can only rearrange the 'fixities and definites' of sense-perception without altering their identity, the 'synthetic and magical power' of the secondary imagination repeats the primal act of knowing by dissolving the elements of perception 'in order to recreate' them, and 'reveals itself in the balance or reconciliation of opposite or discordant qualities'—including the reconciliation of intellect with emotion, and of thought with object: 'the idea, with the image.'" Although Dickey's primal act of knowing presupposes no metaphysical divinity or wish to engage the intellect in any central way, it is clearly "synthetic and magical" in a grandiose manner, especially in its power to reconcile opposites. In Dickey's world, familiar natural elements constantly dissolve and are recreated, even though, in a strange way, they partly retain their normal attributes. His poetic mode of perception gives us the feeling that common things are seen in some new energized state that was previously hidden from view. H. L. Weatherby offers an excellent summary of the recreative effect of Dickey's exchanges with nature that make us "feel that you have discovered the ways things *really* are, as you always knew they must be—what a magnolia tree you have looked at all your life actually is. It is as if you have discovered a new landscape superimposed upon the old one, at once identical with the old one and yet at the same time more nearly coherent and intelligible and consequently more satisfying than the old one."[6]

Dickey's energizing view of nature again bears interesting comparison with Whitman's. In "Roots and Leaves Themselves Alone," a short lyric from *Leaves of Grass*, Whitman's empathic invitation, couched like Dickey's in direct address, delicately engages the reader in a synesthetic genesis of becoming as beautiful and graceful as the lines from "May Day Sermon":

6. M. H. Abrams, "Structure and Style in the Greater Romantic Lyric," in Frederick Hilles and Harold Bloom (eds.), *From Sensibility to Romanticism* (New York, 1965),

ROOTS and leaves themselves alone are these;
Scents brought to men and women from the wild woods,
    and from the pond-side,
Breast-sorrel and pinks of love—fingers that wind
    around tighter than vines,
Gushes from the throats of birds, hid in the foliage of
    trees, as the sun is risen . . .
Frost-mellow's berries, and Third-month twigs, offer'd
    fresh to young persons wandering out in the fields
    when the winter breaks up,
Love-buds, put before you and within you, whoever you are . . .
If you bring the warmth of the sun to them, they will
    open, and bring form, color, perfume, to you;
If you become the aliment and the wet, they will become
    flowers, fruits, tall branches and trees.[7]

To be sure, nature is dynamic for both poets. Whereas Whitman's roots and leaves wind, gush, and unfold, Dickey's animals shine, burst, slide, and shoot. Whereas Whitman's promise of harmony is hypothetical in his conclusion, Dickey's engagement is more direct, assertive, and definite. In Dickey's entrancing world of empathic energy, one need not even move to participate in animal instinct. In his charming poem "Listening to Foxhounds" the poet speculates about an Appalachian hunter who runs not with the hounds but the fox:

When in that gold
Of fires, quietly sitting
With the men whose brothers are hounds,

You hear the first tone
Of a dog on scent, you look from face
To face, to see whose will light up.

When that light comes
Inside the dark light of the fire,
You know which chosen man has heard

---

545; H. L. Weatherby, "The Way of Exchange in James Dickey's Poetry," in Calhoun (ed.), *James Dickey,* 56.
    7. Whitman, *Leaves of Grass,* 124.

A thing like his own dead
Speak out in a marvelous, helpless voice
That he has been straining to hear.

Miles away in the dark,
His enchanted dog can sense
How his features glow like a savior's,

And begins to hunt
In a frenzy of desperate pride.
Among us, no one's eyes give off a light

For the red fox
Playing in and out of his scent,
Leaping stones, doubling back over water.

Who runs with the fox
Must sit here like his own image,
Giving nothing of himself

To the sensitive flames,
With no human joy rising up,
Coming out of his face to be seen.

And it is hard,
When the fox leaps into his burrow
To keep that singing down,

To sit with the fire
Drawn into one's secret features,
And all eyes turning around

From the dark wood
Until they come, amazed, upon
A face that does not shine

Back from itself,
That holds its own light and takes more,
Like the face of the dead, sitting still,

Giving no sign,
Making no outcry, no matter
Who may be straining to hear.   (*P*, 53–54)

For the man who runs with the fox, "no human joy" rises out of his
face as the hounds give chase. "When the fox leaps into his burrow"
and is safe, this face does not reflect but somehow absorbs light from
the human fire into his "secret features." This face "holds its own

light," and like the hiding fox, makes no sound even though its human companions "whose brothers are hounds" are "straining to hear" some sign of discovery and communion from the dogs. By siding with the fox, this outsider is expelled from the fraternity of his companions and becomes as secretive and mysterious as the hidden fox who experiences a kind of light underground which differs radically from "that gold / Of fires" where the other hunters sit. The expelled hunter thus empathically goes "below" the glittering surfaces of the poem to enter the realm of animal instinct.

## SURFACES

In a manner that strongly resembles the method in "The Movement of Fish," the poem "Listening to Foxhounds" employs one of the central paradoxes of Dickey's vision: an approximation of a feeling of the depth of animal instinct without the poet actually entering those depths. That is, his nature poems are poems of surfaces that are never broken. We infer the depths he speaks of, and this inference in many ways better evokes the feeling of dark, natural forces than does direct representation. Granted, Dickey's poems take place in ominous nocturnal settings such as meadows, forests, lakes, or dark green groves of suburban pines at night, twilight, and dusk, but it is his magical descriptions of surfaces, often mixed with golden objects such as shadows and owl's eyes, that conjure a sense of primitive nature and the irrational. In "The Water-Bug's Mittens," a lecture given at the University of Arizona, Dickey mentions his preference for surfaces when speaking of Pound's *Cantos:* "It is just these 'surfaces, presented with great exactitude,' that I find the Ezra Pound that I can most truly, effectively, and permanently use. . . . These passages have had for me . . . a shock of *possibility:* the possibility of catching an observable or imaginable part of the world in fresh, clean language that would be simple without being thin and ordinary."[8]

Dickey's animated surfaces often give rise, like those of the romantics, to radical changes in state of the lyric speaker. Of the English

8. James Dickey, "The Water-Bug's Mittens," in *Night Hurdling* (Bloomfield Hills, Mich., 1983), 40–41.

romantics, Abrams notes that "the best Romantic meditations on a landscape . . . all manifest a transaction between subject and object in which the thought incorporates and makes explicit what was already implicit in the outer scene. And all the poets testify independently to a fact of consciousness which underlay these poems, and was the experiential source and warrant for the philosophy of cognition as an interfusion of mind and nature." Unlike the English romantics, as I mentioned earlier, Dickey's nature has no universal soul or primal intelligent substance that gives warrant to his animating principle or accounts for his "interfusion" of self and landscape. In fact, few if any of his lyrics could be called "meditations" in the romantic mode in which the speaker's mental activity is central. If he does "think," Dickey seldom speculates for long; and instead of sublimating his "aching joys" and "dizzy raptures" (Wordsworth's terms) into sober thought, he cultivates extraordinary sensations or states of excitement that grant him his greatest emotional access to nature. Dickey's transactions with nature are not only more thorough (and less intellectual) than the romantics, but his exchanges result in a deeper access to power. Wordsworth can use poetic song to recollect youth:

> . . . if the song be loth to quit
> Those recollected hours that have the charm
> Of visionary things, those lovely forms
> And sweet sensations that throw back our life,
> And almost make remotest infancy
> A visible scene . . . [9]

But, in "Sleeping Out at Easter," Dickey does not perform a mental act of recollection. Instead, he instinctually sees and touches the earth so that he gains a darker sympathy with the primal "source of all song":

> My animal eyes become human
> As the Word rises out of the darkness
> Where my right hand, buried beneath me,
> Hoveringly tingles, with grasping
> The source of all song at the root.   (P, 17)

9. Abrams, "Structure and Style in the Greater Romantic Lyric," in Hilles and Bloom (ed.), *From Sensibility to Romanticism*, 547; "The Prelude," in *The Poetical Works of Wordsworth*, 129.

In his own attempts to catch the surfaces of the world within "a shock of possibility," Dickey develops an expansive view of nature that strongly resembles that of the so-called prospect poems of the English romantics. In "Grongar Hill" the eighteenth-century poet John Dyer sits above the vale of town, and as he surveys the view below, he emotionally follows the surface movement of nature to a joyous conclusion:

> And see the rivers how they run,
> Thro' woods and meads, in shade and sun,
> Sometimes swift, sometimes slow,
> Wave succeeding wave, they go
> A various journey to the deep,
> Like human life to endless sleep!
> Thus is nature's vesture wrought,
> To instruct our wand'ring thought;
> Thus she dressed green and gay,
> To disperse our cares away.

Wordsworth initiates his own meditation at Tintern Abbey from a similar external perspective:

> The day is come when I again repose
> Here, under this dark sycamore, and view
> These plots of cottage-ground, these orchard-tufts,
> Which at this season, with their unripe fruits,
> Are clad in one green hue, and lose themselves
> 'Mid groves and copses. Once again I see
> These hedge-rows, hardly hedge-rows, little lines
> Of sportive wood run wild: these pastoral farms,
> Green to the very door; and wreaths of smoke
> Sent up, in silence, from among the trees!

And Shelley, of course, in "Ode to the West Wind," follows the wind over the earth as he incants: "Be thou me, impetuous one! / Drive my dead thoughts over the universe / like withered leaves to quicken a new birth!"[10]

Given Dickey's penchant for celestial points of view, especially his cinematic perspective used when he follows the seabird in "Reincar-

<hr />

10. "Grongar Hill," by John Dyer, in Noyes (ed.), *English Romantic Poetry and Prose*, 15; "Tintern Abbey," in *The Poetical Works of Wordsworth*, 91; "Ode to the West Wind," in *Shelley's Poetry and Prose*, 223.

nation II" and the trout in "May Day Sermon," many of his poems issue from surveys of natural surfaces which resemble the prospective strategies of his romantic predecessors. This especially important romantic element in his mystical methodology can be found in poems ranging from "Falling" in which the stewardess sees "the huge partial form of the world . . . lose its evoked master shape" to "The Birthday Dream" which begins "at the worst place in the hills above the city" (*P*, 295, 288). Dickey's lyrics often follow a natural terrain to some new vision which engages the speaking subject with his world in a rejuvenating way. In "Near Darien" Dickey uses the wind and the surface of the sea to discover an "infinite breath" which later becomes a mystical bond of "man and wife breathing together":

> It may be the sea-moving moon
> Is swayed upon the waves by what I do,
> I make on the night no shade,
> But a small-stepping sound upon water.
> I have rowed toward the moon for miles,
> Till the lights upon shore have been blown
>
> Slowly out by my infinite breath . . .
>
> And the wind springs into the sea,
> And for miles on the calming surface
> The moon creeps into its image.   (*P*, 45)

Dickey's empathic response to the sea finds much in common with Wordsworth's youthful relation to nature. Nature's fluid surfaces in "The Prelude" give the poet a lesson couched in opposites which are analogized to the movements of water:

> Ye Presences of Nature in the sky
> And on the earth! Ye Visions of the hills!
> And Souls of lonely places! can I think
>
> A vulgar hope was yours when ye employed
> Such ministry, when ye through many a year
> Haunting me thus among my boyish sports,
> On caves and trees, upon the woods and hills,
> Impressed upon all forms the characters
> Of danger or desire; and thus did make
> The surface of the universal earth

With triumph and delight, with hope and fear,
Work like a sea? [11]

Even when Dickey is on the ground, he seems to be up in the air, moving perpetually on a circuit of redemptive motion so that all his nature lyrics look like prospect poems. In "Hedge Life," although the poet speaks from the "prospect" of hedge creatures close to the earth, he is curiously "above" things. Not only does he follow a movement like Shelley's animating wind but his perspective resembles Dyer's topographical survey (though on a smaller scale) while the feeling he evokes from nature has a delicate passivity to it, not unlike Words-worth's "tranquil restoration" received on the banks of the Wye:

> We wait
> With crowded excitement
>
> For our house to spring
> Slowly out of night-wet to the sun; beneath us,
> The moon hacked to pieces on the ground.
> None but we are curled
>
> Here, rising another inch,
> Knowing that what held us solid in the moon is still
> With us, where the outside flowers flash
> In bits, creatures travel
>
> Beyond us like rain,
> The great sun floats in a fringed bag, all stones quiver
> With the wind that moves us.    (P, 261)

As elements in Dickey's own version of "the correspondent breeze," which Abrams, speaking of the romantics, terms "not only a prop-erty of the landscape, but also a vehicle for radical changes in the poet's mind," breath and air seem everywhere in his graceful universe, not only dematerializing objects but ready at any moment to expand into some larger continuum of motion which subsumes the surface-movement of particulars.[12] In "Dover: Believing in Kings," Dickey uses breath imagery to align himself with the powers of nature and

11. "The Prelude," in *The Poetical Works of Wordsworth*, 130.
12. M. H. Abrams, "The Correspondent Breeze: A Romantic Metaphor," in M. H. Abrams (ed.), *English Romantic Poets: Modern Essays in Criticism* (London, 1975), 37.

thus establish a certain regal territory of sovereignty: "Birds drifted in my breath as it was drawn / From the stressing glitter / Of water" (P, 91). In "Pine," air becomes the medium of exchange for synesthetic perception:

> Air the most like
> Transfusion expands and only
> There it is fresh
> From overhead, steep-brewing and heavy from deep
> Down upcoming new
> To the lungs like a lean cave swimming—
> Throat-light and iron
> Warm spray on the inside face
> Cutting often and cooling-out and brow
> Opening and haunting freshly.   (TCM, 41)

Even when minute, the surface of Dickey's natural topography may expand into a place of cosmic storms and a new world. In "Dust" the poet finds a maelstrom in the mere movement of dust particles with the miraculous whirling result that the dust later becomes Edenic matter, suitable for the creation of children:

>                          the individual motes
> All with a shape apiece      wool fragments
>
> Small segments
> Of rope tricks   spirochetes boring into the very
> Body of light . . .
>
> I have closed my eyes and changed them into forms
> Of fire . . .
>
> That danced about the raising of our hands
> Unable to get in—
> to a human form at this time
>
> But ready
> For children we might raise and call our own   (P, 228–29)

The biblical analogue that underlies "Dust" easily leads us to see the prophetic role of breath and air in this poetry, the animating and rejuvenating power of the breath of the Holy Spirit (or poet!) to infuse dead matter with the life-giving principle of creation. Although Dickey postulates no intellectual design behind nature, he could not be closer to Wordsworth than in his view of the function of his correspondent breath, a principle that in the first book of "The Prelude" gives "to forms and images a breath / And everlasting motion."[13]

We find preoccupation with "exact" surfaces and with animal instinct similar to Dickey's in the neoromantic Ranier Maria Rilke's wonderful spring poem, "From an April":

> Again the forest is fragrant.
> The soaring larks lift up
> aloft with them the sky that to our shoulders was heavy;
> one still saw the day through the branches, indeed, that it was empty—
> but after long, raining afternoons
>    come the gold-besunned
>       newer hours,
> before which fleeing on far housefronts
>       all the wounded
> windows fearfully beat with wings.
>
> Then it grows still. Even the rain goes softer
> over the quietly darkening glint of the stones.
> All sounds duck entirely away
> in the glistening buds of the brushwood.

Like Dickey, Rilke penetrates the surfaces of nature in a gently empathic manner by using animals as vehicles of transport to a realm unseen yet powerfully felt. Rilke's larks "lift up" the sky "that to our shoulders was heavy," after which "come the gold-besunned / newer hours" which drive away "wounded / windows" as if they were insects. Unlike Dickey, Rilke takes us to a world where motion and sound cease entirely. For, after "the rain goes softer" all sounds disappear "in the glistening buds of the brushwood." Rilke's empathic method takes us through several senses to a state where we see not only that the sky is empty but where sensation itself is emptied of content.[14] Dickey, of course, is less radical. He penetrates appearance only to return to his underlying principle of motion which carries him back perpetually in its own great circle to the surface of things then down through nature once more.

13. "The Prelude," in *The Poetical Works of Wordsworth*, 129.
14. "From an April," in *Translations from the Poetry of Ranier Maria Rilke*, trans. M. D. Herter Norton (New York, 1938), 41.

Like Rilke and Dickey, Whitman is also a poet of surfaces. In this passage from "Song of Myself," his empathic movement resembles Dickey's in scope, delicacy, and the assumption of music as his vehicle of communion:

> The smoke of my own breath;
> Echoes, ripples, buzz'd whispers, love-root, silk thread,
>     crotch and vine;
> My respiration and inspiration, the beating of my heart,
>     the passing of blood and air through my lungs;
> The sniff of green leaves and dry leaves, and of the shore,
>     and dark color'd sea-rocks, and of hay in the barn . . .
> The play of shine and shade on the trees as the supple
>     boughs wag;
> The delight alone, or in the rush of the streets, or along
>     the fields and hill-sides;
> The feeling of health, the full-noon trill, the song of me
>     rising from bed and meeting the sun.

Like Dickey, Whitman seldom journeys to darker worlds. Even in "The World Below the Brine," he focuses on natural surfaces where light plays and where we find the external movements of sea-life whether they be "sluggish existences . . . close to the bottom" or the "sperm-whale at the surface."[15] If Dickey is to be criticized for failure to court the darker emotions below the "shine and shade" of nature, then so must Whitman. It is more interesting, I think, to note that both poets prefer to move in a more expansive, outgoing, optimistic direction instead of dwelling in the sloughs of depression where neither light nor air can meet the sun.

ANIMALS AND SURFACES

Like many romantics, Rilke retains his human voice during the empathic process as does Dickey even when he momentarily adopts the persona of a rabid dog in "Madness" or that of the man-bird in "Reincarnation II." D. H. Lawrence, another neoromantic empathizer concerned with animals and surfaces, is much closer to Dickey in terms of the vital energy he acquires from the primal force of animals. And

15. Whitman, *Leaves of Grass*, 29–30, 260.

like Dickey, Lawrence chooses to speak briefly for his animal in
"He-Goat":

> Sometimes he turns with a start, to fight, to challenge, to
>     suddenly butt.
> And then you see the God that he is, in a cloud of black hair
> And storm-lightning-slitting eye
> Splendidly planting his feet, one rocky foot striking the
>     ground with a sudden rock-hammer announcement.
>
> I AM HERE![16]

Even though Lawrence's extensive detail is designed to gain entrance to the goat's world, this poet is further removed than Dickey
from his subject. Lawrence's poems are always meditations with the
central focus on the human act of perception that keeps us safely at a
distance from unbridled instinct. Dickey, on the other hand, uses his
principle of motion to probe deeper than Lawrence. If degree of empathic entrance is a sign of poetic success, then Dickey is more romantic than Lawrence. In fact, Dickey constantly makes us feel that
we have gone deeper into things than the representational surfaces of
his poems warrant. The effects produced by this movement, coupled
with a voice that offers minimal resistance to such entrance, entail
something the poet values greatly: "What I want more than anything
else is to have a feeling of wholeness . . . a sense of intimacy with the
natural process" (SI, 68).

By repressing the human voice and by focusing on natural detail,
Dickey's poetry of natural motion strongly resembles that of Roethke,
whose "non-mental" mode of "meditation" emerges in this catalog of
animal activity:

As when silt drifts and sifts down through muddy pond-water,
Settling in small beads around weeds and sunken branches,
And one crab, tentative, hunches himself before moving along the bottom . . .
Or a salmon, tired, moving up a shallow stream,
Nudges into a back-eddy, a sandy inlet,
Bumping against sticks and bottom-stones, then swinging
Around, back into the tiny maincurrent, the rush of brownish-white
    water,

16. "He-Goat," in *The Complete Poetical Works of D. H. Lawrence*, ed. Vivian de
Sola Pinto and Warren Roberts (New York, 1967), 381.

Still swimming forward—
So, I suppose, the spirit journeys.

Roethke's analogy of the journey of the spirit (or consciousness) to the movements of small creatures in nature is clear-cut. An imagistic specification of the poet's principle that the movement of all journeys is "forward, after a few wavers" and is a "journey within a journey," this section of the Old Woman's meditation wavers empathically forward on natural surfaces "through muddy pond-water" and "a few bubbles" until it swings with a salmon through an energizing "rush of brownish-white water," thus making journeys within journeys as the woman herself travels upstream in search of another life.[17] Although we are always aware that it is Roethke talking, his natural imagery is so entrancing and his use of the word *I* so restrained that when he proclaims his presence we are surprised to find a human voice in this vegetal welter of spiritual change. Dickey greatly admires this aspect of Roethke's poetry. He states:

> There is some mindless, elemental quality in the sound of his voice, something primitive and animistic, something with the wariness and inhuman grace of the wild beast, and with it another thing that could not be and never has been animal-like. His poems are human poems in the full weight of that adjective: poems of a creature animal enough to enter *half* into unthinking nature and unanimal enough to be uneasy there, taking thought at what the animal half discerns and feels. This position, which at times seems triumphantly an extraordinary kind of wholeness impossible to animals and possible to men only on rare occasions, is the quality that Roethke has caught in his best poems. (*BB*, 150)

At times Dickey's voice seems so "unthinking" that his empathic stance also resembles that of "a creature animal enough to enter *half* into unthinking nature." Unlike Roethke, however, Dickey is quite comfortable in this kind of relation. Instead of Roethke's tensions and explosions, Dickey's vocal rhythms flow as smoothly and gently as the subjects he explores. Howard Nemerov sees this fluid romantic instinctualness plus the mystical strain clearly in Dickey's work: "The intention seems often enough this, a feeling one's way down the chain of being, a becoming the voice which shall make dumb things re-

17. Theodore Roethke, *The Collected Poems of Theodore Roethke* (Garden City, N.Y., 1966), 159, 158.

spond, sometimes to their hurt or death; a sensing of alien modes of experience, mostly in darkness or in an unfamiliar light; reason accepting its animality; a poetry whose transcendences come of its reconciliations. Salvation is this: apprehending the continuousness of forms, the flowing of one energy through everything." [18]

Of all Dickey's animal poems, "The Dusk of Horses" best illustrates his power to enter comfortably into "unthinking nature" through a graceful, hypnotic process, half-human and half-beast, which glides over the surfaces of a natural terrain:

> Right under their noses, the green
> Of the field is paling away
> Because of something fallen from the sky.
>
> They see this, and put down
> Their long heads deeper in grass
> That only just escapes reflecting them
>
> As the dream of a millpond would.
> The color green flees over the grass
> Like an insect, following the red sun over
>
> The next hill. The grass is white.
> There is no cloud so dark and white at once;
> There is no pool at dawn that deepens
>
> Their faces and thirsts as this does.
> Now they are feeding on solid
> Cloud, and, one by one,
>
> With nails as silent as stars among the wood
> Hewed down years ago and now rotten,
> The stalls are put up around them.
>
> Now if they lean, they come
> On wood on any side. Not touching it they sleep.
> No beast ever lived who understood
>
> What happened among the sun's fields,
> Or cared why the color of grass
> Fled over the hill while he stumbled,
>
> Led by the halter to sleep
> On his four taxed, worthy legs.
> Each thinks he awakens where

---

18. Howard Nemerov, "Poems of Darkness and a Specialized Light," *Sewanee Review*, LXXI (1963), 102.

> The sun is black on the rooftop,
> That the green is dancing in the next pasture,
> And that the way to sleep
>
> In a cloud, or in a risen lake,
> Is to walk as though he were still
> In the drained field standing, head down,
>
> To pretend to sleep when led,
> And thus to go under the ancient white
> Of the meadow, as green goes
>
> And whiteness comes up through his face
> Holding stars and rotten rafters,
> Quiet, fragrant, and relieved.   (*P*, 113–14)

The poet's reflection, the perceptions of animals, and the movements of nature become one in this lyric. The poem's structure is nothing less than the structure of how dusk is experienced by horses. Because they possess no reflexive or analytic capacity, the horses' dusk is a spontaneous flow of discrete percepts marked by the disengagement of attribute from substance. That is, for humans who perceive causal relations, dusk occurs when the sun sets. For the horses in Dickey's bestial epistemology, "green flees . . . like an insect" because "of something fallen from the sky." When the color green leaves the field, the grass turns white and magically becomes cloud as color determines the identity of objects, a process which seems to be yet one more variation of Dickey's mystical method of exchanging the qualities of objects by making the essence of a material thing merely one moment in a shared continuum of motion. When the horses sleep, they do not dream but enter the "stalls" of habitual instinct which they have followed for years. When they waken, they perceive not that the sun has risen but that the sun *is* the black color of the rooftop and that "green is dancing in the next pasture." In this mystical mix where substance gives way to the silent flow of color, the sustaining whiteness of the meadow permeates all things in a wonderful, purifying, refreshing way, analogous to the healthful effects of human sleep. As "dusk" settles, one horse thus goes instinctually to sleep in a realm where color unites and rejuvenates all things:

> . . . under the ancient white
> Of the meadow, as green goes

And whiteness comes up through his face
Holding stars and rotten rafters
Quiet, fragrant, and relieved.

## MODES OF RENEWAL

The redemptive freshness at the end of "The Dusk of Horses" brings us to a different set of traits in Dickey's romanticism, traits that center not only on animals but humans as well. Borrowing heavily from M. H. Abrams' brilliant history of romantic commonplaces in *Natural Supernaturalism*, I would like to take three prominent nineteenth-century poetic topics from his chapter entitled "The Poet's Vision: The New Earth and The Old." To discuss "three modes of renovative perception" in the romantic vision, Abrams chooses "freshness of sensation, 'moments' of illumination, and visual transvaluations" in his demonstration of ways the romantics generated perception of a new world, a world in which the "imaginative eye" triumphed over the sheerly optical. I have already noted that the circular nature of Dickey's informing principle of the Absolute of Motion bears striking similarity in its structure and effects to what Abrams calls the "circuitous journey" in romantic poetry. Abrams' three topics will help us to specify in greater detail major experiential effects resulting from Dickey's circular forms and will also assist us in seeing more clearly to what extent he belongs squarely in the romantic tradition of redemptive vision.

Taking the phrase "freshness of sensation" from *Biographia Literaria*, Abrams cites Coleridge's impression when he first heard Wordsworth read his poetry aloud, an impression which nicely fits our placement of Dickey in a context both classical and romantic:

To find no contradiction in the union of old and new; to contemplate the ANCIENT of days and all his works with feeling as fresh, as if all had then sprang forth at the first creative fiat; characterizes the mind that feels the riddle of the world, and may help to unravel it. To carry on the feelings of childhood into the powers of manhood; to combine the child's sense of wonder and novelty with the appearances, which every day for perhaps forty years had rendered familiar . . . this is the character and privilege of genius. . . . And therefore it is the prime merit of genius . . . so to represent familiar objects as to awaken in the minds of others . . . that freshness of sensation which is the constant accompaniment of mental, no less than of bodily, convalescence.

Although Coleridge's reference to "the feelings of childhood" has relevance for us when Dickey transports his readers to a childlike realm of fantasy, what is most important here is the claim that the poet can "represent familiar objects" in a surprising and miraculous way, a way that preoccupied Wordsworth in "The Prelude": "And the world's native produce, as it meets / The sense with less habitual stretch of mind, / Is ponder'd as a miracle."[19]

Freshness of sensation permeates Dickey's world usually by one of two means we have already examined: the animating exchange of properties between objects or the transformation of material things into moments of pure motion. "In the Marble Quarry" is a poem in which "a great pulley" transforms not only the weight of a ten-ton block of marble but also the spiritual heaviness of the speaker as he rises:

> To be waked in North Georgia by the ponderous play
>   Of men with ten-ton blocks
>
>   But no more surprised than I
> To feel sadness fall off as though I myself
>   Were rising from stone
>
>   Held by a thread in midair,
> Badly cut, local-looking, and totally uninspired,
>   Not a masterwork
>
>   Or even worth seeing at all
> But the spirit of this place just the same,
>   Felt here as joy.   (P, 148)

In "Winter Trout" the poet hunts trout with a bow and an arrow "whose head is half-missing." With his useless weapon, he gains some degree of access to worlds usually "closed" to man as he walks

>         . . . upon banks
>
> Shaken with the watchfulness of trout
> Like walking barefoot in sleep

19. Samuel Taylor Coleridge and William Wordsworth, both cited by Abrams in *Natural Supernaturalism*, 379.

> On the swaying tips of a grain field,
> On the long, just-bending stems,
>
> Almost weightless

After he shoots and misses, the speaker freezes his hand trying to re-
trieve the arrow. He then reflects on his experience and arrives at a
new view of nature in the concluding lines:

> I froze my right hand to retrieve it
> As a blessing or warning,
> For breaking into closed worlds . . .
>
>        with the wood upside down
> Balanced perfectly in all its leaves
> And roots . . .
>
> The surface full of gold flakes
> Of the raw undersides of leaves,
> And the thing seen right,
> For once, that winter bought.   (*P*, 128–29)

Once again Dickey has moved from a realistic setting through a
mysterious realm and then back to the real world, which he sees more
accurately than before. Although penalized with a frozen hand for re-
trieving his arrow, the poet momentarily gains access to the "pure
void of shadowy purpose / Where the gods live, attuning the world [of
nature] . . . for the first green [spring] / They ever have lived." When
the speaker imaginatively rises "Into spring" with one of these gods,
he discovers a sight both true and beautiful in the "surface full of gold
flakes / Of the raw undersides of leaves." Without undertaking his
empathic journey from the shifting river bank to the "closed worlds"
of "shadowy purpose," Dickey would never have arrived at "The thing
seen right," his new mode of understanding the incipient movements
of spring which are instinctually felt by the trout under the ice of
winter and which eventuate in a vision of light and harmonious nature in "The wood upside down / Balanced perfectly in all its leaves."

Dickey's methods of effecting freshness of sensation in his exchanges can transform an entire landscape as is the case in "Fox Blood,"
in which an envisioned fox hunt is emblazoned on a blood blister on
the poet's thumb. In an action-filled allegory of animal motion, the
poet's sensations are animated by the fox's running to such an extent

that a bush becomes a "Superhuman door," giving the speaker access to a realm of experience magically alive with animal instinct which he wishes to preserve and retain:

> Blood blister over my thumb-moon
> Rising, under clear still plastic
> Still rising strongly, on the rise
> Of unleashed dog-sounds: sound broke,
> Log opened. Moon rose
>
> Clear bright. Dark homeland
> Peeled backward, scrambling its vines.
> Stream showed, scent paled
> In the spray of mountain-cold water.
> The smell dogs followed
>
> In the bush-thorns hung like a scarf,
> The silver sharp creek
> Cut; off yonder, fox feet
> Went printing into the dark: *there,*
> *In the other wood,*
>
> *The uncornered animal's, running*
> *Is half floating off*
> *Upon instinct. Sails spread, fox wings*
> *Lift him alive over gullies,*
> *Hair tips all over him lightly*
>
> *Touched with the moon's red silver,*
> *Back-hearing around*
> *The stream of his body the tongue of hounds*
> *Feather him. In his own animal sun*
> *Made of human moonlight,*
>
> *He flies like a bolt running home,*
> *Whose passage kills the current in the river,*
> *Whose track through the cornfield shakes*
> *The symmetry from the rows.*
> *Once shot, he dives through a bush*
>
> *And disappears into air.*
> That is the bush my hand
> Went deeply through as I followed.
> Like a wild hammer blazed my right thumb
> In the flashlight and moonlight
>
> And dried to one drop
> Of fox blood I nail-polished in,

That lopsided animal sun
Over the nearly buried
Or rising human half-moon,

My glassed skin halfmooning wrongly.
Between them, the logging road, the stopped
Stream, the disappearance into
The one bush's common, foreseen
Superhuman door:

All this where I nailed it,
With my wife's nailbrush, on my finger,
To keep, not under, but over
My thumb, a hammering day-and-night sign
Of that country.   (*P*, 212–13)

By nail-polishing "one drop / Of fox blood" to his thumb, the poet
converts the sensation of a simple blood blister into a miraculous mi-
crocosm of movement that not only helps the poet to recall the pain
he experienced when he first put his hand into the magical bush but,
more importantly, recaptures the entire welter of exciting sensations
from the hunt itself. As in so many of Dickey's poems, the method
here is to employ a common domestic incident, this time involving
nothing less than nail polish, which gives way to some extraordinary
revitalization of an entire world seldom associated with the initiating
event. Once more Dickey has steeped himself in the romantic tradition of rejuvenating ordinary sensation by energizing the middle section of his narrative with gerundives and metaphors of motion that
jolt all things human when the fox's "track through the cornfield
shakes / The symmetry from the rows." Peace and excitation thus
lead to that natural feeling "of wholeness impossible to animals and
possible to men only on rare occasions" (*BB*, 150) that Dickey so admires in Roethke.

The mystical moments of wholeness in "Fox Blood" give rise to another prominent poetic method which Dickey shares with his romantic predecessors, namely, the presentation of a moment of consciousness whose significance blossoms into a larger feeling of intersection
with timelessness. In "Tintern Abbey," for example, "gleams of half-
extinguished thought" give way to awareness of a relation to nature
more intimate and less sensational than the "aching joys" of youth.
Here are Wordsworth's famous lines, prominent among which are our
terms *nature* and *motion:*

> . . . For I have learned
> To look on nature, not as in the hour
> Of thoughtless youth, but hearing oftentimes
> The still, sad music of humanity.
> Not harsh nor grating, though of ample power
> To chasten and subdue. And I have felt
> A presence that disturbs me with the joy
> Of elevated thoughts, a sense sublime
> Of something far more deeply interfused.
> Whose dwelling is the light of setting suns.
> And the round ocean and the living air.
> And the blue sky, and in the mind of man:
> A motion and a spirit that impels
> All thinking things, all objects of all thought.
> And rolls through all things.[20]

Unlike Wordsworth, instead of providing a relief from rapturous sensation, Dickey's moments of revelation propel the speaker through intense emotion to some flash of awareness of what that moment means. Whereas Wordsworth's reflexive meditations put sensation at a distance, Dickey gains knowledge only by means of "the fretful stir" and "fever of the world," without which past experience would be unidentifiable and recollection could never be ignited. Instead of an intellectual or ideal order lying behind the facade of nature, Dickey's Absolute of Motion transports his speaker to an epiphany that is not so much a reflection but an incandescent explosion of consciousness that a past event intersects with some larger pattern of human experience. In "Root-light, or the Lawyer's Daughter," for example, the poet joyously embraces the intensified confluence of a girl's naked dive, a river, and reflexive flashes of poetic perception as he approximates both the feeling and awareness of a past moment of sexual revelation:

> That any just to long for
> The rest of my life, would come, diving like a lifetime
> Explosion in the juices
> Of palmettoes flowing
> Red in the St. Mary's River as it sets in the east
> Georgia from Florida off, makes whatever child
> I was lie still, dividing

20. "Tintern Abbey," in *The Poetical Works of Wordsworth*, 92.

Swampy states    watching
The lawyer's daughter shocked
With silver    and I wished for all holds
On her like root-light. She came flying
Down from Eugene Talmadge
Bridge, just to long for as I burst with never
Rising never
Having seen her except where she worked
For J. C. Penney in Folkston. Her regular hours
Took fire, and God's burning bush of the morning
Sermon was put on her; I had never seen it where
It has to be. If you asked me how to find the Image
Of Woman to last
All your life, I'd say go lie
Down underwater for nothing
Under a bridge and hold Georgia
And Florida from getting at each other    hold
Like walls of wine. Be eight years old from Folkston ten
From Kingsland twelve miles in the clean palmetto color
Just as it blasts
Down with a body    red and silver buck
Naked with bubbles on Sunday    root
light explodes
Head-down, and there she is.    (*TCM*, 99)

Although there is a gentle side to Dickey's revelations, his moments are less like Wordsworth's than Blake's, or more like an emotional combination of the two writers' visions. Although surrounded by the "jocund din" of nature, Wordsworth's moments of discovery seem subdued and solemn. When a boy, he called to "silent owls" who responded "with quivering peals, / and long halloos and screams," after which the moment of consciousness came over him in silence, a "silence" in which "while he hung / Listening, a gentle shock of mild surprise / Has carried into his heart the voice / Of mountain torrents." On the other hand, Blake's visionary moments give rise to a more energetic revelation that leads to a total transformation of the world around him. One recalls this famous passage from *The Marriage of Heaven and Hell*, which comes closer to Dickey's explosive method: "By degrees we beheld the infinite Abyss, fiery as the smoke of a burning city; beneath us, at an immense distance, was the sun, black but shining; round it were fiery tracks on which revolv'd vast spiders, crawling after their prey, which flew, or rather swum, in the infinite deep, in the most terrific . . . shapes of animals sprung from corruption."[21]

In "Approaching Prayer," after Dickey goes to his dead father's attic and puts on the head of a boar killed by the father, his affections no longer "gently lead" him and he begins to pray very much like Blake:

> I don't know quite what has happened
> Or that anything has,
>
> Hoping only . . .
>    that . . .
> I can say with any
> Other than the desert fathers . . .
>
> PROPHECIES, FIRE IN THE SINFUL TOWERS,
> WASTE AND FRUITION IN THE LAND,
> CORN, LOCUSTS AND ASHES,
> THE LION'S SKULL PULSING WITH HONEY,
> THE BLOOD OF THE FIRST-BORN,
> A GIRL MADE PREGNANT WITH A GLANCE
> LIKE AN EXPLODING STAR
> AND A CHILD BORN OF UTTER LIGHT—    (P, 168)

As we have seen in "Fox Blood," "The Owl King," and "In the Tree House at Night," miraculous conversion is everywhere in Dickey's poetry. At times, simple things undergo transvaluation. In his lovely war poem "The Wedding," silver rings made by soldiers for their wives and gold tiger's head patches sewn on soldiers' jackets are transformed from minor emblems into signs of heroism for American GI's in World War II. Not only does Dickey change objects, his activity itself undergoes conversion in "Walking on Water" when an optical illusion is responsible for a report that the poet was walking on water, though, in fact, he was gliding on a narrow plank on top of the water like "A curious pilgrim hiking / Between two open blue worlds" (P, 39). In "Fog Envelops the Animals," Dickey's conversion of scene and act is more extensive as he hunts in a dreamy fog that embraces both hunter and hunted, making them consubstantial, mysterious, even otherworldly:

21: "The Prelude," *ibid.*, 156; Keynes (ed.), *The Complete Writings of William Blake*, 156.

> I stand with all beasts in a cloud . . .
>
> And I drift forward
> Through the hearts of the curdling oak trees,
> Borne by the river of Heaven . . .
>
> Above my head, the trees exchange their arms
> In the purest fear upon earth.
> Silence. Whiteness. Hunting.   (P, 62–63)

As in "The Dusk of Horses," the poem "Fog Envelops the Animals" begins in a realistic setting and ends in a transformed world where a single attribute pervades agents, scene, and action, binding all elements in a fantastic communion so complete that it may be said to constitute Dickey's version of a scenic apocalypse. He thus transcends difference and fragmentation by making the focus of a poem some unifying property, purpose, or event that somehow warrants the forfeiture of natural probabilities in favor of fantastic laws which miraculously and emotionally seem plausible.

Although Dickey constantly makes his own heavens of animals out of real beasts, he sometimes uses fantastic creatures to create a new world where gentleness transmutes all. In a charming fantasy entitled "Chenille," the poet contrasts two orders of animals, one belonging to machine-made chenille bedspreads, the other the product of the half-demented imagination of an old woman who has invented the beasts on her spreads with a darning needle. Halfway through the night, the natural world is left behind:

> Someone up there kept throwing
>         Bedspreads upon me.
> Softly I called, and they came:
> The ox and the basilisk,
>
> The griffin, the phoenix, the lion . . .
>
> The snake from the apple tree came
>         To save me from freezing . . .
> I lay, breathing like thread,
> An inspired outline of myself,
> As rain began greatly to fall,
> And closed the door of the Ark.   (P, 119–21)

Dickey's fantastic world of warmth and comfort is couched in detail as romantic and exotic as that of Keats in "Endymion":

> Over wide streams and mountains great we went,
> And, save when Bacchus kept his ivy tent,
> Onward the tiger and the leopard pants,
>         With Asian elephants:
> Onward these myriads—with song and dance,
> With zebras striped, and sleek Arabians' prance,
> Web-footed alligators, crocodiles [22]

Dreams and trances predominate in Dickey's poems; like Keats, Dickey constantly uses the dream-as-journey to identify himself with what he loves, whether the object be a chenille unicorn, seabird, or nature itself. Dickey so thoroughly integrates the waking dream with the real world that we may say of him what Northrup Frye claims, when reading "Endymion," about the romantic poet who "does not awaken *from* his dream into a different world: he awakens the dream *into* his world, and releases it from its subjective prison." [23]

## RENEWAL AND THE MACABRE

At times, Dickey's encounters with nature lead not only to love but also to death, or, to put it more accurately, to a more intense experience in life by combining an empathic affection for nature with death. Frye calls this romantic combination of Thanatos and Eros "the Romantic Macabre." Historically embodied in the figure of the demon-lover, this combination results in the view of the "grotesque as exuberant," hinted at by Shelley's "hectic red" wild west wind, which is "Preserver and Destroyer," by Blake's union of heaven and hell, and of course by the "Spectre-Woman" in "The Rime of the Ancient Mariner":

> *Her* lips were red, *her* looks were free,
> Her locks were yellow as gold:
> Her skin was as white as leprosy,
> The Nightmare LIFE-IN-DEATH was she,
> Who thicks man's blood with cold. [24]

In "For the Last Wolverine," Dickey uses an imagined creature for a realistic end, not to effect a gentle harmony of affection but to infuse

---

22. "Endymion," in *The Works of Keats*, ed. Forman, VIII, 198.
23. Northrop Frye, *A Study of English Romanticism* (New York, 1968), 143.
24. *Ibid.*, 52, 62; Ernest Hartley Coleridge (ed.), *The Complete Poetical Works of Samuel Taylor Coleridge* (London, 1912), 194.

poetry with a dangerous energy derived from nature. By addressing the "God of the wildness of poetry" and asking it to combine the world's last wolverine and the world's last eagle, Dickey "prays" as aggressively as Blake by demanding "something gigantic" that will be "beyond reason" and will consume "the timid poem" with rage and the "glutton's internal fire" (*P*, 277). In "Madness," a family dog is bitten by a rabid fox, becomes mad, bites a child, and has to be hunted down like a wild animal. Using the dog as the victim of a ritual hunt, Dickey explodes a tranquil domestic setting into a bizarre tumult of blood and violence. Nature is here transformed by a frenzied pursuit that changes the pastoral Virginia countryside into an arena of death and madness:

> Men    horses    spirits
> Of households leaping crazily beyond
> Their limits, dragging their bodies by the foaming throat through grass
> And beggar-lice and by the red dust
> Road where men blazed and roared
> With their shoulders    blew it down and apart where it ran
> And lay down on the earth of God's
> One foot and the foot beneath the table kicked
> The white mouth shut: this was something
>
> In Spring in mild brown eyes    as strangers
> Cut off the head and carried and held it
> Up, blazing with consequence    blazing
> With freedom saying    bringing
> Help    help    madness    help.    (*TCM*, 45–46)

When violent movement pervades nature, Dickey is never psychically threatened like Roethke, who probes more deeply to "hear underground, that sucking and sobbing" of the roots of plant cuttings. Because Dickey remains on his glittering surfaces, he does not feel, like Roethke, nature's subterranean "urge" and "wrestle" deep down in "my veins, in my bones." In Dickey's tree house poem, his "green graceful bones fill the air / With sleeping birds" (*P*, 67), but his direction is always expansive and outward, away from any realm that may entrap or suffocate. Danger is certainly imminent in both poets. In Roethke's famous greenhouse poems, plant shoots ominously hang "down long yellow evil necks, like tropical snakes," and even delicate orchids are "Adder-mouthed" and seem poised to strike. Comparing

Dickey with Roethke, Monroe Spears distinguishes the bestial and expansive impulses in Dickey: "When the basic Dionysian preoccupations (the sense of the more than human and the non-human; metamorphosis and transfiguration) operate in proper balance with the Apollonian elements ['openness and accessibility'] we have been describing, the results can be 'the elevated imagining of the spiritual meaning of such unions of the two natures in myths like those of the centaur or of Leda and the swan.'"[25] When Dickey's agents are threatened by nature, we feel less a primal anxiety than a hypnotic deliverance via either frenzied victimage or melodic transport. The latter marks Dickey's Edenic method in "The Poisoned Man":

> When the rattlesnake bit, I lay
> In a dream of the country, and dreamed
> Day after day of the river,
>
> Where I sat with a jackknife and quickly
> Opened my sole to the water.
> Blood shed for the sake of one's life
>
> Takes on the hid shape of the channel,
> Disappearing under logs and through boulders.
> The freezing river poured on
>
> And, as it took hold of my blood,
> Leapt up round the rocks and boiled over.
> I felt that my heart's blood could flow
>
> Unendingly out of the mountain,
> Splitting bedrock apart upon redness,
> And the current of life at my instep
>
> Give deathlessly as a spring.
> Some leaves fell from trees and whirled under.
> I saw my struck bloodstream assume,
>
> Inside the cold path of the river,
> The inmost routes of a serpent
> Through grass, through branches and leaves.
>
> When I rose, the live oaks were ashen
> And the wild grass was dead without flame.
> Through the blasted cornfield I hobbled,

25. Roethke, *The Collected Poems*, 38–39; Monroe Spears, *Dionysius and the City* (New York, 1970), 259, 257.

My foot tied up in my shirt,
And met my old wife in the garden,
Where she reached for a withering apple.

I lay in the country and dreamed
Of the substance and course of the river
While the different colors of fever

Like quilt patches flickered upon me.
At last I arose, with the poison
Gone out of the seam of the scar,

And brought my wife eastward and weeping,
Through the copper fields springing alive
With the promise of harvest for no one.   (P, 145–46)

After recovering from the rattlesnake bite, the speaker recalls the delirious use of his jackknife in a dreamy process of healing when his own blood took on not only the configurations of the river and surrounding countryside but the "inmost routes of a serpent" as well. When the speaker rises from his sickness, nature itself has become barren as if it were the real victim of the venom: "live oaks were ashen" and "the wild grass was dead." The speaker and his wife are inhabitants, like Adam and Eve after The Fall, of a devastated terrain. This time, Dickey's association with animals has given rise to a disorientation that simultaneously has therapeutic yet disastrous consequences.

The stream of disorientation, healing, and devastation that flows through "The Poisoned Man" brings us to another watershed in our search for Dickey's poetic principles. Although his empathic relation to a nature of perpetual motion still holds in this poem, there is something primitive and dangerous here that we seldom find in English and American nature poets or in lyric poetry at all. For, Dickey's speaker attains personal redemption by aligning himself with the threatening force that caused his crisis, a snake not unlike Blake's "all wonderous serpent clothed in gems and rich array."[26] Instead of running from the source of danger, Dickey courts it, and in so doing, renders all of nature improvident yet somehow still beneficial if not more powerful than before. Although the married couple is severed from their Eden

26. Keynes (ed.), *The Complete Writings of William Blake*, 746.

after the husband receives a withered apple from his wife, the poisoned man is born again in the conclusion as he moves through "copper fields springing alive," though "With the promise of harvest for no one."

Unlike Adam and Eve, there is little sense of loss, guilt, or shame attached to Dickey's agents. They have gained something instead of forfeiting it. In fact the poem presents a number of puzzling moments: the snake at first threatens then rejuvenates its victim by aligning him with the fluid movements of nature; nature, polluted with the snake's venom, is itself redemptively energized then transformed into a realm no longer "natural"; and, the man's disorientation is not disarming but uplifting, therapeutic, exhilarating, and intoxicating in a mood which floods the reconstituted, dreamlike universe of the poem.

We can begin to explain these puzzles by seeing how the world in "The Poisoned Man" strongly resembles the cosmology of the Christian Ophite sect of the third century, a sect that venerated the serpent, rather than cursing him, as the representative of Satan. Here is Saint Hippolytus' description of their belief: "Their cosmos consists of Father, Son, and Matter, each of which three principles contains infinitely many forces. Midway between the Father and Matter, the Son, the Logos, has his place, the Serpent that moves eternally toward the unmoved Father and moved Matter; now it turns to the Father and gathers up forces in its countenance; and now, after receiving the forces, it turns toward Matter, and upon Matter, which is without attribute and form, the Son imprints the ideas that had previously been imprinted upon the Son by the Father." This view is consistent with Dickey's own view of nature. As Joseph Campbell points out in *Creative Mythology*, "Wherever nature is revered as self-moving, and so inherently divine, the serpent is revered as symbolic of its divine life. And accordingly, in the Book of Genesis, where the serpent is cursed, all nature is devaluated and its power of life regarded as nothing in itself: nature is here self-moving indeed, self-willed, but only by virtue of the life given it by a superior being, its creator."[27] With no Supreme Being present in Dickey's world, and because he is so ingrained

27. St. Hippolytus, cited by Joseph Campbell in *Creative Mythology* (New York, 1968), 155, *ibid.*, 154.

in the principles of the Bible, we can easily see how his world view can resemble a primitive variant of a Christian mysticism. In many Gnostic sects, according to Campbell, the serpent reappears after the incident in the Garden of Eden to overturn Moses' moral laws and become a second redeemer. The sexual ecstasy in "May Day Sermon" seems to some degree consistent with this view when the father's Biblical fundamentalism of repression is overturned. And, curiously enough, in "The Owl King," the owl's natural world includes "The serpent taking the shape / Of the stream of life as it slept" and "the snake in the form of all life" (P, 71–72).

Redemption through disorientation, victimage, and the monstrous is, as Abrams points out in "The Disordering of the Senses" in *Natural Supernaturalism*, a modern extension of the old romantic topic of "freshness of sensation."[28] A host of modern writers have also courted perceptual and personal disorientation as a means of rejuvenating their visions and indeed of radically altering reality itself. Whether such disorder occurs in Arthur Rimbaud debauching himself to become a seer or Hart Crane claiming that "when wine redeems the sight," the poet may discover:

> New thresholds, new antinomies! Wine talons
> Build freedom up about me and distill
> This competence—to travel in a tear
> Sparkling alone, within another's will.[29]

We can see from many of Dickey's personal observations that he admires writers who have practiced this extreme method of poisonous redemption. In *Self-Interviews*, he says:

I have drifted into a hard-working hero worship of a few men in literature who represent for me the figure of the totally responsive human being. I think that the further we get into the mechanized world we have created, the more numbing the world is to the sensibilities of people. . . . This seems to be one of the reasons that sex and any kind of artificial stimulation, alcohol or drugs or anything else, are becoming more and more important, because we are able to feel less and less in our own selves. Only extremely strong stimuli can have any effect on us anymore. (*SI*, 74)

28. Abrams, *Natural Supernaturalism*, 412.
29. Waldo Frank (ed.), *The Collected Poems of Hart Crane* (New York, 1946), 89.

To some extent, Dickey believes, this impulse is caused by an over-refined sensibility in writers. It is a sensibility which is both "exhausting" and "exalting" in its capacity for empathic response. Of Keats, Dickey observes: "There is nothing, not even a fly in the room, that he didn't react to in some way. It's exhausting to participate in one's own existence to such a degree as he did. . . . But such is the writer's part . . . to live . . . in that kind of total responsiveness which is extremely painful but also exalting, and in its best, highest reaches gives one the feeling of omnipotence and infallibility, a great, great feeling" (*SI*, 75). And Dickey says that James Agee, who "for all he drank, and despite the shambles of his emotional life, did have this quality of complete participation, of commitment of the self to whatever it was he contemplated" (*SI*, 75).

To redeem us from the numbing world of mechanization, to approximate the feelings of complete participation in the experiences of the intensified man, and to realign modern man with nature, Dickey often resorts to the use of frenzy and the monstrous. The result is not only a feeling of increased intimacy with natural processes but the production of a new (or ancient) reality where conventional moral principles may not apply. Earlier, we saw signs of this "apocalyptic" disorientation in "Madness" and in "May Day Sermon" when the rural Baptist preacher is worked up into "a state of fanatical, Biblical, unbridled frenzy as though pure spirit, beyond good and evil . . . so that the women of Gilmer County" will "throw off the shackles of the Baptist religion and enter into an older world of springtime, pleasure, love, and delight" (*SI*, 184).

Dickey's preference for the attainment of natural holiness through sin and sensation is clearly indicated in interviews and his prose commentary. In conversation with Carolyn Kizer, he puts his principle of perpetual motion into high gear in his disdain for "poets of alienation who feel humiliated by everything and who are endlessly examining" their own motives: "Somebody . . . said that a man running at full speed has neither a brain nor a heart. I'm trying to get into the psychological state of the man running at full speed and see what he does have."[30] Defending Baudelaire's freedom to choose any available sub-

---

30. Dickey quoted in Calhoun (ed.), *James Dickey*, 14.

ject matter, he notes that "the monstrous has always been a part of poetry" (*SI*, 72). Dickey constantly rages against "timid" confessional poetry and calls for "savage delight" and "a poetry of murderous drives" (*S*, 97). He could be no clearer in his desire that a poet be "precise and reckless," in his desire for "fever" and "tranquillity" in verse, while decrying the fact that the "world, the human mind, is dying of subtlety, what it needs in force" (*S*, 85).

Renewal through fever, force, and the monstrous occurs in "Victory," when a drunken sailor on VJ Day in World War II has his entire body tattooed with the design of a snake—another variant of the serpent of the Christian Ophites—that the poet converts from the prince of darkness into a "new prince of peace" for all the living:

> O yes and now he lay low
>
> On my belly, and gathered together the rainbow
> Ships of Buckner Bay. I slumbered deep and he crossed the small
> Of my back   increased
> His patchwork hold on my hip   passed through the V between
> My legs, and came
> Around once more   all but the head   then I was turning   the snake
> Coiled round my right thigh and crossed
> Me with light hands   I felt myself opened
> Just enough, where the serpent staggered on his last
> Colors   needles gasping for air   jack-hammering
> My right haunch burned by the hundreds
> Of holes, as the snake shone on me complete   escaping
> Forever   surviving   crushing   going home
> To the bowels of the living,
> His master, and the new prince of peace.
> (*TCM*, 37)

Dickey's intoxicating imagery of serpentine deformity in "Victory" suggests yet also reverses this moment from "Night the Third" in Blake's "Vala, or the Four Zoas" when Ahania describes to Urizen her vision of what occurred to Luvah and Vala when they were cast down to the lower world:

> "And the vast form of Nature like a Serpent play'd before them;
> "And as they went, in folding fires & thunders of the deep,
> "Vala shrunk in like the dark sea that leaves its slimy banks,
> "And from her bosom Luvah fell far as the east & west

"And the vast form of Nature, like a Serpent, roll'd between.
*"Whether this is Jerusalem or Babylon we know not.*
*"All is Confusion. All is tumult, & we alone are escaped."*[31]

As a form of nature, Dickey's serpent does not roll between men and paradise but coils, crushes, and survives while transforming the sailor with a rainbow of scales until the serpent's power and his victim's are one. Yet the sailor is the serpent's master, for it is the man's body that animates and controls this satanic archetype. In his drunken disorientation, the sailor is able to turn the snake's motion into his own and into a symbol of peace.

Dickey's sense of the monstrous is put to extraordinary effect in "Slave Quarters" when his speaker dreams himself a pre–Civil War slave owner who sleeps with his slave women to rid himself of the sterile gentility of the old romantic South and to take on a primitive sexual vitality that has monstrous moral results:

> . . . let me throw
> Obsessive gentility off;
> Let Africa rise upon me like a man
> Whose instincts are delivered from their chains
> Where they lay close-packed and wide-eyed
> In muslin sheets
> As though in the miserly holding
> Of too many breaths by one ship . . .
>
>                                        What happens . . .
>
> When you learn that there is no hatred
> Like love in the eyes
> Of a wholly owned face? When you think of what
> It would be like   what it has been
> What it is to look once a day
> Into an only
> Son's brown, waiting, wholly possessed
> Amazing eyes, and not
> Acknowledge, but own?   (P, 236–39)

In "The Firebombing," a former bomber pilot who flew missions over Japan in World War II can feel, years later, no guilt for those he killed because his only recollection consists of the spectacular vision

31. Keynes (ed.), *The Complete Writings of William Blake*, 294.

of his bombs turning Japan into an earthly inferno. Dickey's message is clear, especially for our age of modern weaponry—namely, that technology places such distance between soldier and target that victims are never seen. Indeed, the visual aspect of carnage is beautiful. Man has now assumed the power of the gods, and his action carries no guilt with it. Instead, one witnesses a terrible, beautiful, literal apocalypse—an "aesthetic evil":

> Reflections of houses catch;
> Fire shuttles from pond to pond
> In every direction, till hundreds flash with one death.
> With this in the dark of the mind,
> Death will not be what it should . . .
> The death of children is ponds
> Shutter-flashing; responding mirrors; it climbs
> The terraces of hills
> Smaller and smaller, a mote of red dust
> At a hundred feet; at a hundred and one it goes out.
> That is what should have got in
> To my eye
> And shown the insides of houses, the low tables
> Catch fire from the floor mats,
> Blaze up in gas around their heads
> Like a dream of suddenly growing
> Too intense for war . . .
> O death in the middle
> Of acres of inch-deep water! (P, 185–86)

In "May Day Sermon," after the country girl is beaten by her Bible-reading father who has discovered she has a lover, she puts a hatchet in the father's head and an ice pick through his eye, and the entire countryside is converted into a vortex of unearthly energy, primitive and sacred, extending to humans and animals alike:

> Often a girl in the country,
> Mostly in spring   mostly bleeding   deep enough in the holy Bible
> Belt   will feel her arms rise up   up   and this not any wish
> Of hers   will stand, waiting for word . . .
> And she comes down   putting her back into
> The hatchet   often   often   he is brought down   laid out
> Lashing   smoking   sucking wind: Children, each year at this time
> A girl will tend to take an ice pick in both hands   a lone pine
> Needle . . .

> and it is easy for a needle to pass
> Through the eye of a man bound for Heaven   she leaves it   naked goes
> Without further sin through the house . . .
>         comes onto the porch on cloud-feet   steps down and out
> And around to the barn . . .
>         in May, often a girl in the country
> Will find herself lifting wood   her arms like hair rising up
> To undo locks   raise latches   set gates aside   turn all things
> Loose   shoo them out   shove   kick   and hogs are leaping ten
> Million years back through fog   cows walking worriedly   passing out
> Of the Ark   from stalls where God's voice cursed and mumbled
> At milking time   moving   moving   disappearing   drifting
> In cloud . . .   (P, 5–6)

Of the romantic poets, the one holding the view closest to Dickey's dark dreamy vision of nature sanctified by violence is Coleridge, especially in these famous lines from "Kubla Khan":

> But Oh! That deep romantic chasm which slanted
> Down the green hill athwart a cedarn cover!
> A savage place! as holy and enchanted
> As e'er beneath a waning moon was haunted
> By woman wailing for her demon lover!
> And from this chasm, with ceaseless turmoil seething,
> As if this earth in fast thick pants were breathing,
> A mighty fountain momently was forced:
> Amid whose swift half-intermitted burst
> Huge fragments vaulted like rebounding hail,
> Or chaffy grain beneath the thresher's flail:
> And 'mid these dancing rocks at once and ever
> It flung up momently the sacred river.
> Five miles meandering with a mazy motion
> Through wood and dale the sacred river ran,
> Then reached the caverns measureless to man,
> And 'mid this tumult Kubla heard from far
> Ancestral voices prophecying war! [32]

Savage, "holy and enchanted," Coleridge's animated nature is clearly sexual and threatening as it seethes, breathes in "fast thick pants," and explodes outward like Dickey's snake from "May Day Sermon." However, what makes Coleridge's chasm dangerous is the fountain's

32. Coleridge (ed.), Poetical Works of Coleridge, 297–98.

power, which issues such force that it produces a river whose electric current energizes the entire landscape. Unlike Dickey, Coleridge uses no explicit act of violence to charge his setting even though Kubla hears the prophecies of war; the poem's metaphors alone accomplish this. Dickey's characters suffer pain, violate social taboos, even die violently. Of course, these items occur spectacularly in "The Rime of the Ancient Mariner," a poetic paradigm of ritual violence that will be discussed later. Yet Dickey seems to be alone among romantic empathizers and nature poets in his use of victimage to refresh, transform, and restore nature to an Edenic state in which we can all find "holiness learned in the barn" and thus conclude with his Baptist preacher saying:

> Listen O daughters   turn   turn
> In your sleep   rise with your backs on fire   in spring   in your socks
> Into the arms of your lovers:   every last one of you, listen one-eyed
> With your man   in hiding   in fog where the animals walk through
> The white breast of the Lord   muttering   walk with nothing
> To do but be   in the spring laurel in the mist and self-sharpened
> Moon   walk through the resurrected creeks   through the Lord
> At their own pace   the cow shuts its mouth and the Bible is still
> Still open at anything   we are gone   the barn wanders over the earth.
> (*P*, 13)

Just as "The Owl King" led us from Dickey's Neoplatonism to his romanticism, so his poems of intoxication and the monstrous, especially "May Day Sermon," lead us from romanticism to a different set of terms. For, unlike the romantics, Dickey uses explicit violence to produce effects we seldom associate with poets of the graceful empathic imagination. Even though there is a gentle component in the world of "May Day Sermon," it is violence—by ice pick and axe—that reconstitutes both setting and agents in excessive, orgasmic, even barbaric ways. After she kills her father, the country girl acquires an Edenic condition, innocent and natural, as she "naked goes / Without further sin through the house" (*P*, 9). In this dynamic sacrificial vision, Dickey's harmonious methods of mystical transport and cosmic music give way to the intoxicating power of the preacher's incantation that seems not merely recitation of a narrative or even preaching. Instead, the woman preacher is a kind of ancient exorcist who casts out the demons of repression by invoking the demons of sexual instinct and blood sacrifice, which are as blind and unyielding in their compulsive powers of regeneration as are the seasons of nature. The biblical lord of the girl's father is swept away by the savage god of "blood consciousness," to use D. H. Lawrence's term, and woe be to anyone in spring who stands in the way of the sanctity of this primal force. With primitivism as our working hypothesis, let us now turn to that dark aspect of Dickey's imagination that, in the poet's own words, "is absolutely untouched by anything civilized" (SI, 69)

## 4. PRIMITIVISM, or motion, magic, and ritual:

Once every people in the world believed that trees were divine,
and could take a human or grotesque shape and dance among the
shadows; and that . . . almost all things under the sun and moon
. . . were not less divine and changeable. They saw in the rainbow the still bent bow of a god thrown down in his negligence
. . . and when a sudden flight of wild ducks, or of crows, passed
over their heads, they thought they were gazing at the dead
hastening to their rest; while they dreamed of so great a mystery
in little things that they believed the waving of a hand, or of a
sacred bough, enough to trouble far-off hearts, or hood the moon
with darkness.

—W. B. YEATS

The blood *hates* being KNOWN by the mind. It feels itself
destroyed when it is KNOWN.
  And on the other hand, the mind and the spiritual consciousness of man simply *hates* the dark potency of blood-acts: hates
the genuine dark sensual orgasms, which do, for the time being,
actually obliterate the mind and the spiritual consciousness,
plunge them in a flood of suffocating darkness. . . .
  Blood-consciousness overwhelms, obliterates, and annuls
mind-consciousness.
  Mind-consciousness extinguishes blood-consciousness, and
consumes the blood.
  We are all of us conscious in both ways. And the two ways are
antagonistic in us.

—D. H. LAWRENCE

There was, thank God, a great voluptuary born to the American
settlements against the niggardliness of the damming puritanical
tradition; one who by the single logic of his passion, which he
rested on the savage life about him, destroyed at its spring that
spiritually withering plague. For this he has remained since buried in a miscolored legend and left for rotten. Far from dead,
however, but full of a rich regenerative violence he remains,
when his history will be carefully reported, for us who have
come after to call upon him.

—WILLIAM CARLOS WILLIAMS

## MAGIC

If, as we have been arguing, miraculous and romantic exchange is
everywhere in Dickey's poetry, we should look even more closely at
what happens when objects and agents come into contact with one

another. Not everything in his world is initially propelled by his Absolute of Motion. At times, his speakers must search out this mystical force to satisfy specific human needs. Because universal redemptive motion emerges through particular items—deer, birds, rivers,
stars, sawgrass—mere contact enables Dickey's agents to acquire remarkable powers to effect ends ranging from the discovery of natural
resources to the postponement of middle age. For Dickey, however, it
is not contact alone but stylized contact by which he aligns himself
with cosmic movement and also acquires the particular qualities of
the mediating object. In "Springer Mountain," a comic poem of hunting and renewal, the poet strips off his clothes while on a hunting trip
and dashes through the woods in pursuit of an imaginary deer. By imitating a buck's movement, Dickey enters into a peculiar dance with
his prey that enables him to turn "younger / at forty than I ever
have been":

> The world catches fire.
> I put an unbearable light
> Into breath skinned alive of its garments . . .
>
> The green of excess is upon me . . .
> He is moving.   I am with him
>
> Down the shuddering hillside moving
> Through trees and around, inside
> And out of stumps and groves
> Of laurel and slash pine,
> Through hip-searing branches and thorn
> Brakes . . .
>
> My brain dazed and pointed with trying
> To grow horns . . .
> For a few steps deep in the dance
> Of what I most am and should be
> And can be only once in this life   (P, 131–32)

The relationship between men and animals in the act of hunting is
terribly important to Dickey: "The main thing is to re-enter the cycle
of the man who hunts for his food. . . . We come from an ancient lineage of people who hunted their food and depended on the meat, skins,
sinews, and gut of animals. . . . I have a great sense of renewal when I
am able to go into the woods and hunt with a bow and arrow, to enter

into the animals' world in this way" (*SI*, 111). The poet does not argue for the rejuvenating relation with his poetic deer. Rather, he proves the efficacy of his rite through its performance, a performance that in "Springer Mountain" bears analogy to anthropologist James George Frazer's account of the action of a Cambodian hunter who, after he has set his nets and taken nothing, removes his clothes, walks off, then returns to his net as if he didn't see it, permits himself to be caught and exclaims, "Hillo! What's this? I'm afraid I'm caught."[1] According to Frazer, the net is certain to be effective after this.

Not only does hunting enable Dickey to gain renewal by entering into a primitive relation with his prey, it also activates his romantic capacity for empathic union with the larger forms of nature:

> I go out on the side of a hill, maybe hunting deer, and sit there and see the shadow of night coming over the hill, and I can swear to you there is a part of me that has never heard of a telephone . . . there is a half-dreaming, half-animal part of me that is fundamentally primitive. I really believe this, and I try to get it into poems; I don't think this quality should die out of people. It's what gives us a *personal* relationship to the sun and the moon, the flow of rivers, the growth and decay of natural forms, and the cycles of death and rebirth. (*SI*, 69–70)

Repudiating T. S. Eliot's notion of the poem as "a kind of high-cult *objet d'art*," Dickey tries in an essay entitled "Spinning the Crystal Ball" to predict the direction of new poetry but ends speaking more of his own craft: "I think that the poetry of the future is going . . . back toward basic things and basic-sounding statements about them, in an effort, perhaps a desperate one, to get back wholeness of being, to respond fullheartedly and fullbodiedly to experience . . . if we are lucky in this search, and believe in it enough, we shall at least arrive at a condition of emotional primitivism, of undivided response, a condition where we can connect with whatever draws us" (*S*, 203). Walter Pater clearly found this emotional primitivism in Wordsworth; Dickey so values it that he cites Pater on this great romantic predecessor: "To him every natural object seemed to possess more or less of a moral or spiritual life. . . . An emanation, a particular spirit, belonged not to the moving leaves or water only, but to the distant peak arising sud-

1. Sir James George Frazer, *The Golden Bough* (New York, 1963), 21.

denly, by some change of perspective, above the nearer horizon of the hills, to the passing space of light across the plain, to the lichened Druidic stone even, for a certain weird fellowship in it with the moods of men" (S, 204). Because of Dickey's disinclination to focus on the discursive aspect of this "companionship," his methods are more radically primitive than Wordsworth's and can be seen as extensions of his own romantic topics of exchange. And, though the primal grounds of Dickey's cosmic dance are covert in "Springer Mountain," like the Cambodian hunter, his empathic performance is not without principle.

Dickey acquires his feelings of renewed energy and cosmic rapport by imitating beasts in a primitive process well known in anthropological literature, namely, homeopathic magic. Frazer distinguishes homeopathic from contagious magic. Based on "the law of similarity," homeopathic magic assumes that a magician "can produce any effect he desires merely by imitating it . . . That things which resemble each other are the same." The most common form of this magic is that which employs a model or image of the person or thing to be affected. Thus, "when an Ojebway Indian desires to work evil on anyone, he makes a little wooden image of his enemy and runs a needle into its head or heart." On the other hand, contagious magic is based on the assumption that whatever the magician "does to a material object will affect equally the person with whom the object was once in contact, whether it formed part of his body or not." Contagious magic presumes "that things which have once been in contact with each other are always in contact." In this sort of magic, a severed part of a beast, vegetable, or someone's body becomes the magical medium instead of an imitated image or copy. Thus the "parings of nails, hair, eyebrows, spittle, and so forth of your intended victim" must be incorporated in a contagious rite of revenge.[2]

These two magical principles in Dickey's poetry may also be viewed as specifications of his Absolute of Motion. Because all parts of his universe are so harmoniously attuned to one another, homeopathic and contagious contact seem everywhere. They are in fact intermediary kinds of movement located somewhere between his general principle and the array of common things through which Dickey's univer-

2. *Ibid.*, 12, 15, 12–13, 15.

sal cosmic pulse emanates. By imitating the deer's movements in
"Springer Mountain," for example, the poet homeopathically acquires
and then contagiously transfers his bestial energy to the entire scene
as the "world catches fire" and the "waters of life . . . melt . . . at the
touch of an animal visage." In "A Screened Porch in the Country,"
Dickey's musical movement gives way to a purely magical contact as
night creatures and a country family share a single source of light:

> All of them are sitting
> Inside a lamp of coarse wire
> And being in all directions
> Shed upon darkness,
> Their bodies softening to shadow, until
> They come to rest out in the yard
> In a kind of blurred golden country . . .
>
> The smallest creatures,
> As every night they do,
> Come to the edge of them
> And sing, if they can,
> Or, if they can't, simply shine
> Their eyes back, sitting haunches,
>
> Pulsating and thinking of music.

There is no cosmic music here. When "something weightless /
Touches the screen" of the human porch, "nothing happens" to the
family except that they magically and delicately share joyous animal
instincts which verge on song as the family continues

> To be laid down
> In the midst of its nightly creatures,
> Not one of which openly comes
>
> Into the golden shadow
> Where the people . . .
>                         become
> More than human, and enter the place
> Of small, blindly singing things,
> Seeming to rejoice
> Perpetually, without effort,
> Without knowing why
> Or how they do it.   (P, 96–97)

When reading this poem, one pictures the family hovering inside their porch like moths around some source of light while unseen crickets chirp in unison from out of the surrounding darkness. As the porch light softens to shadow, a zone of magical contiguity is established while the family not only resembles insects in this particular setting but now themselves "enter the place" of "nightly creatures." All moving things, human and otherwise, share a unifying "Heavenly light" that charges this graceful poem with a faint, mysterious glow. Whatever action is here is less mental than magical, less intellectual reflection than the contiguous infusion of the night with a "golden shadow" that is "More than human" in the sense that it is a realm both light and dark and both human and animal at once.

In "A Screened Porch in the Country," Dickey's magical principles are in their simplest and most elementary form. When used for more complex ends, they not only reveal how many of Dickey's romantic principles—especially his empathic transvaluations of agents, objects, and settings—are put into operation but also how his poetry produces emotional compensation for dramatic problems confronted by his speakers. In "The Eye-Beaters," for example, the poet visits a home for blind children in Indiana and listens to a therapist who explains that the children beat their eyes (and thus must have their arms bound with gauze to protect themselves) to try to acquire any sensation at all from their eyes. They know they are supposed to see but cannot, and thus settle for the slivers of light and pain that result when "their fists smash their eyeballs." Staggered by this explanation, Dickey tries to invent a poetic fiction of primitive magical therapy by imagining what kind of images the children acquire with their drastic measures and by using his power as magician-poet to build some sort of vision for them. He likens his images to primitive cave pictures and then imagines the children as hunters of these beasts until an entire primal world emerges, one in which a tribal priest *may* have curative power:

> Lord, when they slug
> Their blue cheeks blacker, can it be that they do not see the wings
> And green of insects   or the therapist suffering kindly   but a
> tribal light old

Enough to be seen without sight? There, quiet children stand
                                                    watching
A man striped and heavy with pigment, lift his hand with color
                                                    coming
From him. Bestial, working like God, he moves on stone he is
                                                    drawing
A half-cloud of beasts on the wall. They crane closer, helping,
                                                    beating
Harder, light blazing inward from their fists   and see   see leap
From the shocked head-nerves, great herds of deer on the hacked
                                                    glory plain
Of the cave wall: antelope   elk: blind children strike for the
                                                    middle
Of the brain, where the race is young. Stranger, they stand here
And fill your mind with beasts: ibex   quagga   rhinoceros of
                                                    wool-
gathering smoke: cave bear   aurochs   mammoth: beings that
                                                    appear

Only in the memory of caves   (*TCM*, 48)

Whereas in the real world the children beat their eyes for vision, in
Dickey's imagination they strike magically "for the middle / Of the
brain, where the race is young." By populating their dark realms with
a catalogue of beasts, the poet establishes the fantastic possibility of
"brain blood, as vision" (*TCM*, 51)—another Lawrentian analogue in
Dickey—that is, the possibility that the children may see by means of
their contagious contact with "stampeded bones" and "the color red /
For blood" that the poet converts into "beast-paint" and then into "a
picture on the [cave] wall" (*TCM*, 51). Even so, this magician-poet
knows his efforts are futile, knows in fact that this therapy is not for
the blind children but for himself:

> *O stranger, those beasts and mother-figures*
>                                               *are all*
> *Made up by you. They are your therapy. There is nothing inside*
>                                               *their dark,*
> *Nothing behind their eyes but the nerve that kills the sun above*
>                                               *the corn*
> *Field   no hunt no meat no pain-struck spark no vision   no pre-*
>                                               *history*

*For the blind    nothing but blackness forever    nothing but a new*
                                                                            *bruise*
*Risen upon the old.    (TCM, 50)*

At the end of the poem, the speaker fully realizes the limits of his
magic and leaves sadly "in perversity and the sheer / Despair of invention" (*TCM*, 52).

Doomed as it is to practical failure, Dickey's attempt at magical
healing in "The Eye-Beaters" brings us to two other major aspects of
his primitive universe of motion, namely, naturism and animism. Because Dickey so often imitates and makes contact with natural objects, it is easy to entertain the naturistic assumption that he believes
(or wishes) that the things of nature are somehow alive with spirits
and wills of their own. Like many romantics, Dickey personifies natural things; however, he pushes the process one step further in that external things give off peculiar powers independent of the speaker insofar as his landscapes dazzle with their own animating energy. In
"The Lode," the poet jams images together in a manner reminiscent
of Gerard Manley Hopkins until a complex of objects fuse and give off
a peculiar force independent of the speaker that floods his entire
consciousness:

>                rain, and its nailed smoke—
>           Cobbled, snailing surfaces,
>   Jammed drops at a dead-level stroke    gravity's slow
>           Secretional slashes on this house—
>           Lost laterals, rinses . . .
>
>           When all sucked-up sun-water is falling
>           Potently, modestly, like this . . .
>           I am in it in every position.    (*PU*, 42)

In many ways, the magical pulsations in Dickey's objects resemble
the energies emanating from the primal world of D. H. Lawrence:

>       But long ago, oh, long ago
>       Before the rose began to simper supreme,
>       Before the rose of all roses, rose of all the world, was even in bud,
>       Before the glaciers were gathered up in a bunch out of the
>           unsettled
>               seas and winds . . .

> There was another world, a dusky, flowerless, tendrilled world
> And creatures webbed and marshy,
> And on the margin, men soft-footed and pristine,
> Still, and sensitive, and active,
> Audile, tactile sensitiveness as of a tendril which orientates and
>     reaches out,
> Reaching out and grasping by an instinct more delicate than the
>     moon's as she feels for the tides

Like Dickey, Lawrence senses a magical internal force in natural things. From out of the "unfolded rose" emerges—if we can "cross the frontiers" of our sterile mechanized culture—a "lost, fern-scented world" filled with "creatures webbed and marshy." In his poem "Figs," he claims that the fig "is a very secretive fruit" that flowers "inward and womb-fibrilled" and that gives us access to a dark, mysterious, universal realm of procreation. Lawrence's universe is like that of the Etruscans', in which "all was alive" and every object "had its own peculiar consciousness": "To the Etruscan all was alive; the whole universe lived; and the business of man was himself to live amid it all. . . . The whole thing was alive, and had a great soul, or *anima:* and in spite of one great soul, there were myriad roving, lesser souls: every man, every creature and tree and lake and mountain and stream, was animate, had its own peculiar consciousness. And has it to-day."[3]

In the opening lines of "On the Coosawattee," Dickey and a companion travel by canoe through a Lawrentian landscape in which the things of nature are so alive that they touch and animate each other until the entire setting vibrates with magical warmth and light:

> Into the slain tons of needles,
> On something like time and dark knowledge
> That cannot be told, we are riding
> Over white stones forward through fir trees,
> To follow whatever the river
> Through the clasping of roots follows deeply . . .
>
> Heavy woods in one movement around us
> Flow back along either side . . .
> Small stones in their thousands turn corners

---

3. "The Rose," in *The Complete Poetical Works of D. H. Lawrence,* 285–86; "Figs," *ibid.,* 282; D. H. Lawrence, *Etruscan Places* (New York, 1963), 49.

> Under water and bear us on
> Through the glittering, surfacing wingbeats
> Cast from above . . .
>
> Each light comes into life . . .
>
> The stones beneath us grow rounder
> As I taste the fretted light fall
> Through living needles to be here
> Like a word I can feed on forever.

At first Dickey's fluid landscape invites us to entertain his principle of mystical motion as a descriptive hypothesis. A more precise explanation, however, is that while the poet follows the movement of the river, his Absolute of Motion manifests itself through physical things and gives them a magical power. Magic thus becomes once again a mediating principle between Dickey's cosmic motion and his speaker who, though he follows "whatever the river . . . follows deeply," does so "Through the clasping of roots." As he goes deeper into the forest, the speaker experiences the perpetual principle of motion in its particularized form in the "nerves in the patches of tree-light" which "shake like the wings of angels" and in "Heavy woods in one movement around / Flow back along either side." Motion is so contagious here that "Small stones in their thousands" come alive as if in a fairy tale as they "turn corners / Under water and bear us on" (*P*, 122–23).

When accelerated, Dickey's mixtures of animated objects galvanize an event, charging an entire setting with forces that interact in a dazzling plenitude of motion. Here is a spectacular moment from "Falling" in which the plunging stewardess gives and receives superhuman power from the magical forces surrounding her:

> . . . she slow-rolls over   steadies out   waits for something great
> To take control of her   trembles near feathers   planes head-down
> The quick movements of bird-necks turning her head   gold eyes
>        the insight-
> eyesight of owls blazing into the hencoops   a taste for chicken
>        overwhelming
> Her   the long-range vision of hawks enlarging all human lights
>        of cars
> Freight trains   looped bridges   enlarging the moon racing slowly

Through all the curves of a river     all the darks of the midwest blazing
From above   (*P*, 295–96)

Rather than producing effects issuing unilaterally from the empathic
powers of his speaker's imagination, Dickey's romantic exchanges
with animals are really the products of extensive series of magical
metaphors that blend a dramatized particular movement (a fall, for
instance) with the contagious energy from their local animating
mixtures.

Insofar as his universe is populated with objects that seem to have
their own principles of motion, his world becomes as magical as that
of a fairy tale in which frogs turn into princes or stewardesses into
primal earth-mothers who subsume all forms of life. Dickey's optative
magic operates in a primitive world of personification very much like
that of Yimantuwinyai, a hero of the Hupa Indians:

> When he came to Orleans Bar he found two women had come into exis-
> tence there . . . Yimantuwinyai wanted in someway to meet them. Picking
> up a stick he wished it would become a canoe and it did. Then he wished
> for a lake and the lake was there. Putting the canoe in the water he trans-
> formed himself into a child and seated himself in it. At earliest dawn the
> women came along and saw him there. They started to catch the canoe and
> secure the baby, but the boat avoided them. They made the circuit of the
> lake wading or swimming after it. When they were about to catch it, the
> water broke out of the banks and they failed.[4]

The world of this mythic character is less compliant than Dickey's—
both the water and the boat fail to yield to human will. Yet the Hupa
method of personification conveys the fairy tale quality of Dickey's
world, which seems religious in the sense that some spirit of movement inhabits inanimate objects and gives each its own life. Dickey is
aware of this religious impulse in his poetry; he says that "the religious sense, which seems to me very strong in my work in some weird
kind of way, is a very personal kind of stick-and-stone religion. I would
have made a great Bushman or an aborigine who believes that spirits
inhabit all things" (*SI*, 79).

Even though expansion and diffusion characterize the general direc-

---

4. Earle Pliny Goddard (ed.), *Hupa Texts* (Berkeley, 1904), 125.

tion of Dickey's poetic action, his mode of attention when he beholds single objects strongly resembles Ernest Cassirer's description of primitive enthrallment:

> Thought does not dispose freely over the data of intuition, in order to relate and compare them to each other, but is captivated and enthralled by the intuition which suddenly confronts it. It comes to rest in the immediate experience; the sensible present is so great that everything else dwindles before it . . . it is as though the whole world were simply annihilated. . . . The ego is spending all its energy on this single object, lives in it, loses itself in it. Instead of a widening of intuitive experience, we find here its extreme limitation; instead of expansion that would lead through greater and greater spheres of being, we have here an impulse toward concentration . . . intensive compression. This focusing of all forces on a single point is the prerequisite for all mythical thinking and mythical formulation.[5]

A brief list of Dickey's images supports the accuracy of this description and bears close analogy to Lawrence's animated objects. For instance, Dickey loses himself in concentrated contemplation of a wasp:

> Sealed and sweeping depth
> Is part of me now, and I ride it, gone bright inside in the dark
> Of the raised, rounded quarry and its cool;
> I am reined-in and thriving with the wasp:
> I meet now vibrantly with him
> And unbearably at the broad window   (PU, 25)

Or, the "intensive compression" of sunflowers leads him inside the object:

> Smoking well-heads of blossom,
> Anti-matter and easement, we huddle down
> Unfolding, and balance-bloom is final
> This year, over the unstirring plow.   (PU, 30)

Even domestic items take on animistic traits, seem to shine, and provide magical entrance to the past when the poet drives through a section of Atlanta known as Buckhead when he tries to go home again:

> First of all, going home, I must go
> To Wender and Roberts' Drug Store, for driving through I saw it
> Shining   renewed   renewed
> In chromium, but still there . . .

5. Ernest Cassirer, *Language and Myth* (New York, 1946), 32–33.

> Let me drive around Buckhead
> A few dozen times    turning    turning in my foreign
> Car till the town spins    whirls till the chrome vanishes
> From Wender and Roberts'    the spittoons are remade
> From the sun itself    the dead pages flutter the hearts rise up, that lie
> In the ground, and Bobby Laster's backbreaking fingers
> Pick up a cue-stick    (*TCM,* 17, 19)

When coupled with the poet's general principle of expansive motion, his compressed "magical" attention to single things offers another explanation of one of his poetic strategies of movement, namely, the peculiar in-and-out effect we noted in "May Day Sermon." Expansion and compression thus constitute one of his basic methods of exchange, allowing for thorough and complete mystical penetration of setting and objects by Dickey's speakers.

While primarily naturistic, Dickey's vision is at times animistic in the sense that spiritual beings, invisible to our eyes, pay mysterious visitation to the human world. In "The Being" a succubus-like entity descends upon a sleeper:

> It glides, glides
> Lightly over him, over his chest and legs.
> All breath is called suddenly back
>
> Out of laughter and weeping at once.
> His face liquefies and freezes
>
> Like a mask. He goes rigid
> And breaks into sweat from his heart
> All over his body
>
> In something's hands.   (*P,* 155)

The identity of this ghostly being is not revealed. We know it only in terms of its power to alter the character of the man it visits. After the being "reaches down under / His eyelids," the man receives a strange power of renewal and of awareness as a result of this visitation:

> He blazes back with his eyes closed,
> Given, also, renewed
>
> Fertility, to raise
> Dead plants and half-dead beasts

> Out of their thawing holes,
> And children up,
> From mortal women or angels,
> As true to themselves as . . .
>
>     he is now, seeing straight
> Through the roof   wide   wider
>
> Wide awake.   (*P*, 156)

The principle behind this poem bears analogy to the description by a Sioux chief of how a shaman receives his power: "To the Holy Man comes in youth the knowledge that he will be holy. The Great Mystery makes him know this. Sometimes it is the Spirits who tell him. The Spirits come not in sleep always, but also when man is awake. When a Spirit comes it would seem as though a man stood there, but when this man has spoken and goes forth again, none may see whither he goes."[6] "The Being" is thus an animistic initiation of a shaman whose magic is bestowed upon him in a rite of communion by means of the movement of the spirit of his tribe.

In the poem "The Bee," Dickey animistically invokes the spirits of "Dead coaches" who "live in the air" to give him the speed from his days as a college football player in order to save his young son, who has accidentally stumbled out on to a California highway while trying to get away from a bee:

> To the football coaches of Clemson College, 1942
>
> > One dot
> > Grainily shifting   we at roadside and
> > The smallest wings coming   along the rail fence out
> > Of the woods   one dot   of all that green. It now
> > Becomes flesh-crawling   then the quite still
> > Of stinging. I must live faster for my terrified
> > Small son   it is on him. Has come. Clings.
> >
> > Old wingback, come
> > To life. If your knee action is high
> > Enough, the fat may fall in time   God damn
> > You, Dickey, *dig*   this is your last time to cut
> > And run   but you must give it everything you have

---

6. Joseph Campbell, *Primitive Mythology* (New York, 1959), 243.

Left, for screaming near your screaming child is the sheer
Murder of California traffic: some bee hangs driving

Your child
Blindly onto the highway. Get there however
Is still possible. Long live what I badly did
At Clemson   and all of my clumsiest drives
For the ball   all of my trying to turn
The corner downfield   and my spindling explosions
Through the five-hole over tackle. O backfield

Coach Shag Norton,
Tell me as you never yet have told me
To get the lead out   scream whatever will get
The slow-motion of middle age off me   I cannot
Make it this way   I will have to leave
My feet   they are gone   I have him where
He lives   and down we go singing with screams into

The dirt,
Son-screams of fathers   screams of dead coaches turning
To approval   and from between us the bee rises screaming
With flight   grainily shifting   riding the rail fence
Back into the woods   traffic blasting past us-
Unchanged, nothing heard through the air-
conditioning glass   we lying at roadside full

Of the forearm prints
Of roadrocks   strawberries on our elbows as from
Scrimmage with the varsity   now we can get
Up   stand   turn away from the highway   look straight
Into trees. See, there is nothing coming out   no
Smallest wing   no shift of a flight-grain   nothing
Nothing. Let us go in, son, and listen

For some tobacco-
mumbling voice in the branches   to say "That's
a little better,"   to our lives still hanging
By a hair. There is nothing to stop us   we can go
Deep   deeper   into elms, and listen to traffic die
Roaring, like a football crowd from which we have
Vanished. Dead coaches live in the air, son   live

In the ear
Like fathers, and *urge*   and *urge*. They want you better
Than you are. When needed, they rise and curse you   they   scream

When something must be saved. Here, under this tree,
We can sit down. You can sleep, and I can try
To give back what I have earned by keeping us
Alive, and safe from bees: the smile of some kind

Of savior—
Of touchdowns, of fumbles, battles,
Lives. Let me sit here with you, son
As on the bench, while the first string takes back
Over, far away     and say with my silentest tongue, with the man-
creating bruises of my arms     with a live leaf a quick
Dead hand on my shoulder, "Coach Norton, I am your boy."
    (P, 279–80)

To get the "slow-motion of middle age off," the poet not only appeals to the demonlike coaches who "rise and curse you" and "scream / When something must be saved," he homeopathically imitates the motion of the bee itself when he says to himself, "old wingback, come / To life." The lives of poet, son, coaches, and bee mingle contagiously as all sing and scream while the speaker himself flies and his feet magically disappear.

The belief that the sound of an insect is an effective vehicle for communion with the dead is not unique to Dickey. In his discussion of animism, E. B. Tylor gives a quiet account of the primitive grounds of Dickey's poetic screaming, which also suggests the principles underlying "A Screened Porch in the Country": "One special conception . . . defines the spirit-voice as being a low murmur, chirp, or whistle, as it were the ghost of a voice. The Algonquin Indians of North America could hear the shadow-world of the dead chirp like crickets. The divine spirits of New Zealand dead, coming to converse with the living, utter their words in whistling tones . . . These ideas correspond with classic Western descriptions of the ghostly voice, as a 'twitter' or 'thin murmur.'"[7] Dickey does not at first hear his dead coaches through the bee. Only by virtue of one of his magical exchanges, in this case, the shared screaming, does the practical measure of the insect-as-medium produce the desired result. When the father tackles the son, screaming, saving, invoking, and redemptive diving flood together in this ritual-by-ordeal that magically enables the poet to feel

7. E. B. Tylor, *Primitive Culture* (London, 1929), 453.

the presence of the spirit of a dead coach in a leaf and to become himself once again the son of his athletic father: " 'Coach Norton, I am your boy.' "

In "The Eye-Beaters" and "The Bee," Dickey's magic is sheerly practical. His aim is to effect results not obtainable any other way; as a result, he appeals to emotional needs in his audience that are both primitive and modern. Bronislaw Malinowski describes the emotional appeal of magic for primitive man in a way that describes Dickey's poetic disposition:

> We find magic wherever the elements of chance and accident, and the emotional play between hope and fear have a wide and extensive range. We do not find magic wherever the pursuit is certain, reliable, and well under control of rational methods and technological processes. Further, we find magic where the element of danger is conspicuous . . .

> The integral cultural function of magic . . . consists in the bridging-over of gaps and inadequacies in highly important activities not yet completely mastered by man . . . magic supplies primitive man with a firm belief in his power of succeeding; it provides him also with a definite mental and pragmatic technique wherever his ordinary means fail him. It thus enables man to carry out with confidence his most vital tasks, and to maintain his poise and his mental integrity under circumstances which . . . would demoralize him by despair and anxiety, by fear and hatred, by unrequited love and impotent hate.[8]

To miss the magical principles and emotional purposes underlying Dickey's animistic incantation in "The Bee" is to miss nothing less than the causal grounds for Dickey's method of protective, ritual control and thus the structure of the poem itself.

In another charming lyric of magical protection, "To His Children in Darkness," Dickey secretly enters the bedroom of his two sleeping sons where like a primitive priest he imitates tree and beast in order to breathe "Eternal life / Upon a soul / In deepest sleep":

> To one, I have
> Like leaves grown here,
> And furl my wings
> As poplars sigh,

8. Bronislaw Malinowski, *Myth in Primitive Psychology* (New York, 1926), 82.

And slowly let
On him a breath
Drawn in a cloud,
In which he sees
Angelic hosts
Like blowing trees
Send me to earth
To root among
The secret soil
Of his dark room.

The other hears
A creature shed
Throughout the maze
The same long breath
As he conceives
That he no more
Desires to live
In the blazing sun,
Nor shake to death
The animal

Of his own head . . .

My sons, I bring
These beings home
Into your room.
They are. I am.    (P, 94–95)

It is not clear what sort of "god or beast" Dickey resembles here; he
has grown leaves yet also can "furl [his] wings." Even so, the fact that
a god is both animal and vegetable presents no problem to the primitive mind. Frazer extensively documents how the corn spirit appears
in the form of many different animals.[9] The poet is a caster of spells,
or shaman, who claims to be possessed by a superhuman spirit whose
power he appropriates. The shaman does not work through divination
by appeasing the gods but rather by acquiring through magical methods the very powers of the gods that he imparts to his tribe or family.
By bringing mythical beings into his sons' room, Dickey as poet-god
gains mysterious knowledge of the dark room, discovers "what lies /

9. Frazer, *The Golden Bough,* 518ff.

Behind all words," and imparts "Eternal life" on his children now sleeping in a sanctified soil where a god may strike root.

In his long poem "A Folksinger of the Thirties," Dickey adds the element of victimage to sympathetic magic when a hobo-folksinger is caught riding a freight train by railroad detectives and nailed Christ-like to the side of a boxcar as a warning to others. As the crucified folksinger travels cross-country, he becomes supersensitized through pain and magically gains knowledge of the location of precious natural resources:

> Through the landscape I edged
> And drifted, my head on my breast . . .
> And went flying sideways through
> The country, the rivers falling
> Away beneath my safe
> Immovable feet,
> Close to me as they fell
> Down under the boiling trestles,
> And the fields and woods
> Unfolded. Sometimes, behind me,
> Going into the curves,
> Cattle cried in unison,
> Singing of stockyards
> Where their tilted blood
> Would be calmed and spilled.
> I heard them until I sailed
> Into the dark of the woods,
> Flying always into the moonlight
> And out again into rain
> That filled my mouth
> With a great life-giving word,
> And into the many lights
> The town hung up for Christmas
> Sales, the berries and tinsel,
> And then out again
> Into the countryside.
> Everyone I passed
>
> Could never believe what they saw . . .
> I lifted my head and croaked
> Like a crow, and the nails
> Vibrated with something like music

> Endlessly clicking with movement
> And the powerful, simple curves.
> I learned where the oil lay
> Under the fields,
> Where the water ran
> With the most industrial power,
> Where the best corn would grow
> And what manure to use
> On any field that I saw   (*P*, 150–51)

Once again, Dickey's mystical and romantic habits are evident. Through a combination of movement and music, the singer penetrates the surface of nature and comes into sympathetic contact with underlying sources of power. As he flies "sideways through / The country," rain fills his mouth "With a great life-giving word" such that he can say of any field he sees:

> If riches were there,
> Whatever it was would light up
> Like a bonfire seen through an eyelid
> And begin to be words
> That would go with the sound of the rails.

Yet, because "in the end he knew it all / Through pain," what is also crucial to his increased status is that he "hung for years" on the box-car (*P*, 151). When seen by people as the train went by, he presents a bizarre if not monstrous sight.

One imagines the singer as an extraordinary effigy of Christ-crucified that stuns all who see it, a public martyr displayed as warning not only to the "boys who would ride the freights" but as a sign of something even more terrible. Terror electrifies Dickey's gentle landscape and converts the singer from a victim of railroad "yard bulls" into a sacred monster, the living incarnation of a primitive principle of violence, whose magic renders him kingly and prophetic.

Yet the speaker's power issues less from magic than from victimage. Paradoxically, he becomes godly by being a victim, or to put it more concisely, a scapegoat who draws evil and violence to himself in an instantaneous rush of transference and at the same time transforms this violence into a state of stability and fruitfulness that results in a "future of profits and commerce." Dickey's speaker acquires godlike

knowledge and status less because of his empathic powers than because of his trial-by-ordeal of kingly victimage that gives him magical
insight. The animating incident is the conversion of the folksinger
into a capitalistic god by means of homeopathic imitation of crucifixion based on the scapegoating mechanism that René Girard calls the
"surrogate victim."[10] Precisely how this device operates in Dickey's
poetry is the subject of our next section. Most of Dickey's most spectacular contributions to American poetry consist of lyric dramatization of "ritual violence." While we continue our interest in Dickey's
magical ontology, let us now turn to his poetic principles of primitive
sacrifice.

## THE SACRED

"The Vegetable King" exhibits Dickey's principle of ritual violence in
full bloom. A fantastic ordeal in which violence is self-directed to ensure the safety of his household and his own participation in the rebirth of nature in spring, the poem is, Dickey claims, an attempt "to
mythologize my family" and constitutes his "answer to [T. S.] Eliot's
use of the Osiris myth" (*SI*, 85). In *Self-Interviews* he provides his
own gloss on the myth he wishes to reimbody: "In his notes to *The
Waste Land*, Eliot talks about his deliberate use of Near Eastern fertility rituals. A civilization had, in its early stages, a living victim who
was torn apart and thrown into the nearest body of water. . . . The
living victim was dismembered, thrown into a river or lake, and was
supposed to be gathered together and resurrected when the crops came
up in the spring. . . . My poem is a small, personal commentary on
the same situation Eliot uses for much larger purposes" (*SI*, 90). The
poet then speaks of the rationale for his poem:

> What if I took an ordinary householder in the spring of the year and . . . had
> him sleep in the backyard and dream that he was the one who was dismem-
> bered, thrown into the water, and gathered together again? What if he then
> came back into the house and realized that this hadn't happened to him
> except in a dream? But how could he be sure? Maybe when he returned he
> really *was* the resurrected Vegetable King and the whole spring *had* been

10. René Girard, *Violence and the Sacred* (Baltimore, 1977), 79.

brought by him! The flowers on the table and everything else might have been brought about by his death and rebirth, as the people in the Near Eastern cultures believed. I thought, suppose I take this idea seriously and make part of it dream, part reality?   (*SI*, 90)

Here is the poem:

> Just after the sun
> Has closed, I swing the fresh paint of the door
> And have opened the new, green dark.
> From my house and my silent folk
> I step, and lay me in ritual down.
>
> One night each April
> I unroll the musty sleeping-bag
> And beat from it a cloud of sleeping moths.
> I leave the house, which leaves
> Its window-light on the ground
>
> In gold frames picturing grass,
> And lie in the unconsecrated grove
> Of small, suburban pines,
> And never move, as the ground not ever shall move,
> Remembering, remembering to feel
>
> The still earth turn my house around the sun
> Where all is dark, unhoped-for, and undone.
> I cannot sleep until the lights are out,
> And the lights of the house of grass, also,
> Snap off, from underground.
>
> Beneath the gods and animals of Heaven,
> Mismade inspiringly, like them,
> I fall to a colored sleep
> Enveloping the house, or coming out
> Of the dark side of the sun,
>
> And begin to believe a dream
> I never once have had,
> Of being part of the acclaimed rebirth
> Of the ruined, calm world, in spring,
> When the drowned god and the dreamed-of sun
>
> Unite, to bring the red, the blue,
> The common yellow flower out of earth
> Of the tended and untended garden: when the chosen man,

Hacked apart in the growing cold
Of the year, by the whole of mindless nature is assembled

From the trembling, untroubled river.
I believe I become that man, become
As bloodless as a god, within the water,
Who yet returns to walk a woman's rooms
Where flowers on the mantel-piece are those

Bought by his death. A warm wind springs
From the curtains. Blue china and milk on the table
Are mild, convincing, and strange.
At that time it is light,
And, as my eyelid lifts

An instant before the other, the last star is withdrawn
Alive, from its fiery fable.
I would not think to move,
Nor cry, "I live," just yet,
Nor shake the twinkling horsehair of my head,

Nor rise, nor shine, nor live
With any but the slant, green, mummied light
And wintry, bell-swung undergloom of waters
Wherethrough my severed head has prophesied
For the silent daffodil and righteous

Leaf, and now has told the truth.
This is the time foresaid, when I must enter
The walking house, and return to a human love
Cherished on faith through winter:
That time when I in the night

Of water lay, with sparkling animals of light
And distance made, with gods
Which move through Heaven only as the spheres
Are moved: by music, music.
Mother, son, and wife

Who live with me: I am in death
And waking. Give me the looks that recall me.
None knows why you have waited
In the cold, thin house for winter
To turn the inmost sunlight green

And blue and red with life,
But it must be so, since you have set

These flowers upon the table, and milk for him
Who, recurring in this body, bears you home
Magnificent pardon, and dread, impending crime.   (P, 23–25)

If the folksinger is a partial deity, a Christlike figure transformed by
crucifixion into a prophet of natural resources, the speaker in "The
Vegetable King" is a full-fledged fertility god, "hacked apart" and resurrected "by the whole of mindless nature." Instead of Christ as his
poetic analogue, Dickey uses Osiris, the Egyptian god of agriculture,
who was killed and cut into fourteen pieces by his evil half-brother,
reassembled in linen and bandages like a mummy, then brought to life
by his wife the goddess Isis, after which he reigned with power and
dignity as Lord of the Underworld. According to Frazer, not only was
Osiris a god of the dead who promised life everlasting but also a corn-
god who died and came to life each year. Frazer claims that as "a god
of vegetation Osiris was naturally perceived as a god of creative energy
in general, since men at a certain stage of evolution fail to distinguish
between the reproductive powers of animals and plants." Using his
principles of magic, Frazer accounts for Osiris' powers by noting that
to ensure the growth of corn in ancient Egypt a corn-stuffed effigy of
Osiris was buried in the fields at sowing time along with the seed.
The sympathetic assumption was that if the god had died and risen
again so would the crops. In ritual celebrations of the death and resurrection of the god, the homeopathic (or imitative) principle was carried to extraordinary lengths in other Egyptian ceremonies: "The
Egyptians, with shorn heads, annually lamented over a buried idol of
Osiris, smiting their breasts, slashing their shoulders, ripping open
their old wounds, until, after several days of mourning, they professed
to find the mangled remains of the god, at which they rejoiced."[11]
    Although Dickey's ritual is not as violent as the Egyptians'—his
god is, in fact, bloodless—magical connections certainly underlie the
process of acquisition by which the suburban homeowner becomes
"part of the acclaimed rebirth / Of the ruined, calm world, in spring."
While lying in his "unconsecrated" grove of pines, he sanctifies the
earth by uniting "The drowned god and the dreamed-of-sun" then
emerging reborn from nature's "trembling, untroubled river." Presum-

11. Frazer, The Golden Bough, 442, 435.

ably a variant of the fertile Osirian Nile, Dickey's river is really another of his perpetual circuits of redemptive motion—magical, contagious, cosmic, even amniotic, when he "in the night / Of water lay, with sparkling animals of light / And distance made, with gods / Which move through Heaven." Although one conjectures that these "animals of light" are constellations, this water encompasses both heaven and earth, binding together even the seasons by uniting "wintry" waters with the time of "the silent daffodil." Dickey's amniotic night then gives way sympathetically to "inmost sunlight" which turns "green / And blue and red with life" inside his house and in the colors of flowers set on the table by his wife (*P*, 23–25).

Once again Dickey converts a simple domestic event into something larger. What begins with "a musty sleeping-bag" moves through primitive dismemberment and ends with "Magnificent pardon, and dread, impending crime," terms which respectively signal, Dickey tells us, the speaker's own kingly "resurrection" and "ritual murder" (*SI*, 90). But what is really larger than the principles of magic in this poem is the poet's paradoxical method of "resurrection" by "ritual murder." For, the "flowers on the mantel-piece" result not only from his sympathetic alignment with nature but more importantly are "Bought by his death." To understand fully the mechanics of Dickey's ritual method, we must turn to René Girard.

In his discussion of the initiations of shamans, Girard says:

> If he wishes to acquire the means of ridding men of illness, the apprentice shaman must first expose himself to the full fury of these illnesses. . . . He emerges triumphant from an ordeal that would have killed an ordinary mortal, thus demonstrating that he not only enjoys the protection of Supreme Violence but also shares in its power and can even, to some extent, effect the transformation of "bad" into "good" violence.

> In isolated cultures as far apart as Australia and Asia the initiation culminates in a vision of dismemberment, after which the neophyte awakens or rather, is reborn as a full-fledged shaman.

> Dismemberment is emblematic of triumph and resurrection; it reflects the operation of the surrogate victim, the transformation of maleficent violence into beneficent violence. The neophyte experiences the same metamorphosis as the mythical creatures whose help he will later require in the exercise of his shamanistic functions.[12]

12. Girard, *Violence and the Sacred*, 286.

The tribal shaman, according to Girard, acquires his healing powers by making himself a scapegoat whose victimization transforms contagious reciprocal violence into ritual violence, a process that brings unanimity to a community by focusing social dissension on a single target whose very nature it is to *not* reciprocate the violence done to it. Because of his capacity to effect "the unanimous polarization of hostility that produces the reconciliation" of internal communal violence by transferring it outside the community, the scapegoat is often revered by his attackers even while they condemn him.

That the ritual victim should simultaneously be loved and reviled is no contradiction for Girard. Rather, this paradox is one of the scapegoat's central traits. He is, in Girard's terms, a "monstrous double" who "partakes of all possible differences within the community, particularly the difference between within and without; for he passes freely from the interior to the exterior and back again. Thus the surrogate victim constitutes both a link and a barrier between the community and the sacred" (*i.e.*, reciprocal or unending violence). By using this formulation, we can see why the "sacred king is also a monster. He is simultaneously god, man, and savage beast. . . . Moral and physical monstrosity are thus blended and confused. Like Oedipus, the king is at once stranger and son, the most intimate of insiders and the most bizarre of outsiders; he is an exemplar of enormous tenderness and frightful savagery." Thus, whenever "the restoration of unity is personally attributed to the surrogate victim, he is seen as 'divine,' 'royal,' 'sovereign'" so that the "sacred character of the king" is nothing less than "his identity with the victim."[13]

In addition to magical animism, Dickey's primitive strategy in "The Vegetable King" is one of ritual rebirth based on a process of victimage in which the poet-shaman plays the roles of god, priest, victim, and suburban father all at once. By dreaming himself to be the "hacked apart" Osiris, Dickey becomes a monstrous mummy with "severed head" who receives but does not reciprocate violence. The poet also blurs stable distinctions between men and gods, the living and the dead, the healthy and the mutilated; in so doing, he becomes even more monstrous by threatening the stable social order that depends

13. *Ibid.*, 271, 252, 302, 304.

for its coherence on fixed differences between the two opposites in each of these pairs. At poem's end, when he wakes from his dream and returns to his single human identity, the poet retains the shamanistic power of regeneration that he acquired by entering the world of reciprocal violence that constitutes the middle or dream-section of his rite.

In other words, the poet not only undertakes an ordeal of physical violence but also a more threatening violence that annihilates stable social distinctions by which men identify themselves and on which cultural "order, peace, and fecundity depend." The middle section of "The Vegetable King" is a hallucinatory blur of traits in which a man becomes a god, and the living and dead are joined in a "fiery fable" that if carried into the speaker's suburban home would not ensure domestic tranquility but destroy it. Thus, the speaker goes *away* from the human house to encounter contagious violence that he, as a nonretaliative scapegoat, absorbs and converts into redemptive power by partaking of the sacred and yet bringing to it a principle of closure that is nothing less than his own victimage. Merely by coming close to the sources of unrestrained violence, he takes on its power, then returns with renewed energy to his family and conveys to them a new proportion of protection and danger. Girard says, "Having sown the seeds of death, the god, ancestor, or mythic hero then dies himself," and in "so doing he bestows a new life on men." This process, in T. S. Eliot's "The Family Reunion," bears a remarkable similarity to Dickey's:

> Spring is an issue of the blood
> A season of sacrifice
> And the wail of the new full tide
> Returning the ghosts of the dead
> Those whom the winter drowned
> Do not the ghosts of the drowned
> Return to land in the spring
> Do the dead want to return? [14]

The ritual structure of "The Vegetable King" consists of three parts: the separation of the speaker from his family as he leaves the house to initiate his ritual, the dream in which he acquires his powers by virtue of his proximity to contagious violence, and his waking from the

---

14. *Ibid.*, 49, 255; T. S. Eliot, *The Complete Plays* (New York, 1967), 82.

dream in a rejuvenated state that accompanies the seasonal change from winter to spring. The violence in Dickey's poem is gentle and minimal but nonetheless the fulcrum of his poetic activity, an activity neither discursive nor mental but practical and preventative. His ritual is designed to attract and transform violence long before it reaches a state of uncontrolled or escalating reciprocity. In "A Folksinger of the Thirties," the folksinger similarly acquires his mystical powers because he has been sanctified through crucifixion as a scapegoat and thus becomes a fertility king who "is the catalyst who converts sterile, infectious violence into positive cultural values."[15] By placing the singer's crucifixion on a moving boxcar in the middle of his poem, Dickey not only infects the countryside with the man's power but prevents him from stopping too long and thus overinfecting any single community. The fact that the poem is cast as a recollection with some temporal distance between act and audience also serves structurally to keep sacred violence at arm's length from those it is designed to serve. At the end of the poem, the singer sells his knowledge to the rich and thus remains a kind of capitalistic monster, a stance fully consistent with the double nature of the sacrificial king who has extraordinary capacity for both good and evil but who nonetheless retains the power to draw infectious social tensions to himself.

For Girard, whose critical terms fit Dickey better than any other writer on primitivism, *violence* and *the sacred* are interchangeable. Because of the mechanism of the surrogate victim, the "operations of violence and the sacred are ultimately the same process." We do not worship violence for itself; rather, "Violence is venerated insofar as it offers men what little peace they can ever expect. Nonviolence appears as the gratuitous gift of violence . . . for men are only capable of reconciling their differences at the expense of a third party. The best men can hope for in their quest for nonviolence is the unanimity-minus-one of the surrogate victim." Because we so value "the immense calm produced by the act of generative unanimity, by the initial appearance of the god," a primitive god is

> Nothing more nor less than the massive violence that was expelled by the original act of generative unanimity. . . . Every time the sacrifice accom-

15. Girard, *Violence and the Sacred*, 107.

panies its desired effect, and bad violence is converted into good stability, the god is said to have accepted the offering of violence and consumed it. . . . Successful sacrifice prevents violence from reverting to a state of immanence and reciprocity; that is, it reinforces the status of violence as an exterior influence, transcendent and beneficent. Sacrifice accords the god all that he needs to assure his continued growth and vigor. And it is the god himself who "digests" the bad immanence, transforming it into good transcendence, that is, into his own substance.

Further, the human need for appeasement of the sacred is a permanent part of the human condition: "If we neglect to feed the god, he will waste away; or else, maddened by hunger, he will descend among men and lay claim to his nourishment with unexampled cruelty and ferocity."[16] Whatever Dickey has accomplished in modern lyric method, surely one of his most valuable achievements is to provide poetic models of "beneficent" violence, that is, stylized ways of symbolically transforming immanent violence into emotional conditions of peace and tranquility.

Dickey's most spectacular poem of ritual violence—one of the most remarkable lyrics in American poetry—is "Falling." Because it is difficult to quote sections of this poem to convey its distinctive power and because the piece itself is so extraordinary, included here is the entire six-page poem.

FALLING

*A 29-year-old stewardess fell . . . to her death tonight when she was swept through an emergency door that suddenly sprang open . . . The body . . . was found . . . three hours after the accident.*
—New York *Times*

The states when they black out and lie there rolling   when they turn
To something transcontinental   move by   drawing moonlight out
   of the great
One-sided stone hung off the starboard wingtip   some sleeper next to
An engine is groaning for coffee   and there is faintly coming in
Somewhere the vast beast-whistle of space. In the galley with its racks
Of trays   she rummages for a blanket   and moves in her slim tailored
Uniform to pin it over the cry at the top of the door. As though she blew

The door down with a silent blast from her lungs   frozen   she is black
Out finding herself   with the plane nowhere and her body taking
   by the throat

16. *Ibid.*, 258, 258–59, 266.

The undying cry of the void    falling    living    beginning to be
     something
That no one has ever been and lived through    screaming without
     enough air
Still neat    lipsticked    stockinged    girdled by regulation    her hat
Still on    her arms and legs in no world    and yet spaced also strangely
With utter placid rightness on thin air    taking her time    she holds it
In many places    and now, still thousands of feet from her death
     she seems
To slow    she develops interest    she turns in her maneuverable body

To watch it. She is hung high up in the overwhelming middle of things
     in her
Self    in low body-whistling wrapped intensely    in all her dark
     dance-weight
Coming down from a marvellous leap    with the delaying,
     dumfounding ease
Of a dream of being drawn    like endless moonlight to the harvest soil
Of a central state of one's country    with a great gradual warmth
     coming
Over her    floating    finding more and more breath in what she has
     been using
For breath    as the levels become more human    seeing clouds placed
     honestly
Below her left and right    riding slowly toward them    she clasps it all
To her and can hang her hands and feet in it in peculiar ways    and
Her eyes opened wide by wind, can open her mouth as wide    wider
     and suck
All the heat from the cornfields    can go down on her back with a
     feeling
Of stupendous pillows stacked under her    and can turn    turn as
     to someone
In bed    smile, understood in darkness    can go away    slant    slide
Off tumbling    into the emblem of a bird with its wings half-spread
Or whirl madly on herself    in endless gymnastics in the growing
     warmth
Of wheatfields rising toward the harvest moon.    There is time to live
In superhuman health    seeing mortal unreachable lights far down
     seeing
An ultimate highway with one late priceless car probing it    arriving
In a square town    and off her starboard arm the glitter of water catches
The moon by its one shaken side    scaled, roaming silver    My God
     it is good
And evil    lying in one after another of all the positions for love

Making    dancing    sleeping    and now cloud wisps at her no
Raincoat    no matter    all small towns brokenly brighter from inside
Cloud    she walks over them like rain    bursts out to behold a
    Greyhound
Bus shooting light through its sides    it is the signal to go straight
Down like a glorious diver    then feet first    her skirt stripped
    beautifully
Up    her face in fear-scented cloths    her legs deliriously bare
    then
Arms out    she slow-rolls over    steadies out    waits for something
    great
To take control of her    trembles near feathers    planes head-down
The quick movements of bird-necks turning her head    gold eyes the
    insight-
eyesight of owls blazing into the hencoops    a taste for chicken
    overwhelming
Her    the long-range vision of hawks enlarging all human lights
    of cars
Freight trains    looped bridges    enlarging the moon racing slowly
Through all the curves of a river    all the darks of the midwest blazing
From above. A rabbit in a bush turns white    the smothering chickens
Huddle    for over them there is still time for something to live
With the streaming half-idea of a long stoop    a hurting    a fall
That is controlled    that plummets as it wills    turns gravity
Into a new condition, showing its other side like a moon    shining
New Powers    there is still time to live on a breath made of nothing
But the whole night    time for her to remember to arrange her skirt
Like a diagram of a bat    tightly it guides her    she has this flying-skin
Made of garments    and there are also those sky-divers on TV sailing
In sunlight    smiling under their goggles    swapping batons back
    and forth
And He who jumped without a chute and was handed one by a diving
Buddy. She looks for her grinning companion    white teeth    nowhere
She is screaming    singing hymns    her thin human wings spread out
From her neat shoulders    the air beast-crooning to her    warbling
And she can no longer behold the huge partial form of the world    now
She is watching her country lose its evoked master shape    watching
    it lose
And gain    get back its houses and peoples    watching it bring up
Its local lights    single homes    lamps on barn roofs    if she fell
Into water she might live    like a diver    cleaving    perfect    plunge

Into another    heavy silver    unbreathable    slowing    saving
Element: there is water    there is time to perfect all the fine

Points of diving    feet together    toes pointed    hands shaped right
To insert her into water like a needle    to come out healthily dripping
And be handed a Coca-Cola    there they are    there are the waters
Of life    the moon packed and coiled in a reservoir    so let me begin
*To plane across the night air of Kansas    opening my eyes superhumanly*
*Bright    to the dammed moon    opening the natural wings of my jacket*
*By Don Loper    moving like a hunting owl toward the glitter of water*
*One cannot just fall    just tumble screaming all that time    one must use*
*It*    She is now through with all    through all    clouds    damp hair
Straightened    the last wisp of fog pulled apart on her face like wool
    revealing
New darks    new progressions of headlights along dirt roads
    from chaos

And night    a gradual warming    a new-made, inevitable world of
    one's own
Country    a great stone of light in its waiting waters    hold    hold out
For water: who knows when what correct young woman must take up
    her body
And fly    and head for the moon-crazed inner eye of midwest
    imprisoned
Water    stored up for her for years    the arms of her jacket slipping
Air up her sleeves to go    all over her? What final things can be said
Of one who starts out sheerly in her body in the high middle of night
Air    to track down water like a rabbit where it lies like life itself
Off to the right in Kansas? She goes toward    the blazing-bare lake
Her skirts neat    her hands and face warmed more and more by
    the air
Rising from pastures of beans    and under her    under chenille
    bedspreads
The farm girls are feeling the goddess in them struggle and rise
    brooding
On the scratch-shining posts of the bed    dreaming of female signs
Of the moon    male blood like iron    of what is really said by the moan
Of airliners passing over them at dead of midwest midnight passing
Over brush fires    burning out in silence on little hills    and will wake
To see the woman they should be    struggling on the rooftree to become
Stars: for her the ground is closer    water is nearer    she passes
It    then banks    turns    her sleeves fluttering differently as she rolls
Out to face the east, where the sun shall come up from wheatfields
    she must
Do something with water    fly to it    fall in it    drink it    rise
From it    but there is none left upon earth    the clouds have drunk
    it back

The plants have sucked it down    there are standing toward her only
The common fields of death    she comes back from flying to falling
Returns to a powerful cry    the silent scream with which she blew down
The coupled door of the airliner    nearly    nearly losing hold
Of what she has done    remembers    remembers the shape at the heart
Of cloud    fashionably swirling    remembers she still has time to die
Beyond explanation. Let her now take off her hat in summer air
        the contour
Of cornfields    and have enough time to kick off her one remaining
Shoe with the toes    of the other foot    to unhook her stockings
With calm fingers, noting how fatally easy it is to undress in midair
Near death    when the body will assume without effort any position
Except the one that will sustain it    enable it to rise    live
Not die    nine farms hover close    widen    eight of them separate,
        leaving
One in the middle    then the fields of that farm do the same    there
        is no
Way to back off    from her chosen ground    but she sheds the jacket
With its silver sad impotent wings    sheds the bat's guiding tailpiece
Of her skirt    the lightning-charged clinging of her blouse    the intimate
Inner flying-garment of her slip in which she rides like the holy ghost
Of a virgin    sheds the long windsocks of her stockings    absurd
Brassiere    then feels the girdle required by regulations squirming
Off her: no longer monobuttocked    she feels the girdle flutter    shake
In her hand    and float    upward    her clothes rising off her ascending
Into cloud    and fights away from her head the last sharp dangerous
        shoe
Like a dumb bird    and now will drop in    SOON    now will drop

In like this    the greatest thing that ever came to Kansas    down
        from all
Heights    all levels of American breath    layered in the lungs from
        the frail
Chill of space to the loam where extinction slumbers in corn tassels
        thickly
And breathes like rich farmers counting: will come among them after
Her last superhuman act    the last slow careful passing of her hands
All over her unharmed body    desired by every sleeper in his dream:
Boys finding for the first time their loins filled with heart's blood
Widowed farmers whose hands float under light covers to find
        themselves
Arisen at sunrise    the splendid position of blood unearthly drawn
Toward clouds    all feel something    pass over them as she passes
Her palms over *her* long legs    *her* small breasts    and deeply between

Her thighs    her hair shot loose from all pins    streaming in the wind
Of her body    let her come openly    trying at the last second to land
On her back    This is it    THIS
                                                          All those who find her impressed
In the soft loam    gone down    driven well into the image of her body
The furrows for miles flowing in upon her where she lies very deep
In her mortal outline    in the earth as it is in cloud    can tell nothing
But that she is there    inexplicable    unquestionable    and remember
That something broke in them as well    and began to live and die more
When they walked for no reason into their fields to where the whole
    earth
Caught her    interrupted her maiden flight    told her how to lie
    she cannot
Turn    go away    cannot move    cannot slide off it and assume another
Position    no sky-diver with any grin could save her    hold her in
    his arms
Plummet with her    unfold above her his wedding silks    she can
    no longer
Mark the rain with whirling women that take the place of a dead wife
Or the goddess in Norwegian farm girls    or all the back-breaking
    whores
Of Wichita. All the known air above her is not giving up quite one
Breath    it is all gone    and yet not dead    not anywhere else
Quite    lying still in the field on her back    sensing the smells
Of incessant growth try to lift her    a little sight left in the corner
Of one eye    fading    seeing something wave    lies believing
That she could have made it    at the best part of her brief goddess
State    to water    gone in headfirst    come out smiling    invulnerable
Girl in a bathing-suit ad    but she is lying like a sunbather at the last
Of moonlight    half-buried in her impact on the earth    not far
From a railroad trestle    a water tank    she could see if she could
Raise her head from her modest hole    with her clothes beginning
To come down all over Kansas    into bushes    on the dewy sixth green
Of a golf course    one shoe    her girdle coming down fantastically
On a clothesline, where it belongs    her blouse on a lightning rod:

Lies in the fields    in *this* field    on her broken back as though on
A cloud she cannot drop through    while farmers sleepwalk without
Their women from houses    a walk like falling toward the far waters
Of life    in moonlight    toward the dreamed eternal meaning of
    their farms
Toward the flowering of the harvest in their hands    that tragic cost
Feels herself go    go toward    go outward    breathes at last fully

Not   and tries   less   once   tries   tries   AH, GOD—
    (*P*, 293–99)

In *Self-Interviews* Dickey says that "'Falling' is a record of the way [the stewardess] feels as she falls: panic at first and then a kind of goddess-like invulnerability. . . . I also tried to think of the mystical possibility there might be for farmers in that vicinity, under those conditions" (*SI*, 175). To see how the stewardess' "brief goddess / State" is linked to those midwesterners above whom she falls, we may best read "Falling" not simply as an accidental spectacular fall from a plane but as a ritual reenactment of the primitive practice of killing a god of vegetation to ensure both the perpetuation of crops and the continuation of the human species itself.

Although Dickey's modern ritual is less ghoulish than many primitive sacrifices, his rite bears close analogy in principle and structure to an ancient Aztec process of victimage described by Frazer. The Aztecs offered victims of both sexes. Here is what happened to one slave girl:

> They sanctified a young slave girl of twelve or thirteen years, the prettiest they could find, to represent the Maize Goddess Chicomecohuatl. They invested her with the ornaments of the goddess, putting a mitre on her head and maize-cobs round her neck and in her hands, and fastening a green feather upright on the crown of her head to imitate an ear of maize . . . we are told, in order to signify that the maize was almost ripe at the time of the festival, but because it was still tender they chose a girl of tender years to play the part of the Maize Goddess. The whole long day they led the poor child in all her finery, with the green plume nodding on her head, from house to house dancing merrily to cheer people after the dulness and privations of the fast.
>
> And the end of the festival . . . the priests solemnly incensed the girl who personated the goddess; then they threw her on her back on the heap of corn and seeds, cut off her head, caught the gushing blood in a tub, and sprinkled the blood on the wooden image of the goddess, the walls of the chamber, and the offerings of corn, peppers, pumpkins, seeds, and vegetables which cumbered the floor. After that they flayed the headless trunk, and one of the priests made shift to squeeze himself into the bloody skin . . . they clad him in all the robes which the girl had worn; they put the mitre on his head, the necklace of golden maize-cobs about his neck, the maize-cobs of feathers and gold in his hands; and thus arrayed they led him

forth in public, all of them dancing to the tuck of drum, while he acted as fugleman, skipping and posturing at the head of the procession as briskly as he could be expected to do, incommoded as he was by the tight and clammy skin of the girl and by her clothes, which must have been much too small for a grown man.[17]

Using Girard's principles, I will divide this Aztec rite into three parts that will shed light on the three central procedures of Dickey's ritualistic structure in "Falling," namely, preparation of the victim as a regal "monster" (or scapegoat), her subsequent execution, and finally, the transference of her extraordinary energy to the crops she is supposed to empower. While preparation precedes execution in Frazer's account and in the poem, the process of transference occurs in all stages, though felt most fully in the conclusion of each rite.

Dickey's ritual preparation extends, roughly, from the beginning of the poem until the stewardess hits the ground, which occurs approximately five-sixths of the way through the poem, thus leaving one-sixth for execution and transference. In other words, her fall is that poetic space in which she becomes a goddess not only because she is flying through the air but because she acquires the sacred status of a "monstrous double." For Girard, "sacrificial preparation" consists not only of those ceremonial events that precede the kill; it is, more specifically, the preparation or molding of the victim as an effective scapegoat, a unanimously chosen "double" who paradoxically "should belong both to the inside and the outside of the community . . . any creature chosen for sacrifice must fall short in one or another of the contradictory qualities required of it . . . but never in both at the same time. The goal is to make the victim wholly sacrificeable . . . sacrificial preparation employs two very different approaches. The first seeks to make appear more foreign a victim who is too much a part of the community. The second approach seeks to reintegrate into the community a victim who is too foreign to it."[18]

In what possible sense is Dickey's inoffensive airline stewardess a "monstrous double"? The answer lies in Dickey's extraordinary method of "sacrificial preparation," especially in how he *conceals*

17. Frazer, *The Golden Bough,* 682.
18. Girard, *Violence and the Sacred,* 272.

what Girard calls the "mechanism of unanimity" by which the girl is designated a scapegoat. For, the stewardess is not explicitly but implicitly monstrous. Like the male victims in Dickey's other poems of violence, her role is that of a modern pharmakos, those persons the Greeks used to maintain and expend as offerings in times of crisis. The extraordinary emotional effect of this lyric persuades us that there is more at stake here than the mere accidental death of an anonymous airline employee. Above all, it is the intoxicating, beneficent catharsis of her fatal fall, not merely her personal tragedy, that warrants our inquiry into ritual structure. (If one doubts the momentous transference of primal energy in this poem, its overwhelming mixture of the forces of life and death, I urge the reader to recite the poem aloud or listen to Dickey's spectacular recording on Caedmon Records.)

The central aim of Dickey's ritual preparation is to infect the community with both the stewardess' sacred benevolence and her malevolence. The poem begins innocently enough, looking merely like a factual account of a fall. The journalistic excerpt from the New York *Times* gives the event a literal basis as if to suggest that what follows really happened. To expel the greatest amount of real violence from a real community, the sacrificial act must use a real victim, not merely a fantastic figure who by definition belongs to some other world. After her initial shock at exploding through the plane door, the stewardess slows and develops interest in her fall. Her accident becomes a "marvellous leap with the delaying, dumfounding ease / Of a dream." Yet, for all the extraordinary earthly views that befall her, her situation is "good / And evil"; when her skirt billows up, "her legs are deliriously bare," yet her face is now covered "in fear-scented cloths."

As Dickey distracts us with his amazing description of her descent, he subtly uses his metaphors of exchange to make the woman more than human by aligning her magically with the attributes of animals, a process that gives her "New Powers" while "enlarging" and infecting nature itself. Explicitly, she acquires these powers only by means of the impossible "half-idea" that her lethal fall can be converted into "a fall / That is controlled" or that she will miraculously be handed a parachute or dive safely into some body of water. In reality, these options are not open to her. She realizes the truth of her situation and begins "screaming singing hymns" while "the air" is "beast-crooning to her" in one of Dickey's obsessive mixtures of beauty and terror. As she opens her eyes, the stewardess decides to "use" her fall and encounters "New darks   new progressions of headlights . . . / a gradual warming   a new-made, inevitable world of one's own / Country." Her apocalyptic power is sympathetically sensed by those below as "farm girls are feeling the goddess in them struggle and rise brooding." As a final gesture of existential contempt "to die / Beyond explanation," she takes off her clothes, "noting how fatally easy it is to undress in midair / Near death   when the body will assume without effort any position / Except the one that will sustain it." With death and physical mutilation imminent, she begins to acquire superhuman sexual powers that continue to be conveyed to those below and are described in terms of magical "blood consciousness" as she plummets downward.

At this point in the poem, a peculiar reversal occurs. As the stewardess descends, she *ascends* in power and status; the closer she comes to violent death, the more goddesslike she becomes in terms of a pervasive sympathetic sexual effect which moves upward and outward in the "position of blood unearthly drawn / Toward clouds." By means of his dazzling array of up-down movements, Dickey brings his principle of Absolute Motion to an ecstatic pitch as the poem itself continues to gain incredible acceleration, thus "proving" emotionally that its own universe is dynamically alive with the stewardess' "superhuman" powers. At the moment of the poem's greatest intensity and with one last attempt to control her fall by landing on her back—her most vulnerable but most powerful moment—she suddenly hits the ground, yet continues to live for a short time.

Let us pause for a moment and ask once more: how has the stewardess become a suitable sacrificial victim? To call the stewardess a "monstrous double" who draws communal evil to her at first seems to be a claim far off base; she seems merely the victim of a tragic accident. Yet nowhere in Dickey's poetry is his skill at mixing opposites so brilliant as in "Falling," where his main character is the product of a series of "double" traits that both threaten and absolve the community from spontaneous violence. One key to "doubleness" is the inside-outside mechanism, the capacity of the victim to draw internal chaos to her and then to expel it. Like the sacred king who is "an exemplar of enormous tenderness and frightful savagery," the stewardess is both honored and vilified and, most important, blurs stable social distinctions in a frenzy that itself seems dangerously contagious. A marginal social figure without whom the community may easily continue to function, the airline stewardess threatens the stable difference between gods and humans by becoming, however briefly, a goddess, a hybrid creature who is a member of society and yet clearly outside it, human and yet more than human. Further, like so many of Dickey's agents, she acquires the traits of animals. As she gains the "insight- / eyesight of owls," she blurs the "distinction between man and beast" that Girard claims "is always linked to violence."[19] Although this exchange with animals is beneficial insofar as it produces several of her new powers, it is also threatening in that the stewardess herself becomes part animal. A bestial combination is more dramatically presented in Dickey's poem "The Sheep Child," in which a half-human, half-sheep embryo is the monstrous product of a farm boy who has coupled with a ewe.

The stewardess' sexual power is both benevolent and malevolent. The poet has her remove her clothes not only "to die / Beyond explanation" but more importantly to instill in plants and people below a fertile sexual force curiously mixed with death that has considerable scope. Her sexual power is so comprehensive that she incorporates all brands of sexuality. Thus, while fruitful, her sexual strength is monstrous; it overflows normal bounds and if unchecked would produce a state of Dionysian frenzy hardly conducive to communal stability. Taken briefly as cataclysmic impregnation, her regenerative force verges on chaos and is valuable only insofar as it is controlled; what controls her orgiastic strength is her death. As read aloud by Dickey on record, the poem's last two words, "AH GOD," sound not only like someone's prayerful last breath but also like sexual ecstasy.

The stewardess is also monstrous because she is so *near* death. Throughout the poem, Dickey carefully mixes reminders of her fatal situation. Even when she animates the countryside, it is her death that will generate fertility in "the loam where extinction slumbers in corn tassels thickly." Her imminent death and physical monstrosity

19. *Ibid.*, 252, 128.

constitute, when coupled with her life-giving energy, a threat to blur distinctions between the living and the dead. Her energy lives on, yet she must be separated from the community. Girard asks:

> How can the dead incarnate violence as authoritatively as do the gods?

> Death is the ultimate violence that can be inflicted on a living being. . . . With death a contagious sort of violence is let loose on the community, and the living must take steps to protect themselves against it. So they quarantine death, creating a *cordon sanitaire* all around it. [Through] funeral rites . . . the dying man finds himself in a situation similar to that of the surrogate victim vis-á-vis the community. The grief of the mourner is a curious mixture of terror and hope—a mixture conducive to resolutions of good conduct in the future. The death of the individual has something of the quality of a tribute levied for the continued existence of the collectivity. A human being dies, and the solidarity of the survivors is enhanced by his death.[20]

If one doubts that the violation of stable social distinctions produces the monstrous, we need only recall what happens when Mary Shelley's Frankenstein aspires to godly powers by making a living creature out of parts of the dead. Even when Lewis Carroll's comic creatures in *Alice in Wonderland* produce laughter, we also feel a curious anxiety in their bizarre animal and human behavior, an anxiety that gives way to considerable disorientation for Alice as Carroll consistently mixes conventional rules of behavior, logic, and perception with those in Wonderland until fantasy and reality blur in a hallucinatory frenzy. If one wishes to test further the results of violating stable social differences, we need only think of the taboos surrounding topics such as bestiality, incest, necrophilia, and other sexual activity. Whether in a horror story by Poe or a Hollywood movie, the aesthetic formula for making a credible monster still hinges on the strategic violation of some taboo.

We can now see why the closer the stewardess comes to death the more power she acquires as a "monstrous double," why her physical descent is a ritual ascent. She becomes a goddess—a sacrificial scapegoat—precisely because she is about to die and thus can "exercise functions that are elsewhere the prerogative of the gods."[21] As a muti-

---

20. *Ibid.*, 255.
21. *Ibid.*, 256.

lated victim about to be absolutely expelled from the living, she draws death to her and sends it away from those who are alive. She leaves only her energized clothing which begins "To come down all over Kansas" as a sign of her presence. What is crucial to an effective scapegoat is that it partakes of the internal dissension in a community, transfers that dissension to itself, and thus engenders an intoxicating unanimity among individuals who are at odds with each other. Whether political or psychological, the scapegoating process is perpetually with us. And though well hidden, the dynamics of unanimous victimage animate "Falling" by producing an intoxicating tacit assent by the reader to the "monstrous" fitness of the stewardess as victim.

Although Dickey's poem ends with his victim's death, whereas the Aztec rite incorporates its slaying in the middle, the formal parts of both rituals match closely. First, just as the Aztecs spent considerable time in their ceremony converting a slave girl into a goddess infected with primal vegetal power, so Dickey spends five-sixths of his extraordinary poem in elevating an ordinary airline employee into a goddess by covertly, even festively, mixing opposite attributes in an agent who is simultaneously part of and external to the community she serves. Second, just as the Aztec priests put on the clammy skin of the sacrificed girl and deposited her blood on vegetables to ensure the effective transference of her sacred powers, so Dickey makes sure to perpetuate his victim's power in "fields where the whole earth / Caught her" and in the comic totems of her clothes. For example, her blouse ends up on a lightning rod, an instrument, like the girl herself, designed to transform and control massive energy. And third, both the Aztec slave girl and the stewardess die at "tragic cost" to convert infectious violence into ritual violence to ensure order and tranquility.

If it be argued that I am ignoring the extraordinary descriptive sections of the poem by focusing on the scapegoat mechanism, I do not mean to do so. What interests me is that aspect of Dickey's poetic method that changes the material act of falling from a plane into something quite different, something that accounts for our felt experience that the airline stewardess really is some sort of confluence of extraordinary powers and that her death is much more than another sensational and sympathetic item in a newspaper story.

As brilliantly depicted as the stewardess' various maneuvers are, the even more powerful structure in "Falling" is sacrificial. This structure is necessarily *covert*. The sacrificial mechanism must be concealed to keep its own component of contagious violence at arm's length and to ensure that the victim seems spontaneously chosen. Because all forms of violence are so infectious, anyone who comes near the victim—for instance, an executioner or priest—is likely to be tainted. If the scapegoat's death seems to arise from nature or a god's decree or religious custom or an airplane accident, then the violence associated with the victim issues from no human source and the community runs less risk of pollution. The victim is even more isolated from its worshipers, whose untainted unanimity against it consequently increases. Beautifully camouflaged by the hallucinatory frenzy of the stewardess' acrobatics and our own natural compassion for her plight, the girl's sacrificial doubleness is kept at a distance from those she will benefit because she is in midair and because our attention is distracted by Dickey's spectacular imagery. What is primitive and even more spectacular about this particular fall, is Dickey's ritual structure of preparation, execution, and redemptive regeneration.

## THE SACRED PARADIGM

In his dark preoccupation with the sacred as a literary method, Dickey is scarcely alone among writers, especially those dramatists and novelists steeped in the American southern tradition of ritual violence. Although most of the violence in Faulkner's novels is not redemptive, in "The Old People," seventy-year-old Sam Fathers (whose father was a Chickasaw chief) symbolically anoints Isaac with the blood of the boy's first killed deer as a sign of transition to manhood, a sign of longevity, and a sign of the blood bond between hunter and hunted. The boy

> drew the head back and the throat taut and drew Sam Fathers' knife across the throat and Sam stooped and dipped his hands in the hot smoking blood and wiped them back and forth across my face . . . the white boy of twelve with the prints of the bloody hands on his face . . . [was] marked forever, and the old dark man sired on both sides by savage kings, who had marked him, whose bloody hands had merely consecrated him to that which, under

the man's tutelage, he had already accepted, humbly and joyfully, with abnegation and with pride too; the hands, the touch, the first worthy blood which he had been found at last worthy to draw, joining him and the man forever, so that the man would continue to live past the boy's seventy years and then eighty years, long after the man himself had entered the earth as chiefs and kings entered it.[22]

In Flannery O'Connor's short story "Greenleaf," a tendentious white woman is impaled by the very bull she had asked her hired man to kill. After complaining earlier with characteristic irritability that "I'm the victim . . . I've always been the victim," she drives her car to a pasture near a wood where Mr. Greenleaf, her white-trash employee, had been sent to shoot the ridiculous and heretofore harmless animal. The following passage makes Dickey look almost tame in comparison:

> The bull . . . was crossing the pasture toward her at a slow gallop, a gay almost rocking gait as if he were overjoyed to find her again. . . . She looked back and saw that the bull, his head lowered, was racing toward her. . . . She stared at the violent black streak bounding toward her as if she had no sense of distance, as if she could not decide at once what his intention was, and the bull had buried his head in her lap, like a wild tormented lover, before her expression changed. One of his horns sank until it pierced her heart and the other curved around her side and held her in an unbreakable grip. She continued to stare straight ahead but the entire scene in front of her had changed—the tree line was a dark wound in a world that was nothing but sky—and she had the look of a person whose sight has been suddenly restored but who finds the light unbearable.

In O'Connor's Christian allegory, the sacred reality of the victimage the woman had self-righteously suspected about herself all along comes violently true in this moment of unbearable light. Her sight is redeemed but at terrible cost. In the story's last lines, she seemed "to be bent over whispering some last discovery into the animal's ear."[23]

Although one can find similar uses of stylized violence in dramatists such as Tennessee Williams and Lillian Hellman and in novelists such as Walker Percy and Barry Hannah, the incidence of redemptive victimage in poets—southern or otherwise—is rare. Although the modern exception of Robert Penn Warren springs immediately to

22. "The Old People," in *Uncollected Stories of William Faulkner*, ed. Joseph Blotner (New York, 1975), 201–203.
23. Flannery O'Connor, *The Complete Stories* (New York, 1971), 333.

mind, the fullest example of a lyric of ritual sacrifice may be found in Coleridge's "The Rime of the Ancient Mariner," though few of its commentators have featured the scapegoating mechanism, much less the conception of the monstrous double, as an integral part of their analyses. Even those readers who partially use primitive principles to explain the structure of the poem would do well to expand their use of anthropological terms. To further examine the wider value of the sacrificial principle, I would like to discuss several prominent readings of this poem.

In his reading of the first half of "The Rime of the Ancient Mariner" as an activity of "daemonic vengeance," John Livingston Lowes addresses the issue of structure by noting Wordsworth's observations about the poem that "the events having no necessary consequence do not produce each other." Centering on the problem of how the killing of an albatross could initiate such widespread consequences, Lowes's response is that "within *that* world, where birds have tutelary daemons and ships are driven by spectral and angelic powers, consequence and antecedent are in keeping." By using the principle of the scapegoat, Lowes might have added that in a world of primitive fantasy on shipboard where civilized codes of jurisprudence do not operate, the killing of an omen of good luck may easily precipitate calamity. Girard states that "the sacred embraces all those forces that threaten to harm man or trouble his peace. Natural forces and sickness are not distinguished from the threat of a violent disintegration of the community."[24]

After the Mariner kills the albatross and the ship stalls without wind while the sailors suffer from thirst, what would be a more natural event than to try to appease nature by designating the Mariner as the cause of their travail? However, because the sailors themselves are accomplices in the crime insofar as they initially approve the Mariner's act, the scapegoating process backfires, and the sailors become the victims of their own contagious victimage. What Lowes calls Coleridge's "ethical component," the Mariner's crime, gives "the illusion of inevitable sequence to that superb inconsequence" and is nothing

---

24. John Livingston Lowes, *The Road to Xanadu* (Boston, 1927), 300; Girard, *Violence and the Sacred*, 58.

other than the initiating spark that sets into motion a train of primitive methods exercised by the sailors to relieve their situation by placing the Mariner at the center.[25] In our terms, the poem is a narrative
lyric of partially effective victimage because it represents a state of affairs in which violence so exceeds all attempts at control that even
the scapegoat principle is ineffective. The Mariner is condemned forever to repeat his sacrificial role as he tells his tale to any listener he
can entrance. Thus, Lowes's contention that the Mariner's suffering is
valid only within the fantastic dreamlike world of the poem runs
counter to our reading of the narrative as the demonstration of primitive principles that are very much social mechanisms operating in
ritual and symbolic thought in modern and primitive cultures.

Eschewing Robert Penn Warren's view of the poem merely as a symbolic presentation of Coleridge's theological views of sin, punishment, and redemption, Edward Bostetter believes that the moral conception behind the Mariner's shooting of the albatross is "primitive
and savage" and that one of the instruments of revenge, the "lonesome
Spirit from the South Pole," is "less a Neoplatonic daemon than a
kind of primitive totem-force." The poem's pattern of sin and redemption for Bostetter is less Christian than something more universal. He
writes, "Just as the poem is molded and shaped by Coleridge's fears, so
it makes its appeal to the irrational fears that lurk not far beneath the
surface of modern consciousness. No matter how emancipated from
the magical view of the universe modern man may be intellectually,
he can never free himself from it emotionally or from the values associated with it. He is never quite able to eradicate the uneasy fear that
it might turn out to be true." In this critic's view, the religious commonplaces in the poem are merely superficial; they "give an aura of
sweet reasonableness and religious authority to an experience essentially negative and irrational; and satisfy the longing to believe that in
spite of our fears the universe is ultimately benevolent and reason-
able, and if we behave properly will leave us alone."[26]

Interesting as it is, Bostetter's definition of the "magical" character

25. Lowes, *The Road to Xanadu*, 300.
26. Edward Bostetter, "The Nightmare World of 'The Ancient Mariner,'" in Alun R.
Jones and William Tydeman (eds.), *Coleridge: The Ancient Mariner and Other Poems*
(London, 1973), 188–89, 195, 195–96.

of the Mariner's universe requires specification. In general, he sees this world as an aberration of one governed by divine law; it is "the Christian universe gone mad." What Coleridge "wanted to believe in and increasingly devoted his intellectual energies to asserting was a universe of order and benevolence in which man possessed freedom of will and action to mold his own destiny; what he feared was a universe in which he was at the mercy of arbitrary and unpredictable forces. 'The Rime' envisions such a universe. The Mariner's act is a compulsive sin which strips away the illusion of freedom and reveals just how helpless he is."[27] From a theological point of view, this universe may indeed be "arbitrary and unpredictable." From a primitive viewpoint, we are less surprised. We can say more accurately that in a world of radically generative violence in which ritual victimage is one of the few methods of control, the sequence of events in "The Rime of the Ancient Mariner" is neither arbitrary nor unpredictable. The poem's structure certainly involves a process of sin, punishment, and temporary redemption. Yet the action occurs on ship, away from the world of a civilized judicial system. With few external controls, not only does the society of sailors become tribal, but nature itself seems transformed when reciprocal violence begins and distinctions between life and death are blurred by the "Nightmare LIFE-IN-DEATH" and by the ship's "ghastly crew" of animated corpses. In an inflammatory world without a fixed judiciary where we find the blurring of stable cultural distinctions, chaos, and the scapegoating of the Mariner for so slight a crime, these events are as predictable as the ritual patterns of escalation and control in *Oedipus* and even *Macbeth*.

To the history of commentary on "The Rime of the Ancient Mariner," ranging from Wordsworth to George Whalley, we can also add the scapegoat principle to supplement several well-known remarks. To Wordsworth's complaint about the poem's lack of necessary sequence, we may add that the poem reflects the consequences of a sacrificial crisis when natural distinctions are blurred and the scapegoat is used to set things aright. Second, to Wordsworth's claims that the poem is defective because the Mariner has no "distinct character" and that "he does not act, but is continually acted upon,"[28] we would

---

27. *Ibid.*, 194.
28. Wordsworth quoted in Jones and Tydeman, 30.

counter that the Mariner, like the airplane stewardess, needs no fully developed characterization for him to function as vehicle for projected wrongs. Indeed, a fuller psychological profile might detract from his priestly role, just as at religious ceremonies further information about the "personality" of the priest would not only shift the focus of events but also jeopardize the unanimity of his selection were he to seem too sympathetic. It is in the very nature of the scapegoat as a nonreciprocating victim to remain to some degree passive.

To those commentaries that find the killing of the albatross incommensurate with the Mariner's suffering, we need only add that this is a primitive world of escalating contagion, not a universe of fixed moral principles. To even as discerning a modern critic as Whalley, we might use the scapegoating mechanism in a reading of *Oedipus* to specify his claim that "there is a sternness and inexorability of Greek tragedy in the paradox that an act committed in ignorance of the laws governing albatrosses and genii *must* be punished in the most severe manner." The contradictory nature of a ritual victim *is* the aesthetic and historical formula for its emotional efficacy. And, finally, to those critics like the infamous Mrs. Barbauld who can find no "moral" in the poem, we may side with the poet himself, who claimed that "the poem had too much" by arguing that the poem is "symbolic," *i.e.,* that it is "characterized by a translucence of the special in the Individual or of the General in the Especial" because of the particular dramatization of universal primitive processes.[29]

We can push our own inquiry further by noting that "The Rime of the Ancient Mariner" may be read as the ritual preparation of a victim, although in this case the victim is not sacrificed. Instead, he is doomed eternally to repeat the tale of his own monstrosity to whomever will listen. The Mariner is priest, penitent, god, and goat as his hypnotic glittering eye pulls the Wedding Guest into a fantastic world so filled with magical contagion that even the Mariner's extensive suffering cannot bring violence to an end. The Mariner is thus an imperfect scapegoat; because he does not die, his therapeutic power is limited. Just as his tale must continue, so does the mimetic reciprocity of his demonic universe over which he has limited control.

29. George Whalley, "The Mariner and the Albatross," in Jones and Tydeman, 175; Wordsworth quoted *ibid.,* 30.

## SACRIFICIAL PREPARATION

Coleridge's lyric of imperfect victimage brings us back to one more look at Dickey's own methods of ritual preparation. To round out our inquiry into Dickey's sacred principles, we need to examine several other aspects of the poetic method by which he makes monsters, aspects which at first seem extraordinary if not outrageous but are actually integral to the structure of primitive sacrifice. "The Fiend" is a lyric of sacrificial preparation that does not include execution. The poem depicts a homicidal sex maniac who monstrously infects the suburbs as he stalks the women who are his prey.

At first glance, Dickey seems to be mitigating, if not celebrating, the actions of a pervert. Even though he stalks through backyards and carries a knife, the fiend does not resemble a psychopath. Instead, he seems harmless yet also godly. He is a "worried accountant not with it" who, when he returns to the sidewalk after peeping from a tree, looks like "a solid citizen." He has "a super-quiet hand" to calm watchdogs. As he peers at a shopgirl, he appears to have divine extrasensory vision, plus a power of touch that takes strength from nature. During his pursuit, he gains mystical powers through "the godlike movement of trees," which mirror his sexual passion as the trees are "stiffening with him." Yet, at the point of his greatest power, his most threatening moment, the poem ends with an explicit image of weakness and a reminder of the fiend's aberrative character:

                                        the light
Of a hundred favored windows   gone wrong somewhere in his glasses
Where his knocked-off panama hat was   in his painfully vanishing
    hair.   (P, 230–33)

Rather than condemn the poet for a sensibility as perverse as the fiend's, we might recall a romantic topic mentioned earlier—renewal through the monstrous—and add to it our primitive principles. To be sure, the fiend is a moral monster, yet he is also a kind of king, "conferring immortality while it lasts" on his victims with a look. Like the speaker in "The Vegetable King," the fiend is a double agent, both monster and sacred king. Tender and frightening, cunning and insane, lover and killer, the fiend blurs differences between these opposites while embodying a vast range of "good" and "bad" traits. In short, his is the double face of a creature who draws evil to him then transforms it by virtue of his fitness as scapegoat.

Dickey does not complete his ritual; the fiend is not slain, for this is a poem of preparation of a monster, not its execution. At poem's end, this monster is about to move from speculation to action. The principle of closure here is nothing less than the inferred atrocity of what he is about to do, leaving us with the intense desire to annihilate him before he succeeds. Although the body of the poem uses Dickey's representative methods of motion and empathic entrance to contaminate society with the fiend's potential evil, the concluding lines convince us with no doubt whatsoever that the subject is a monster; as such, his execution would clearly cleanse the community of the mighty poison so powerfully understated in the innocuous details of his appearance. Although the fiend is not the victim here, his status is that of a suburban savage, dazzlingly prepared for unanimous victimage by Dickey's obsessive mixtures. What makes this poem glitter with evil is the suspenseful danger of the fiend's potential act and the intoxicating unanimity we feel in the poet's convincing portrayal of a frightening power that is out of control.

RITES OF PASSAGE

If any poet's habits of construction are especially apposite for dramatizing rites of passage in lyric form, Dickey's are. His universe is so much one of transition and exchange that almost all his speakers seem to be undergoing personal or cosmic metamorphosis. Whether the airline stewardess in "Falling" flies from life to death or the suburban father changes with the seasons in "The Vegetable King," Dickey's mystical primitivism contains elements that powerfully integrate the three major phases Arnold Van Gennep identifies as *rites de passage*, namely, separation, transition, and incorporation.[30] At times Dickey's poems may focus on one or all three of these stages. "The Hospital Window" centers on separation as the poet leaves a hospital where his father is deathly ill. "Drinking from A Helmet" focuses on

30. Arnold van Gennep, *The Rites of Passage* (Chicago, 1975), 11.

transition when the young GI changes identities just as he changes helmets in combat. And "Springer Mountain" is clearly a rite of incorporation of the hunter with his prey.

"Dover: Believing In Kings" incorporates all three of these phases. An extraordinary sixteen-stanza poem with a complex system of one- and two-line refrains, the lyric is a fantasy about an American tourist who lands in Dover with his pregnant wife. The speaker imagines himself a king and his unborn son a prince in a tale of swordplay and death, in which the speaker buries his father, inherits a crown, and conceives a son, all in a gerundive chant marked by swooping sea gulls and mystical movement. At the end of the poem, in a series of rhetorical questions, the poet asks himself who this new king really is, while partially answering the question with the statements enclosed within his interrogative syntax.

> Yet who is *he?* Whom does he face, in reflection?
> The stained-glass king,
> Or the child, grown tall, who cried to earth and air,
> To books and water: to sun and father and fire
> And nothingness to come and crown him, here?
> Or are they, both of them, and neither . . .
> *In a movement you cannot imagine*
> *Of England, the king smiles, climbing: running.*   (*P*, 93)

Is the face in the mirror the father or son, newly crowned king or prince? The answer lies, somewhat ambiguously, in the last line. The face is that of the smiling king. Yet also, to put it another way, it is "both of them, and neither, / This straw-headed knave, in blue-printed blue-jeans" (*P*, 93). The reflection is the speaker-as-father who can see in his own image his unborn son. The poem is a fantastic rite of passage for the speaker who formalizes his own new role as a father by establishing a regal lineage that encompasses past and future. Because the speaker is not restricted to the limitations of natural time, his mystical climbing and running integrate his new family into a fantastic whole: dead father, wife, son, and self. Consequently, many sides of the contradiction are possible. The mirrored image is both king and child, and neither, for Dickey's rhetoric of exchange allows him to align his speaker with his people in a single personage who encompasses several different aspects of self and family. The poem thus separates the speaker from his old self while simultaneously integrating him into a new identity as father and family man.

One of the poet's most affectionate rites of passage occurs in an epiphany experienced by a boy at a carnival. In *Self-Interviews*, Dickey tells us that "The Celebration" is based on an actual incident involving himself and his parents at Lakewood Park near Atlanta. Even though the speaker's revelation does not occur until the concluding lines, the boy is already in movement in the poem's first two words: "All wheels." Surrounded by a carnival of motion that includes a roller coaster, gambling wheels, and bumper cars, he spies his parents acting like young lovers and follows them to the Ferris wheel. Like Ezekiel's wheel, this "Wheel of wheels" begins to spin with light and movement until it approximates the celestial motion of the origin of life itself, a universal circularity in which the boy recognizes "the whirling impulse / From which I had been born" (*P*, 202). As the result of another of Dickey's connections of a particular event with Absolute Motion, the speaker suddenly appreciates his gift of life, and his bond with his parents grows clearer and stronger. The poem thus celebrates a gentle yet momentous moment of awareness, transition, and incorporation in a young man's life.

When violence is involved in an agent undergoing transition, that agent at times takes on a monstrous character, physically and emotionally. In "The Scarred Girl," a car accident turns a once-beautiful girl into someone frighteningly different as she waits in a hospital bed:

> For her calm, unimagined face
> To emerge from the yards of its wrapping,
> Red, raw, mixed-looking but entire . . .
>
> To confront the pale glass it has dreamed
> Made whole and backed with wise silver,
> Held in other hands brittle with dread,
> A doctor's, a lip-biting nurse's
>
> Who do not see what she sees . . . (*P*, 139)

In "Mangham" a high school math teacher suffers a stroke in class but continues to teach. Even as he is dying, Mangham bizarrely, comically, and heroically forestalls his separation from the living by

> . . . explaining for my own good, from the good
> Side of his face, while the other
> Mixed unfelt sweat and ice water, what I never
> Could get to save my soul: those things that, once
> Established, cannot be changed by angels,
> Devils, lightning, ice or indifference:
> Identities! Identities!   (*P*, 225)

Even as he clings to his old identity, the teacher is part of the dead, a character halfway between two realms who becomes a prophetic monster as "his cracked voice was speaking / of perfection, sphere-music, / through the stroke which blazed in his mind" (*P*, 225). Although he celebrates Mangham's tenacity, Dickey primitively makes him the subject of dangerous change in a poem of separation and transition that animates the "dark night of the adolescent mind" with a cracked music of life and death.

"The Shark's Parlor" is Dickey's best depiction of a rite of passage centering on violence. Two young boys go shark hunting on an island off the coast of Georgia and hook a hammerhead that almost demolishes the house to which they secured their line. In the process, they comically become hunters and almost the hunted. Analysis of this poem will be deferred until the last chapter for two reasons. First, I wish to examine one of Dickey's best poems in considerable depth, and second, I wish to show how my four critical hypotheses, used in conjunction rather than separately, can be used in a comprehensive yet precise fashion.

FOUR HYPOTHESES: A SUMMARY

At this point in our inquiry, we have distinguished four different kinds of activity in Dickey's universe: mysticism, Neoplatonism, romanticism, and primitivism. As we saw, his mysticism is characterized by a kind of universal motion permeating objects and agents, allowing each to exchange attributes so thoroughly that all entities seem to be mere moments in a continuum of perpetual flux. His Neoplatonism is a variant of his mystical motives that bear such an extraordinary correspondence to the rhythms of song and music that his events and agents seem governed by cosmic principles of melody. When the poet's objects of exchange are animals and the things of nature, his movement seems more concrete; its power bears close analogy to the empathic unity the romantic poets have traditionally sought in nature. At the same time, Dickey's romantic poems have placed an emphasis on sensation, sometimes violent, as a method of renewal and redemption. And finally, from a primitive perspective, Dickey's empathic world seems so alive that the things of nature seem to have their own indwelling spirits. When victimage enters his poetic equation, his methods of redemption and exchange are closer to tribal methods of ritual than to the romantic topics of monstrosity.

It may reasonably be argued that my divisions are artificial, that none of Dickey's poems are purely mystical or romantic or primitive, and that Dickey's art may best be served not by a differentiation of poetic principles but rather by a synthetic approach that combines lines of inquiry to show the full methodology of a particular poem. I fully agree. Yet, before we can see Dickey's vision as a concrete whole, it seems to me necessary to separate out as clearly as possible the central structural strategies in his universe and to specify these strategies by aligning them historically with similar methods used by other distinguished poets. We may thus establish formal grounds for locating Dickey in a number of different traditions to see not only how he fits in these categories but, more importantly, how he differs from them. We may then judge his achievement by seeing what he has added to his methodological predecessors or by seeing how he has modified their practices.

For example, we may fruitfully read "May Day Sermon" with its intoxicating rhythms and imagery as a reindividuation of the romantic topic of disordering the senses to produce an apocalyptic revitalization of sexual energy in spring. Yet, if we add primitive principles, we have an even more precise reading. Performed by a Baptist preacher who as a modern shaman entrances herself and her flock, "May Day Sermon" becomes a fertility rite designed to restore earth and women to a "natural" state of fruitfulness by purging the community of evil through the scapegoating of the country girl's father. By means of blood sacrifice, the earth is sanctified through violence because the

repressive sexuality of the Bible is expelled along with its representative. Not only is human instinct revitalized, but nature itself seems
to become a festival of energy. Once the victim has been claimed,
nothing perverse remains: the realms of beast and man remain distinct, the dead have been separated from the living, and thus the frenetic energy that came to violent culmination around the father's victimage begins to subside as the poem ends. The poem has partaken of
the hallucinatory energy of reciprocal violence long enough to use
that energy to rejuvenate its setting so that at its conclusion the audience can return to a feeling of order and tranquility.

By using my hypotheses, I hope to have shown that Dickey's art
bears similarity to a number of esteemed writers, that his methods are
complex and worthy of study, and that one may do well to look to dis-
ciplines other than literary history to discover how he constructs his
poems. As I mentioned in my introduction, the commonplaces of anthropology constitute an extremely fruitful area in which to find
terms to discuss this poet. In fact, the central problem in this entire
study has been one of invention of a critical method. While research-
ing this project, when I set out to discuss Dickey as a mystic, I probed
the literature of mysticism and was surprised to find that most discus-
sions of mystical methods in literature were themselves mystical in
the sense that they were imprecise repetitions of general expressions
surrounding mystical experience and were even less serviceable as ho-
listic hypotheses to be used to account for major elements of lyric expression such as imagery, action, and emotional effect. I found it necessary to try to understand mysticism as a literary method before
deciding whether Dickey was mystical or not. Thus my rationale for
isolating mysticism itself as a poetic strategy.

Now that the hypothetical strands have been separated, we can begin to combine them. My procedure at this point bears analogy to Aristotle's method in the *Poetics*. After using his four causes analyti-
cally to generate the constituent parts of his subject in the first five
chapters of his inquiry, he then combines his elements in the famous
definition in Chapter Six, and from then on, his method is synthetic
as he tests his formulation against the range of extant works nomi-
nally called tragedies. From this point in my study, I would like to fol-

low his lead by using all four of my hypotheses synthetically to offer as full an explanation as possible of three central elements in Dickey's art: the speaker, representation techniques, and diction. I then wish to read "The Shark's Parlor" in the last chapter to show how my principles can work in combination in a particular analysis to reveal the wide range of strategies informing one of Dickey's poems.

# II / Agent

Magnifying and applying come I,
Out bidding at the start the old cautious hucksters,
Taking myself the exact dimensions of Jehovah,
Lithographing Kronos, Zeus his son, and Hercules his grandson,
Buying drafts of Osiris, Isis, Belus, Brahma, Buddha. . . .
With Odin and the hideous-faced Mexitli and every idol and
     image,
Taking them all for what they are worth and not a cent more.
                              —WALT WHITMAN

Ye gods, come and accept this wine and drink.
Ye ghosts, come and accept this wine and drink. . . .
Spirit of the earth, come and accept this wine and drink.
Spirit of pools, come and accept this wine and drink.

Stand behind me with a standing, and let me be possessed with a
     good possession . . .

If anyone is sick, let me be able to tend him . . .

Do not let my eyes come covered over.
Do not let my ears become closed up.
                              —ASHANTI SHAMAN

  We fear!
  We fear the elements with which we have to fight in their fury
to wrest our food from land and sea.
  We fear cold and famine in our snow huts.
  We fear the sickness that is daily to be seen among us. Not
death, but the suffering.
  We fear the souls of the dead, of human and animal alike.
  We fear the spirits of earth and air.
  And therefore our fathers, taught by their fathers before them,
guarded themselves about with all these old rules and customs,
which are built upon the experience and knowledge of generations. We do not know how or why, but obey them that we may
be suffered to live in peace.
                              —ESKIMO HUNTER

Granted Dickey's primitivistic disposition, his lyric speaker is very
much a modern man. Whether suburbanite or bomber pilot, folksinger or football fan, he is a person whose initial field of action is

mid-twentieth-century middle America. Although this speaker assumes a myriad of identities, ranging from a lifeguard to a poisoned
man, his poetic voice is the same throughout all Dickey's lyrics. His
identities are merely circumstantial and reflect less a three-dimensional psychological character than an agent whose nature is determined by the specific function he performs. In "Power and Light,"
when a telephone lineman drinks whiskey in his basement after a day
of climbing power poles, the speaker is really the cosmic Dickey who
claims that "in the deep sway of underground among the roots / That
bend like branches    all things connect    and stream / Toward light
and speech" (P, 256–57). And in the long poem "The Zodiac" narrated
by a drunken Dutch sailor, the speaker is none other than what Dickey
calls his "I-figure" (S, 155), who attempts an apocalyptic vision that
will link him to the stars.

Certainly one of the most representative stances for Dickey is his
experience as a modern soldier. Whether recalled or directly por-
trayed, events in the Pacific theatre in World War II are very much alive
for this poet, often revealed through his striking mixtures of terror
and joy. In "The Performance," he recalls a fellow GI who was decapi-
tated by the enemy and comically imagines that the man might have
done a series of acrobatic tricks to amaze his executioners. When the
poet slides into the seat of a "rusted halftrack" underwater at the end
of the war in "The Driver," we see his mystical motives in operation
as boundaries begin to dissolve and he sees the "uneasy, lyrical skin
that lies / Between death and life, trembling aways" (P, 169). Perhaps
Dickey's experience with war is a personal motive for his impulse to
protect his family and the country for which he feels so strongly. In
"The War Wound," he tells a wound in the heel of his hand

> to burn like a poison
> When my two children threaten themselves,
> Wall-walking, or off the deep end
>                         Of a country swimming pool    (P, 223)

In fact, we may speculate that Dickey's early experience with the
lightning-like transitions of life and death in war may have led to his
primitive view of the interconnecting of these two realms. In "Horses
and Prisoners," the poet recalls how prisoners in the Philippines lived

on horsemeat then imagines a bizarre life-giving race for them with "Each footstep putting forth petals, / Their bones light and strong as the wind" (*P*, 171). And, in "Drinking From A Helmet," a young GI grows into manhood by inheriting the spirit of a dead colleague when he puts on the man's helmet.

Although he often weighs issues of considerable consequence, Dickey's speaker is not discursive. He is a man of practical action for whom knowing and doing are inseparable. Instead of thinking his way through problems, Dickey *performs* solutions or dramatizes a crisis in terms that are actional and sensory, not intellectual. He decries confessional poems, which he finds "flat and non-committal and rather complacent" as if they were all "written by the same rather synthetic, flat-speaking, neurotic, and quietly desperate person" (*S*, 51). Like his invented beast in "For the Last Wolverine," which is half-wolverine and half-eagle, Dickey prefers that his voice "Rise beyond reason over hills / of ice SCREAMING    that it cannot die" (*P*, 277). At times, his over-reliance on explosive sensation results in a speaker who has little to say and who relies on a formless diffusion of energy to communicate his cosmic connection. However, when Dickey has his materials under control, usually by virtue of a plotlike structure or an interesting exchange with nature, the specific function of his speakers becomes clear and moving.

In another sense, however, Dickey has no speakers at all. No matter how social this poet's roles nor how realistic his settings and situations, so powerful are his principles of motion and exchange that his speakers threaten to dissolve at any moment into the activities they undergo or the landscapes in which they perform. This chapter will examine the romantic topic of radical assimilation of self and object in Dickey, while noting still another paradox in his agents. That is, despite their modernity, his agents constantly invite us to return to our romantic and primitivistic vocabulary, especially with regard to their roles as hero and shaman. What is certainly modern is Dickey's sense of humor, whether present in poems that are fully comic in nature or in ironies that bind us to the speaker with an implicit understanding that his primitive practices have only emotional, not practical, solutions for the crises they confront.

## The Romantic "I"

M. H. Abrams notes that, as an effect of their confrontations with landscapes, "the distinction between self and not-self tended to dissolve" for many romantic poets. Citing Coleridge, Abrams goes on to say:

> The reintegration of the divided self (of "head and heart") and the simultaneous healing of the breach between the ego and the alien other (of "subject and object") was for Coleridge a profound emotional need which he translated into the grounds both of his theory of knowledge and his theory of art . . . he specifically defined art as "the reconciler of nature and man . . . the power of humanizing nature, of infusing the thoughts and passions of man into every thing which is the object of his contemplation." It is "the union and reconciliation of that which is nature with that which is exclusively human."[1]

For a truly pantheistic poet, the union of self and nature is a transformation of self, even a dissolution of self into something else. Pushing this assimilative process further than Abrams, Geoffrey Hartman states that he does not believe that in many instances the romantics wished "for a mere return to the state of nature" but for an overcoming of alienated self-consciousness seen by the likes of Shelley, Keats, and Blake "as a kind of death-in-life, as the product of a division in the self." According to Hartman, the romantics' preoccupation with the solitary lyric reflects a need to transcend and heal breaches in the mind resulting from the rise of analytic thought: "The Romantic 'I' emerges nostalgically when certainty and simplicity of self are lost." For Hartman, imagination becomes a kind of bridging faculty, the central problem of which is "whether myth-making is still possible, whether the mind can find an unselfconscious medium for itself or maintain something of the interacting unity of self and live."[2]

If any modern American poet has successfully addressed himself to these issues by making poetic "myths" that, like those of Wordsworth, convert "the solipsistic into the sympathetic imagination,"[3] it is James

1. M. H. Abrams, "Structure and Style in the Greater Romantic Lyric," in Frederick Hilles and Harold Bloom (eds.), *From Sensibility to Romanticism* (New York, 1965), 547.
2. Geoffrey Hartman, *Beyond Formalism* (New Haven, 1970), 300, 303, 304, 302.
3. *Ibid.*, 303.

Dickey. Given his romantic thrust for self-unity, Dickey's dislike for the confessional poets who self-indulgently glory in their neuroses and solitary pains becomes even more understandable. The age of anxiety may be part of the current human condition that confronts Dickey in his work, but it is most certainly *not* the place he wishes to be. As we have seen throughout this study, Dickey persistently avoids poetic strategies—especially extended speculation and analysis—that interfere with his throwing off the husk of self-consciousness, Blake's "mind-forged manacles" that separate self and other.

Whether Dickey changes "places into the spirit / I had as a rack-ribbed child" to "rail at my lust of self" (*P*, 34) in "The Other," or whether he finds in "the scrambling animal weight / Of lust" the means to change from "a thing half-beast . . . To the wholly human" (*P*, 268) in "Sustainment," he is constantly preoccupied with the restoration of a splintered self by means of instinctual experience. Because his poetic action is not meditative, his reflective lyric ego is less distant from his objects of consciousness than more discursive poets, and appears most often as a narrative rather than philosophic "I." Nonetheless this "I" is far enough from its object to require assimilation. Not only does Dickey personally feel a "loss of intimacy with the natural process" (*S*, 68), but he wants a "total responsiveness" in order to achieve, like Roethke, "an extraordinary kind of wholeness impossible to animals and possible to men only on rare occasions" (*BB*, 150).

Dickey is also well aware that his poetic "I" is not really himself. In "The Self as Agent," he says that the poet is well aware that "the conditions by which he is limited and delimited in the poem are, in fact, nothing like the same ones that shape his actual life" (*S*, 157). The I-figure at the beginning of composition is "nebulous, ectoplasmic" then later an "expressive possibility" (*S*, 157, 164). Dickey heartily approves of Keats's conception of "negative capability" and claims that the poetic self is "fluid and becomes what is most poetically profitable for it to become, in the specific poem in which it comes to exist. Poems are points in time when the I-figure congeals and takes on a definite identity and ascertainable qualities, and the poet is able to appear, for the space of the poem, as a coherent and stabilizing part of the presentation, observing, acting, and serving as a nucleus of the inities and means and revelations of the poem" (*S*, 160). One of the poetic means the I-figure serves for Dickey is to provide an agent "for dramatic expression . . . of emotional truth, a humanly dramatic and formally satisfying truth" present not "in the real world of fact but in a kind of magical abstraction, an emotion-and-thought-charged personal version of it" (*S*, 163–64).

If "an extraordinary kind of wholeness" is difficult "in the real world of fact," Dickey can, with remarkable ease and grace, heal the fragmented relation between self and nature with his I-figure. Given his emphasis on communal and familial topics, his preference for magical contact rather than analytic division, and his preoccupation with interpenetrating modes of movement, we can see how his agent disappears into and out of its subject. If the I-figure feels pain at his mother's illness in "Buckdancer's Choice," Dickey solves the solitary problem by building a continuum of song that transcends death by uniting mother and son with joy rather than anguish. If the I-figure feels the need to protect his sons in "To His Children in Darkness," the isolating anxiety of the speaker is overcome by a bond of ritual expulsion of evil by a father who sanctifies his son's room by making himself into a beast fit for scapegoating. If, in Dickey's ritual ceremonies, the dancer and the dance seem one, then this poet, even more thoroughly than his romantic predecessors, has overcome analytic alienation by constructing myths that unite him socially and magically without, as Hartman says, "sacrifice to abstraction."[4] To specify in even greater detail how Dickey binds his speaker to landscape, we will return once more to our primitivistic vocabulary.

SHAMAN AND HERO

If the ghostly visitation of a spirit upon a sleeper in "The Being" is a variation on a shamanistic rite of initiation, "Remnant Water" shows the poet trying fully to carry out his holy office by redeeming the death of a pond. As Dave Smith rightly observes of this poem, Dickey is "the shamanistic genius of the place."[5]

---

4. *Ibid.*
5. Dave Smith, "The Strength of James Dickey," *Poetry,* CXXXVII (1981), 354.

                                    one carp now knowing grass
                        And also thorn-shucks and seeds
              Can outstay him . . .
              A hundred acres of cancelled water come down
                        To death-mud shaking
          Its one pool    stomach-pool    holding the dead one diving up
        Busting his gut in weeds    in scum-gruel glowing with belly-white
Unhooked . . .
                        Here in the dry hood I am watching
              Alone, in my tribal sweat    my people gone my fish rolling
                        Beneath me    and I die
                        Waiting    will wait out
                        The blank judgment given only
In ruination's suck-holing acre    wait and make the sound surrounding NO

                        Laugh primally: be
              Like an open-gut flash    an open under-
                  water eye with the thumb
              pressure to brain the winter-wool head of me,
        Spinning my guts with my fish in the old place,
                  Suffering its consequences, dying,
                        Living up to it.    (*TCM*, 108–109)

Standing next to a pool that was once a "hundred acres" of water, alone in his "tribal sweat," the poet-fisherman watches his catch roll belly-up in the remnants of the "slain lake." Just as the dying carp knows that grass and "thorn-shucks and seeds / Can outstay him," so the poet dies "Waiting" with only his word, "the sound surrounding NO," to prevent the loss of the "gone depths." Yet he has no effective power. All he has is sympathetic magic and a primal laugh whereby hunter and hunted join spirits as the speaker is: "Spinning my guts with my fish in the old place, / Suffering its consequences, dying, / Living up to it" (*TCM*, 108–109).

To be sure, Dickey is not alone in the neoprimitivist romantic tradition when he evokes through poetry the "genius loci" in his visionary landscape. In "The Marriage of Heaven and Hell," Blake notes: "The ancient Poets animated all sensible objects with Gods or Geniuses, calling them by the names and adorning them with the properties of woods, rivers, mountains, lakes, cities, nations, and whatever their enlarged & numerous senses could perceive . . . choosing forms of worship from poetic tales." For Geoffrey Hartman, the English romantics' uses of the genius loci signaled a "new structure of fusion." He states: "To invoke the ghost in the landscape is only preparatory to a deeper, ceremonial merging of the poet's spirit and the spirit of place." This "merging" is a "mode of ritual identification" involving "a divinity and a notary," a mode that centers on the problem of self-identification, especially in a time of crisis: "Whenever the question of persona arises in a radical way, whenever self-choosing, self-identification, becomes a more than personal, indeed a prophetic, decision—which happens when the poet feels himself alien to the genius of country or age and destined to assume an adversary role—poetry renews itself by its contact with what may seem to be archaic forces."[6]

Dickey's feeling for the need of "archaic forces" resembles the melancholy of an old Omaha Indian who reflects on the spoiling of the landscape.

> When I was a youth, the country was very beautiful. Along the rivers were belts of timberland, where grew cottonwood, maple, elm, ash, hickory, and walnut trees, and many other shrubs. . . . In both the woodland and the prairies I could see the trails of many kinds of animals and could hear the cheerful songs of many kinds of birds. When I walked abroad I could see many forms of life, beautiful living creatures which *Wakanda* [the Supreme Being] had placed here. . . . But now the face of all the land is changed and sad. The living creatures are gone. I see the land desolate and I suffer an unspeakable sadness. Sometimes I wake in the night and I feel as though I should suffocate from the pressure of this awful feeling of loneliness.

Like that of the Omaha wiseman, the central problem that confronts the poet in "Remnant Water" is that of loss but also pollution, pollution of matter and soul. This situation is movingly expressed by Assiniboin Chief John Snow.

> We believe that the Creator made everything beautiful in his time. We believe that we must be good stewards of the Creator and not destroy nor mar His works of creation. We look upon stewardship . . . in . . . respect for the beauty of the land and of life in harmony with the succession of the sea-

6. Geoffrey Keynes (ed.), *The Complete Writings of William Blake* (Oxford, 1972), 153; Hartman, *Beyond Formalism*, 322, 326, 335.

sons, so that the voices of all living things can be heard and continue to live and dwell among us. If an area is destroyed, marred, or polluted, my people say, the spirits will leave the area. If pollution continues, not only animals, birds, and plant life will disappear, but the spirits will also leave. This is one of the greatest concerns of the Indian people.[7]

Not only does Dickey face the loss of a natural resource in his poem but also the loss of the benevolent spirits—the animating principles of man's connection with nature—that once dwelled in the "cancelled water." To restore the sacred spirits that ensure both the source of food and man's harmony with the earth, the poet uses the shamanistic medicine of sympathy, ecstasy, and the chant. By means of jammed images ("Grass-wind") and run-on lines ("gone depths duly arriving / Into the weeds"), the poet's diction fuses natural forces in the setting, energizing and inspiriting the scene with magical contact that produces an intensity (or shamanistic ecstasy) the speaker achieves as he "howls" with loss. This ecstasy is characteristic of this poet, and Dickey uses it to generate what anthropologist Ernest Arbman calls a "total suggestive absorption in the object of belief." Thus Dickey suffers *with* his dying fish; by "Living up to it" in the final line, he clearly signals his primal responsibility in trying to bring his own live soul into the inanimate object and by sympathetic magic into the entire "slain lake." When he utters the "sound surrounding no," Dickey's mythic strategy resembles that of the heroic vision of a warrior of the Hicarilla Apaches known as "The Killer of Enemies" mentioned by Joseph Campbell in *Hero With a Thousand Faces:* "Listen to what I say. The world is just as big as my body. The world is as large as my word. And the world is as large as my prayers. The sky is only as large as my words and prayers. The seasons are only as great as my body, my words, and my prayer. It is the same with the waters; my body, my words, my prayer are greater than the waters."[8]

In many ways, the fish in "Remnant Water" becomes the poet-shaman's "sacred animal," the material manifestation of a localized spirit that allows the shaman access to an unchanging world not sub-

7. Melvin Gilmore, *Prairie Smoke* (New York, 1929), 36; John Snow, *The Mountains Are Our Sacred Places* (Toronto, 1977), 145.
8. Ernest Arbman, *Ecstasy or Religious Trance* (Norstedts, Sweden, 1963), xv; Joseph Campbell, *Hero With a Thousand Faces* (New York, 1953), 319.

ject to physical decay. This poem is a key to Dickey's other relationships with animals. Among the Buriat shamans of Siberia, Campbell notes, "the animal or bird that protects the shaman is called *Khubilgan*, meaning 'metamorphosis,' from the verb *khubilku*, 'to change oneself, to take another form.'" And in *Shamanism*, Mircea Eliade observes: "All categories of shamans have their helping and tutelary spirits. . . . The presence of a helping spirit in animal form, dialogue with it in a secret language, or incarnation of such an animal spirit by the shaman (masks, actions, dances, etc.) is another way of showing that the shaman can forsake his human condition, is able, in a word 'to die.'" By suffering, dying, and "living up" to his fish, Dickey redeems the death of the lake by gaining access to the magical world of permanent substance. Eliade states: "From the most distant times almost all animals have been conceived as psychopomps that accompany the soul into the beyond or as the dead person's new form. Whether it is the 'ancestor' or 'initiatory master,' the animal symbolizes a real and direct connection with the beyond. . . . The tutelary animal not only enables the shaman to transform himself; it is in a manner his 'double,' his alter ego. This alter ego is one of the shaman's 'souls,' the soul in animal form or, more precisely, the 'life soul.'" By ecstatically "Spinning my guts with my fish," the poet can thus reanimate and restore things to an Edenic condition: "While preparing for his ecstasy and during it, the shaman abolishes the present human condition and, for the time being, recovers the situation as it was at the beginning. Friendship with animals, knowledge of their language, transformation into an animal are so many signs that the shaman has re-established the 'paradisal' situation lost at the dawn of time."[9]

Because the trancelike ecstasy not only distinguishes the shaman from other members of his tribe but also is the source of his magical power,[10] we will spend a moment examining the ecstatic aspect of Dickey's speaker. And, while it is interesting to note how many marks of shamanistic ecstasy are found in this poet, our task is really to show how these marks are wholly consistent with this poet's romantic and primitive principles. Of course, everything depends on what

9. Joseph Campbell, *Primitive Mythology* (New York, 1959), 257; Mircea Eliade, *Shamanism*, trans. Willard Trask (Princeton, 1972), 91–93, 93–94, 99.
10. Eliade, *Shamanism*, 499–506.

we mean by *ecstasy*. To some extent, the topic of Dickey's ecstasy has already been covered in the section on mysticism insofar as many descriptions of mystical experience coincide with descriptions of shamanistic ecstasy. However, when anthropologists use phrases like "dazzling inner clairvoyance or illumination" and "a peculiar, strictly organized and intensively clear, conscious and realistic visionary state of dream" to describe estatic states of mind, we learn less which is new about our own subject than when the issue centers on ends and means.[11]

One thing the shaman must be able to do is to initiate his trance at will; whether the methods include drum, rattle, or drugs, music is a crucial element. Recalling for us Dickey's Neoplatonic impulse, N. Kershaw Chadwick notes: "The use of music is undoubtedly due partly to the practical necessity of couching prophecy in the most impressive and far-reaching vehicle of expression, partly to a desire to reach the spirits, who are assumed to be far away, and to 'publish' orally in the most impressive form. But it is also ritual in purpose, for music is the language of spirits, and the principal means of communication between the spirits and humanity."[12] Dickey's ecstatic music issues from his rhythmic strategies: his frenetic long lines divided by ceasura, his hypnotic anapests, and his pervasive gerundives. When used to communicate with the dead or to inspirit a location, Dickey's trance becomes not neoplatonic but priestly, as in "Into the Stone":

> Elsewhere I have dreamed of my birth,
> And come from my death as I dreamed;
>
> Each time, the moon has burned backward.
> Each time, my heart has gone from me
> And shaken the sun from the moonlight.
> Each time, a woman has called,
> And my breath come to life in her singing.   (*P,* 47)

Even in this, one of his earliest lyrics, Dickey's speaker seems shamanistic in Eliade's sense insofar as his ecstasy is "induced by his ascent to the sky or descent to the underworld."[13] Not only has his

---

11. Arbman, *Ecstasy or Religious Trance,* 297.
12. Campbell, *Primitive Mythology,* 257; N. Kershaw Chadwick, *Poetry and Prophecy* (Cambridge, England, 1952), 45.
13. Eliade, *Shamanism,* 499.

chant enabled him to communicate with a kind of spirit world ("The dead have their chance in my body"), but it also transports him to a magical world where he experiences a "light vision" based on fantastic laws when "The sun is shaken from the moonlight." Dickey's trance entails a journey entailing a new vision and new powers, powers that, unlike those of the solipsistic mystic, are intended to be shared with the residents of this world.

In addition to the journey, another prominent mark of the shaman is the suffering of personal disorientation which gains him unusual powers.[14] Joseph Campbell characterizes the first stage of the "shamanistic crisis" as "a spontaneously precipitated rupture with the world of common day, revealed in symptoms analogous to those of a serious nervous breakdown: visions of dismemberment, fosterage in the world of the spirits, and restitution." Although they suffer no internal crises resembling neurosis (as is the case with many shamans), Dickey's speakers continually confront real problems of such magnitude that they are forced to break from the everyday world to undergo what Campbell calls "the standard path of mythological adventure": "A hero ventures forth from the world of common day into a region of supernatural wonder: fabulous forces are there encountered and a decisive victory is won: the hero comes back from this mysterious adventure with the power to bestow boons on his fellow man." Based on the three stages in rites of passage (separation-initiation-return), Campbell's paradigm of the heroic journey fits well into Dickey's version of the shamanistic crisis, which is a kind of perpetual trial-by-ordeal, a heroic adventure to a "fateful region of both treasure and danger . . . a distant land, a forest, a kingdom underground, beneath the waves, or above the sky, a secret island, lofty mountaintop, or profound dream state; . . . a place of strangely fluid and polymorphous beings, unimaginable torments, superhuman deeds, and impossible delight."[15]

In "Approaching Prayer," the poet converts his father's attic into just such a region of primitive adventure: "The universe is creaking like boards / Thumping with heartbeats / And bonebeats." By put-

14. Paul Radin, *Primitive Religion* (New York, 1957), 107.
15. Campbell, *Primitive Mythology*, 265; Campbell, *Hero With a Thousand Faces*, 30, 58.

ting on the father's sweater, the spurs of his gamecocks, and the head
of a boar killed by him, the son not only experiences "unimaginable
torment" and "impossible delight" but also establishes a magical connection with his dead father:

> My father's sweater
> Swarms over me in the dark.
> I see nothing, but for a second
>
> Something goes through me
> Like an accident, a negligent glance,
> Like the explosion of a star
> Six billion light years off . . .
>
>         I nearly lift
> From the floor, from my father's grave
> Crawling over my chest   (P, 166–67)

His father's attic thus becomes another of Dickey's circuits of redemptive motion, a realm at the foundation of many mythic world views.
The poet's goal is to obtain a vision like that of Old Testament prophets, namely, to get

>       to the hovering place
> Where I can say with any
> Other than the desert fathers—
> Those who saw angels come   (P, 167)

In Dickey's world and in the world of the ancients, the principle is the
same: "All the visible structures of the world—all things and beings—are the effects of a ubiquitous power out of which they rise,
which supports and fills them during the period of their manifestation, and back into which they must ultimately dissolve. This is the
power known to science as energy, to the Melanesians as *mana*, to the
Sioux Indians as *wakonda*, the Hindus as *shakti*, and the Christians
as the power of God."[16] Only with this peculiar power can Dickey finally answer "what questions men asked / In Heaven's tongue, Using
images of earth / Almightily" (P, 168).

When Dickey dons the costume of an animal like the "lord of the
animals" engraved on the walls of the Paleolithic caves at Montes-

---

16. Campbell, *Hero With a Thousand Faces*, 257.

quieu-Avantes in the Pyrenees, he becomes not only a shaman but also a god, "an epiphany of the divine being itself." As Campbell notes, such a figure "is taboo. He is a conduit of divine power. He does not merely *represent* the god, he *is* the god; he is a *manifestation* of the god, not a representation."[17] When he puts on the boar's head in "Approaching Prayer" and when he puts on a helmet in "Armor," Dickey assumes a new and primitive character plus remarkable powers of unification:

> When this is the thing you put on
> The world is pieced slowly together
> In the power of the crab and the insect.
> The make of the eyeball changes
> As over your mouth you draw down
> A bird's bill made for a man.   (*P*, 81)

While "breathing deep through [his] sides like an insect in armor," he gains a strength which enables him to give life to his dead brother "who shall wake and shine on my limbs / As I walk, made whole" into a realm where he begins "living forever" (*P*, 81–82). Not only has the poet gained a godlike immortality through his animal ritual and through communion with the dead, but he himself becomes divine. By dying in "Drowning With Others," he reenacts an ancient rite of redemption that also generates his magical chant as if it were a gift of sea gods:

> If I opened my arms, I could hear
>
> Every shell in the sea find the word
> It has tried to put into my mouth.
> Broad flight would become of my dancing,
> And I would obsess the whole sea,
>
> But I keep rising and singing
> With my last breath.   (*P*, 85)

At times, as in "The Poisoned Man" and "The Firebombing," Dickey's speaker assumes a dangerous character who is diseased yet achieves miraculous vision or who, like the scapegoat, draws evil to himself in a startling way. In "Diabetes" the poet-as-diabetic ignores his doctor's

17. Campbell, *Primitive Mythology*, 311.

warnings, opens a beer, and with his blood sugar rising discovers "Sweetness everywhere." In "Blood" the speaker wakes up hungover in bed and discovers not only "Blood blood all over / Me and blood" (*TCM*, 30) but also a bleeding girl he does not know and has never seen before. In "The Sheep Child" the poet speaks for an embryo, half-human, half-sheep, that is "pickled in alcohol" in a jar in an Atlanta museum. After a farm boy has coupled with a ewe, the creature from two worlds comes momentarily to consciousness as a mythic beast with a bizarre yet striking vision, achieved by the violent breaking of the taboo against bestiality:

> *I woke dying,*
>
> *In the summer sun of the hillside, with my eyes*
> *Far more than human. I saw for a blazing moment*
> *The great glassy world from both sides . . .*
> *My hoof and my hand clasped each other,*
> *I ate my one meal*
> *of milk, died*
> *Staring.   (P, 253)*

Although Dickey's poem is shocking to the modern western mind, coitus with animals plays a prominent part in initiation rites in New Guinea and in curative magic in other primitive cultures, Arnold van Gennep notes.[18]

Whether his speaker moves "at the heart of the world" in his tree house or discovers the primal "Word" in "Sleeping Out At Easter," Dickey's shaman-hero becomes both magician and priest when he conveys his powers to others. Borrowing E. O. James's distinctions from *The Nature and Function of Priesthood*, we may say that Dickey is a magician in that he "acts exclusively on his own authority and initiative . . . by occult methods," as is the case in "Eye-Beaters." Yet he is also priestly insofar as he "supplicates and conciliates forces superior to himself, guards the sacred tradition in his care" and acts "as the representative of the community in its relation with the gods and the unseen world," as we have seen in "Falling" and "The Vegetable King."[19] All of these traits are combined in his roles as shaman and

18. Arnold van Gennep, *The Rites of Passage* (Chicago, 1975), 173.
19. E. O. James, *The Nature and Function of the Priesthood* (London, 1955), 33.

hero, and are reflected in his continuous sense of the world as sacred. No better summary of Dickey's speaker's religious attitude can be found than Rudolf Otto's description of "The Holy," a feeling Paul Radin believes to be at the root of shamanistic experience:

> The feeling . . . sweeping like a gentle tide, pervading the mind with a tranquil mood of deepest worship . . . thrillingly vibrant and resonant, until at last it dies away and the soul resumes its "profane," non-religious mood of everyday experience. It may burst in sudden eruption up from the depths of the soul with spasms and convulsions, or lead to the strangest excitements, to intoxicated frenzy, to transport, and to ecstasy. It has its wild and demonic forms and can sink to an almost grisly horror and shuddering. . . . It may become the hushed, trembling, and speechless humility of the creature in the presence of—whom or what? In the presence of that which is a *Mystery* inexpressible and above all creatures.[20]

## THE COMIC

In many ways, Dickey's speaker resembles a comic shaman, a character known in primitive mythology as the trickster. Such a figure is, Campbell tells us, a "fool, and a cruel, lecherous cheat, an epitome of the principle of disorder," though "he is nevertheless the culture-bringer also." Surviving in carnival customs, this figure gives "the character of topsy-turvey day to the feast." He is a kind of comic scapegoat, according to Carl Jung: "The trickster is a collective shadow figure, an epitome of all the inferior traits of character in individuals."[21] While such a creature is scarcely a god or superhuman, he can function, like Proteus the shape-shifter or Prometheus the thief of fire, as a kind of intermediary between the everyday world and the gods.

To be sure, Dickey's comic speakers are less divine. Nonetheless, even as fully contemporary men, they perform mock heroic acts that allow the poet to straddle the realms between living and dead in a way that humorously threatens certain taboos yet provides insightful contact as well. In "In the Lupanar at Pompeii," the poet "As tourist, but mostly as lecher" visits the ancient ruins of a house of ill repute in Pompeii, seeking "out the dwelling of women / Who all expect me,

---

20. Radin, *Primitive Religion*, 160; Rudolf Otto, *The Idea of the Holy* (London, 1931), 12–13.
21. Jung quoted in Campbell, *Primitive Mythology*, 273, 274.

still, because / They expect anybody who comes." As he sits "in one
of the rooms / Where it happened again and again," the poet's comic
spirit gives way to his empathic imagination as he feels how Mt. Vesu-
vius exploded, killing the residents of the house. By reliving the death
of these women, Dickey gains an awareness of the ephemeral nature
of passion and concludes with a mixture of pathos and dark comedy:

> We never can really tell
> Whether nature condemns us or loves us
> As we lie here, dying of breath . . .
> Believing the desperate dead
> Where they stripped to the skin of the soul
> And whispered to us, as to
> Their painting, observing selves:
> "Passion. Before we die
> Let us hope for no longer
> But truly know it."   (P, 84)

Another mock-heroic encounter, this time in defense of his beloved
craft, is "False Youth: Autumn: Clothes of the Age." The middle-aged
balding poet, wearing a fox hat and denim jacket, walks into a redneck
barbershop and meets with considerable scorn from the customers.
As he gets up to leave, however, a single word emblazoned on the back
of his jacket assures us that victory is his.

> Three red foxes on my head, come down
> There last Christmas from Brooks Brothers
> As a joke, I wander down Harden Street
> In Columbia, South Carolina, fur-haired and bald,
> Looking for impulse in camera stores and redneck greeting cards.
> A pole is spinning
> Colors I have little use for, but I go in
> anyway, and take off my fox hat and jacket
> They have not seen from behind yet. The barber does what he can
> With what I have left, and I hear the end man say, as my own
> Hair-cutter turns my face
> To the floor, Jesus, if there's anything I hate
> It's a middle-aged hippie. Well, so do I, I swallow
> Back: so do I    so do I
> And to hell. I get up, and somebody else says
> When're you gonna put on that hat,
> Buddy? Right now. Another says softly,
> Goodbye, Fox. I arm my denim jacket

On and walk to the door, stopping for the murmur of chairs,
And there it is
                    hand-stitched by the needles of the mother
Of my grandson    eagle riding on his claws with a banner
            Outstretched as the wings of my shoulders,
                    Coming after me with his flag
                    Disintegrating, his one eye raveling
                        Out, filthy strings flying
            From the white feathers, one wing nearly gone:
                    Blind eagle but flying
            Where I walk, where I stop with my fox
Head at the glass to let the row of chairs spell it out
            And get a lifetime look at my bird's
One word, raggedly blazing with extinction and soaring loose
In red threads burning up white until I am shot in the back
            Through my wings    or ripped apart
                    For rags:

*Poetry.*  (*TCM*, 119–20)

Self-deprecating irony is one of Dickey's strongest tools. Although he fully realizes that poetry constitutes no force but that of confusion or further ridicule from the barbershop crowd, the poet playing hippie defiantly displays his banner anyway. When Dickey self-consciously engages in many of his mythic roles, he uses irony to signal to his reader that he too knows that primitive magic doesn't really work but that he is trying to use poetry to help himself and his people out of a desperate situation or to ensure their protection. At the same time, irony signals a pathetic disproportion between ends and means; that is, although this modern shaman's magic is ineffective and he knows he is doomed to failure, nonetheless his attempt is emotionally heroic. In "The Eye-Beaters" the "half-broken light" that "flickers with agony" in the head of a blind child can never be converted poetically in satisfactory vision. In "Remnant Water" the fisherman can never restore the "slain lake"; only by "Suffering [the fish's] consequences" can the poet do anything at all. And when attempting to revive the ghosts of his past in "Looking for the Buckhead Boys," Dickey is fully modern as he realizes that his rejuvenation is a far-distant goal; he concludes by asking one of his old pals, now a gas station attendant, not to fill up his heart with memories of the dead but merely to fill his car up with fifty cents worth of gas.

Whether he skates "like an out-of-shape bear to [his] Chevrolet" (*P*, 292) after an ice storm in "False Youth: Two Seasons" or when he tells us that "the rain reached [his] underwear" (*TCM*, 106) in "Rain Guitar," Dickey's straightforward sense of humor is ingratiating and entertaining. His narrator seldom takes himself too seriously and at times is capable of a completely farcical performance as in "Cherrylog Road," the saga of the poet's teen-aged tryst in the surrealistic setting of a country junkyard. Couched in the imagery of its location, the poem describes with innocence and charm the encounter as the poet and his girl "clung, glued together, / With the hooks of the seat springs / Working through to catch us red-handed" (*P*, 136). In "Encounter in the Cage Country," the poet in sunglasses visits a zoo and comically stalks a panther from the safe side of the animal's cage. When the speaker draws a make-believe gun from his hip, the "bite-sized children broke / Up  changing their concept of laughter" (*P*, 274). But none of this fazes the beast behind the bars, who takes the moves of the man in green glasses with deadly seriousness. At the end of the poem, the poet speaks for the panther whose words are comic and something else: "*your moves are exactly right / For a few things in this world:  we know you / When you come, Green Eyes, Green Eyes*" (*P*, 275).

# III / Techniques of Representation

It was her voice that made
The sky acutest at its vanishing. . . .
She was the single artificer of the world
In which she sang.
                                    —WALLACE STEVENS

That is the usual method, but not mine—
    My way is to begin with the beginning;
The regularity of my design
    Forbids all wandering as the worst of sinning,
And therefore I shall open with a line. . . .
Narrating somewhat of Don Juan's father,
And also of his mother, if you'd rather.
                                    —BYRON

He holds him with his glittering eye—
The Wedding-Guest stood still,
And listens like a three year's child:
The Mariner hath his will.
                                    —COLERIDGE

            Oh sir, she smiled, no doubt,
Whene'er I passed her; but who passed without
Much the same smile? This grew; I gave commands;
Then all smiles stopped together. There she stands
As if alive. Will't please you rise? We'll meet
The company below, then. I repeat,
The Count your master's known munificence
Is ample warrant that no just pretense
Of mine for dowry will be disallowed;
Though his fair daughter's self, as I avowed
At starting, is my object. Nay, we'll go
Together down, sir.
                                    —BROWNING

Was it a vision, or a waking dream?
    Fled is that music: Do I wake or sleep?
                                    —KEATS

Having examined four central kinds of action and the role of the speaker in Dickey's world, we may now discuss how this poet dramatizes his materials. In his own comments on his poetry, Dickey is well

159

aware of the relation of representation strategies to his particular vision. In *Sorties* he notes:

> Someone said of my poetry that it attempts to win back for poetry some of the territory that poetry has unnecessarily relinquished to the novel. That is accurate. I like very much the emphasis on narrative that this implies, but above all the emphasis on *action* of some kind. . . . I want, more than anything else, for the poem to be an experience—that is, a *physical* experience—for the reader. It must be a completed action, and the plunging in of the reader into this action is the most difficult and the most desirable feat that the poet can perform. Nothing can be more important than this: it is the difference between poetry of reflection and poetry of participation. (*S*, 58–59)

In an explanation of how he effects immediate reader involvement in this "poetry of participation," Dickey restates his preference for the "narrative element, the poem with a definite beginning, a definite middle, and a definite end" (*S*, 61), in which there is "something that moved from an event or an action through something else, and resolved into something else, and resolved into something else, so that there was a constant sense of change in the poem; sometimes the change might even be circular and the same at the end as it was at the beginning. I liked to make use of the element of time in a poem instead of having a conventional lyric approach in which a moment of perception, of extreme sensibility, is presented" (*SI*, 48). He also says, "What I want most for the poem to be for the reader is a kind of *adventure*. He should start out on it, continue, and then, end. But the sense of adventure, certainly with a good deal of *peril* entailed in it, is paramount" (*S*, 101).

In this poet's world of perpetual motion and imminent violence, time and change are important constituents. Without a continuum of dramatic action in which to present crisis and confrontation, to send his heroes on some sort of journey, or to entail some series of stages of ritual process, Dickey would have no grounds by which to engage his reader in a "physical experience," that is, one that gives us the sense of "being a particular creature at a particular time and place" (*S*, 59). Dickey's focus on particularity naturally leads him to a concern with telling a story: "In most of my poems, I want a sense of story. There are two ways to do this basically. One way is for the story to be obvious; that is, for there to be a beginning, middle, and end in that order. The other way is for the story to be implicit, and there are a million ways of doing this" (S, 49).

If we assume that in many of Dickey's poems there is an implicit story (some pattern of action involving time and a change in an agent's fortune), then the ways that story is presented become relevant topics for our inquiry. Further, because Dickey himself distinguishes obvious and implicit ways of presenting his lyric stories, we will follow his lead in trying to develop his line of inquiry. Although we cannot examine the "million" ways of implicit storytelling, we can fruitfully use terms for analysis of narrative fiction to see how Dickey makes his mystical and primitive principles so strikingly vivid to modern readers.

Narrator and Action

Because lyric action is so much a matter of the speaker's center of consciousness, we may best begin by tracing the relations of Dickey's narrator to his stories. Although Dickey's poetic voice is constant throughout all his lyrics, the specific connection of speaker to action differs greatly in his poetry and reveals the remarkable variety of ways this poet focuses on different aspects of his tales.

Dickey may choose to concentrate on physical or verbal action. In "Springer Mountain," in order to approximate his narrator's rejuvenating physical exuberance, the poet emphasizes the man's sensory experience and his act of running like a deer through the woods in an animal dance seen as a counterforce to his body-softening middle age. In "The Shark's Parlor," although the shark capture seems central, the poem's primary activity is the narrator's recounting the venture, not literally but verbally and symbolically as a statement against his own mortality. Sheer verbal representation is more clearly present in "For the Last Wolverine" where the poet's hybrid creature could exist only in his imagination, not as a natural thing. The entire poem is a verbal imperative to the sacred "wildness of poetry."

Dickey may exhibit the narrator as personally involved or uninvolved in the process depicted. Although the girl's perception presented in "The Scarred Girl" is extremely poignant, the speaker is in no way personally involved. The representation focuses entirely on the girl's plight and the pathos of her recalling the view in the windshield through which she crashed. On the other hand, when Dickey wants to implicate his speaker intimately with what is going on, he may choose to place the narrator directly in a setting when, for example, he is in bed with a woman in "Adultery." Through direct address and the precarious sexual situation, the immediacy and intensity of effect is much more forceful than if the representation had issued from an uninvolved third person.

In Dickey's poetry, the narrator may be physically present or absent from the scene, simply imagining himself to be present. In "Falling" the speaker could not have been present with the woman during her fall. Instead, Dickey uses one of his most interesting methods of omniscient narration, that of the point of view of a movie camera—his modern variation of the prospect poem—to conceive imaginatively what the girl in reality could never have done under realistic conditions. He seems thus to be with her cinematically, capturing extensive detail of the event, as she defies death with her grandiose and futile gesture. In "Buckdancer's Choice" the speaker remembers himself outside his mother's sickroom listening to her whistle. In the actual reminiscence, however, a nostalgic feeling results because things take place after the fact from an unspecified location. In "Sustainment" the location of the past event is the same as that in which the narrator now addresses his lover, although he was not present at the prior accident involving a woman and a horse that simply serves as an occasion for his thought.

Another closely related dimension of the poet's placement of narrator is temporal. Throughout Dickey's work, the narrator always speaks in the present, although he may or may not depict something from the past. In poems such as "Power and Light," "The Summons," and "A Dog Sleeping at my Feet," in which emphasis on the immediate moment is paramount, the action and representation fully coincide point for point in the present. Sometimes a past event is represented, after which the narrator assigns it a current significance, as in "The Shark's Parlor" and "Horses and Prisoners." In each of these, the past meaning of the recounted incident is seen as enduring through time to the present. In the completely fictive realm, time may be of no significance at all. The beast in "For the Last Wolverine" needs no spatial or temporal location. As explicitly indicated in the poem, it exists only in the poet's mind.

Under this temporal dimension fall certain techniques for distancing Dickey's narrator from his action, a distancing that gives drama to Dickey's poems as he tries to close the gap between speaker and object. For instance, essential to the bomber pilot's anxious lingering guilt in "The Firebombing" are twenty intervening years between his war experience and his present condition. Similarly, in "In the Tree House at Night," the narrator's desire to recover his dead brother's spirit presupposes considerable distance between his immediate intention and the fragments of the past he is trying to revive. Greater proximity between past and present is found in "The Lifeguard," in which at night and still in shock, the guard recounts his failure that day to save a child from drowning. At this point, even more futilely, he swims back to the fatal spot and searches, recovering nothing. To make the guard's hopeless gesture seem likely, the poet restricts the time between the drowning and the present, lest the speaker's stunned hallucinatory state wear off. The time placement also makes it likely that no one else would be at the lake at night so that the guard would be alone for his second attempt. Dickey may depict two past events at different times with each having different emotional functions. In "The Leap," the narrator's apparently pleasant reminiscence of the girl's past leaping in grammar school is reversed by our discovery that he has just read a newspaper account of her suicidal leap from a hotel window. Both distant and recent past events are ultimately subsumed as parts of the speaker's overall stunned reaction to her tragedy.

At times the poet presents the past or present as fictive, even though realistic elements are used in the representation. One of Dickey's most important devices is the dream, which he uses in "The Vegetable King" to establish a realm apart from his family where his self-engendered mythical violence can be cultivated without threatening those he loves. As a state of induced hallucination, dreams in Dickey's poems produce surrealistic states that give the poet magical and prophetic contact with the gods whose powers he wishes to assume. His extensive use of fantasy is a clear sign of his impulse to construct a new reality in which benevolent wholeness, not possible in the everyday world, can be achieved through poetic means. Even when his mode of vision is fantastic, realistic detail may be abundant, as in the historical description of the Old South in "Slave Quarters."

When Dickey wants to present an extraordinary moment in someone's life or to approximate the feeling of someone undergoing an extensive process, he usually employs natural probabilities in convincingly possible situations. Such is the case with his perception of the scarred girl and the detailed capture in "The Shark's Parlor." On the other hand, Dickey may use natural probabilities within an entirely fantastic event. Once the "fact" of such an event is accepted, the agents are subject to natural laws for the duration of the poem. Except for the half-human, half-bird perceptions of the subject, this subordination to the laws of nature is true of "Reincarnation II" and is consistently the case throughout "Slave Quarters." In "For the Last Wolverine," however, all parts of the event issue explicitly from the poet's hyperbolic imperative. Dickey may also combine natural and hyperbolic probabilities in an impossible physical act that he tries to present as possible. By making the airline stewardess subject to gravity and inevitable physical destruction and by using the distractions of sexual and macabre elements, the poet focuses attention away from the natural improbabilities in her poetic fall, for example, the degree of control she would have while falling at such a speed.

Dickey may let events speak for themselves or he may comment on them. If he does comment, he may do so intermittently or assign a single section of the poem to this function. In "A Folksinger of the Thirties," the incidents following the singer's crucifixion to the side of a boxcar are perfectly clear, needing no comment. Equally clear is his assertion that while traveling through the country in such remarkable fashion, he became supersensitized by the pain. When the poet does use commentary, it is usually kept at a minimum, interspersed among a series of perceptions or moments in some process. Commentary is most direct and extensive in "In the Lupanar at Pompeii," where throughout the second half of the poem, the narrator-tourist speculates outright on "the marvel of lust" and on what he is doing:

> For we who must try to explain
> Ourselves in the house of this flesh . . .

> We never can really tell
> Whether nature condemns us or loves us  (*P*, 84)

Or, the commentary may be appended after the event's depiction, as is the case in "The Shark's Parlor," in which the concluding seven lines are devoted exclusively to signifying the present meaning of the capture of the shark for the narrator.

The representation may be exhibited in sharp detail or may be sketched simply with a few hard-edged images. When Dickey wants to make a scene, act, or agent seem convincing, he tends to use considerable, often minute, detail to infect magically the landscape he is trying to draw. For example, in "The Fiend," the poet achieves bizarre effects by combining the description of the lurking sexual psychopath with extensively detailed, familiar suburban household and apartment imagery, thus delineating the full monstrosity of the culprit. On the other hand, when Dickey wants to focus on a single aspect or quality rather than build an elaborate context, he keeps detail to a minimum. Such is the case in "Knock," where only enough detail is present to make clear that two unidentified lovers in bed have been jolted in the middle of the night by a mysterious and forceful knock at their door. Trying to approximate their moment of fear, the poet sketches the scene by simply letting the room's door and bed register the couple's shock. Extensive description would only detract from the piercing sense of terror that Dickey wants to produce.

A poem's central action or its parts may be depicted fully with little left to inference and implication, or only a fragment of it may be shown with the rest for us to fill in. When the drunken soldier in "Victory" is elaborately tattooed with a snake design, there is no need for inference. The entire story is contained in the representation, whereas in "In the Tree House at Night," we must infer the narrator's motivation by piecing together his remarks about his dead brother. For Dickey, intensity and immediacy of effect are usually produced by leaving little to inference. When he wants a more sedate, eerie, or suspenseful quality to his action, he requires inference, most often by leaving an expository element unclear.

As indicated in the chapter on agent, Dickey may speak through his I-figure or he may use a persona. In spite of his use of different speakers, the voice behind all his poems is Dickey's literary "self." Even so, his selection of pseudoidentities is wide, ranging from a power lineman to the sheep-child. Most of these identities are either general social roles (for example, a soldier, father, power lineman) or determined solely by a particular incident (for example, a poisoned man). Each speaker is chosen to make probable what the poetic subject is doing, given the peculiarity of circumstances in which such persons find themselves.

Whatever role his narrators take, Dickey may present the speaker as fully aware of the meaning and implication of his act, or he may be struggling toward its significance. In "The Vegetable King," the narrator knows what he is doing and why. In "Approaching Prayer," the speaker is uncertain what his eccentric activity (putting on his dead father's old sweater and a boar's head) really means. As he says: "I don't know quite what has happened / Or that anything has" (P, 167). His aim is to do something extraordinary to generate cosmic vision, whatever the results. Somewhat differently, the disoriented guard in "The Lifeguard" acts more from helpless instinct than conscious calculation when futilely swimming back to where the child drowned. A narrator fully aware of his action would be improbable within the circumstances of the poem.

These devices by no means exhaust the technical richness of Dickey's representational methods. These techniques may be used in different combinations depending on the emotional requirements of individual poems. For instance, in "Slave Quarters," an unidentified narrator imagines himself intimately involved in extraordinarily detailed, historically based events at which he could not possibly have been present. In verbalizing his physical activity, he is subject to natural probabilities, is fully aware of the implications of his imagined acts, and leaves little to inference while extensively commenting throughout on what he is doing. The entire poem exhibits the feeling of a man searching for primal instincts and in the process imaginatively and monstrously producing a son he also owns. In "The Heaven of Animals," another unidentified but uninvolved narrator comments on the sheerly physical cyclic relation in the animal world between hunter and hunted. Speaking from a completely generalized location and using moderate detail—just enough to substantiate his thesis—he is fully aware of what he says and leaves little to inference. It is a poem of a man universalizing a process that he finds embodied in the particular landscape he is viewing.

## SUSPENSE

To engage and focus the attention of his readers, Dickey's use of suspense is crucial in his narratives. By arousing our curiosity through the uncertainty of what we wish to know or by the delay of what we know will happen, Dickey strategically molds and shapes our anxiety as does any good storyteller, parceling out information bit by bit about agents, instruments, scenes, antecedent circumstances, even the very issue of the poem itself.

In "The Night Pool," for instance, by keeping the source of light mysterious, Dickey gives an eerie quality to the location, action, and relation of the narrator and a woman. One assumes the two are lovers, though their relation is sketched simply, giving agents, scene, and act a "darkly bright" quality like the unnamed pervading "element." The poem begins:

> There is this other element that shines
> At night near human dwellings, glows like wool
> From the sides of itself, far down:
>
> From the deep end of heated water
> I am moving toward her, first swimming,
> Then touching my light feet to the floor
>
> Rising like steam from the surface
> To take her in my arms   (P, 222)

Whatever this element may be, it is important enough for the poet to assert its presence and influence several lines later:

> There is this other element, it being late
> Enough, and in it I lift her, and can carry
> Her over any threshold in the world.   (P, 222)

By not specifying the nature of the element, Dickey gives the word a certain grammatical opacity by which it seems to reflect the hazy dreamlike ambience of lights from the apartments at night. What ac-

tually produces the scenic atmosphere, however, are the concrete, specific images (for example, steam from the pool, the wool analogy, window light) that surround and qualify the abstract word *element*. The
poet's refusal to name the pervasive substance makes the ambience all
that more mysterious. One might call this intentional obscurity "suspense of scenic quality" or even "suspense of subject." What Dickey
wants to do is not develop a theme or idea but evoke a magical atmosphere in which objects themselves are animated not by human consciousness but by an unknown indwelling power.

   Another device is suspense of agent, found in "The Other." In this
poem, the speaker invokes a spirit with several synonymous identities indicated as "like Apollo," a "brother," a "king-sized shadow," a
"body-building angel," and "another body for my life" (*P*, 34–36). Suspense is involved to the extent that the continuous assignment of
titles to the Other beclouds momentarily its exact nature, as does the
title of the poem. One comes to identify the thing by its function as
an alter ego of rejuvenation that the poet implores and seeks as he ritu-
ally cuts down a dead tree, an act that he sees as symbolically effective
against aging. For, as the poem closes, the dead tree casts "down its
foliage with the years" (*P*, 36). In "Madness," for three-quarters of the
poem, Dickey holds in suspense the narrator's identity along with his
relation to the action. It is uncertain whether the narrator is the dog
itself or some unspecified, omniscient third person. Finally, at the
seventy-fifth line, the dog is shot; the narrative continues uninterrupted, and an impersonal, possessive pronoun assigned to the dog
provides the conclusive differentiating sign. The suspense over, our
anticipation is replaced by natural sympathy for the animal's plight,
while the continuous representational confusion has already contrib-
uted effectively to the poet's vertiginous approximation of the dog's
rabid condition.

   Dickey also uses what we may call implicit plot or perhaps suspense of antecedent circumstances, in which the reader is initially
unsure of the narrator's personal background, which contains the motivation for his present act. This motivation must be gathered piece-
meal from the immediate reflection in order to construct the narrator's full intention. For instance, in "In the Tree House at Night," we
find in the speaker's past a dead brother who apparently helped build

the house and whose memory (or spirit) the narrator is trying to retain by sleeping there. Another example of this kind of suspense used even more extensively is found in the transformational poem "Reincarnation II," in which the representation begins with the unidentified subject flying instinctively over the arctic. For nearly half the poem, one is not sure who or what is flying until signs finally provide evidence that the seabird was once an office worker. When we discover what is happening, the poet's magical imagery has already carried us emotionally into its fantasy.

The suspense of agent device is sometimes combined with the poet's intentional omission of antecedent circumstances or with ambiguity about the location of the depicted activity. In "Blood" the narrator wakes up hungover with a profusely bleeding woman next to him. He has no idea who she is, how she has come to be there, or if he is responsible for her condition. The representational strategy seems to be twofold: first, by making the circumstantial evidence obscure, the poet focuses on the shock value of the blood imagery; and second, the poem is essentially one of unresolved anticipation. That is, the central point is that there is no available resolution to the narrator's questioning. There is only the fact of the woman's presence. With no immediate explanation forthcoming, the impact of the fact is all the more shocking. In "Adultery," we find a variation of this strategy. Dickey identifies his subjects only as an adulterous couple in bed in a cheap hotel. He then draws a correspondence between the hopeless banality of the wallpaper and the ultimate futility of their relation. Just as their love cannot come to fruition, so they seem to be as sad and anonymous in their "hazardous meeting" as the wallpaper characters surrounding them.

Dickey's most widely used device for creating suspense centers on his lineal strategies. What might be called syntactic or semantic suspense occurs when he uses line endings, stanza breaks, or breath spaces to frustrate momentarily the completion of a perception, thought, or statement in order to emphasize certain parts of a grammatical unit, to multiply meanings within it, or to arouse interest through brief delay of the unit's construction. Examples of this use of suspense are found in this selection from "The Leap." After reminiscing about his former classmate's leaping ability as a girl, Dickey reverses the emotional tone of the poem by producing a sense of impending change with line endings and a stanza break in the complex introductory clause that begins the periodic sentence:

> If I said I saw
> In the paper where Jane MacNaughton Hill,
>
> Mother of four, leapt to her death from a window
> Of a downtown hotel, and that her body crushed-in
> The top of a parked taxi, and that I held
> Without trembling a picture of her lying cradled
> In that papery steel as though lying in the grass,
> One shoe idly off, arms folded across her breast,
> I would not believe myself.   (P, 284)

Syntactic suspense is especially important in the creation of Dickey's magical metaphors. A brief list of images shows how the poet fuses qualities from one object with another by combining items as he moves from the end of one line to the beginning of another. In just a few lines from "Falling" we find: "she has this flying skin / Made of garments"; "her skirt / Like the diagram of a bat"; and "all small towns brokenly brighter from inside / Cloud" (P, 295).

SCALE

The last representational problem we will treat is scale. Scale is the structural strategy that centers on how much or to what extent something should be represented. The problem of scale besets the novelist or playwright when he asks: How long should a certain scene run? Which character traits should be emphasized, which minimized? How much dialogue is appropriate at this point in the plot? Somewhat similar questions may be asked by a poet, though we must remember that in a lyric the artist is clearly working with a more compressed form. Still, one may ask: How should suspense be employed when one has only thirty lines instead of thirty pages? How can reversals be effectively constructed in a relatively short space? How much detail is required to make a particular circumstance or mental condition seem authentic? Like all aspects of representation, scale is primarily a function of the poem's emotional effect and the probabilities issuing from the narrator's situation and behavior. Scale affects every part of the representation and constitutes one of the most immediate ways of directing our attention, of maximizing and minimizing the impact of specific parts, and eventually of shaping the kind and intensity of effect of the whole poem.

Because so many of Dickey's poems are long and because of his extensive use of a storylike structure, scale is an especially important issue. However, one difficulty in analyzing scale lies in its radically particular character. That is, the scale of any part of a poem is entirely relative to the particular emotional requirements of the particular poem. Thus, adequate analysis of Dickey's handling of scale should entail close scrutiny of a number of poems plus the size of many elements (for example, imagery, detail, narrative voice) and could easily run to treatise length. To compress this topic without oversimplifying the issue, I will look briefly at one poem for its suspenseful revelation of descriptive detail, detail that in its cumulative order of presentation very nearly constitutes the poet's entire strategy of storytelling.

In "False Youth: Autumn: Clothes of the Age," Dickey's comic poem of confrontation, the poet enters a redneck barbershop in Columbia, South Carolina. Dressed like "a middle-aged hippie," he wears a fox hat on his head and a jacket on which has been sewn an eagle flying with a banner in his claws. On the banner is a single word: *Poetry.* His back as yet unseen by the customers in the shop, the poet takes considerable abuse for his outlandish dress, gets up in anger, puts on his jacket, and then, as his method of revenge, lets the boys in the shop get a full view of the eagle and its "One word, raggedly blazing with extinction and soaring loose / In red threads burning up white" (*TCM*, 119–20).

The most important representational strategies in the first half of the poem consist of expository elements plus some dialogue, whereas the second half is almost all descriptive detail. Detail is maximal in the conclusion, not only to give us a vivid picture of the eagle but more importantly to constitute an emotional force powerful enough not only to offset but to obliterate the sarcasm of the customers. By extensively characterizing the eagle with ferocious imagery, Dickey builds to a resounding comic irony that reverses the dramatic situation in favor of the poet and his craft. Of course, no one believes that poetry can really do battle effectively with these good ol' boys, but for the moment, their scorn has changed to something else. Not only are the rednecks silenced, they are amazed!

Dickey's conclusion issues both from the suspenseful confrontation with the shop customers and his strategic revelation of two other elements of suspense, namely, the identity of the object on his back and the word on the banner. When we discover what these items are, our surprise, abetted by extensive serial detail and ironic depreciation, provides the mock-heroic charm that wins the day against the adversaries. In fact, in a strange and enchanting way, Dickey's emblem provides him a comic rejuvenation, "blazing with extinction" like the oxymoronic power of the poetic eagle that really has no power. The poet's clothes give him a "ragged" youth and imagistically turn his arms into "wings" even though he may be "shot in the back" or "ripped apart / For rags" (*TCM*, 119–20). Crucial to his poetic conflict is his strategy of scale of detail, which not only describes the objects in his world but raises the intensity of action the way the formula of the hero-to-the-rescue does in drama by using surprises and reversals.

# IV / Diction

The eye of a vagabond in metaphor
That catches our own.
                    —WALLACE STEVENS

The greatest thing by far is to have a command of metaphor. This
alone cannot be imparted by another; it is the mark of genius, for to
make good metaphors implies an eye for resemblances.
                    —ARISTOTLE

Metaphor is a semi-surreptitious method by which a greater variety of elements can be wrought into the fabric of experience. . . .
What is needed for the wholeness of an experience is not always
naturally present, and metaphor supplies an excuse by which
what is needed may be smuggled in.
                    —I. A. RICHARDS

We find poetic truth struck out by the collision rather than the
collusion of images.
                    —C. DAY LEWIS

Suppose he does beat the last breath from a lively meaning, he
never escapes from himself without giving us more than we'd
ever dare ask.
                    —THEODORE ROETHKE ON DYLAN THOMAS

    A springful of larks in a rolling
Cloud and the roadside bushes brimming with whistling
    Blackbirds and the sun of October
              Summery
        On the hill's shoulder
                    —DYLAN THOMAS

Dickey's language is as much a function of his general lyric vision and
underlying principles as are his techniques of representation. Given
the distinctively mystical, romantic, and primitive kinds of experience he wishes to exhibit, one can understand why this poet chooses
familiar, concrete, and tactile terms that consist so often of analogues
of natural processes and things. Were he to employ a vocabulary of abstract or exotic words, he would lose the peculiar magical and animistic contact with the universe he cultivates. Instead of an ornate or

173

esoteric diction that would render his forms emotionally remote, Dickey usually presents a verbal—though not always syntactic—simplicity that permits his narrative lines to emerge cleanly and powerfully. When his poetry is obscure, it is not because of ambiguity of language but because of intentional obfuscation of an expository element or because of an inadequately developed conception for the poem as a whole. What he wants in his diction is explicitly stated in *Self-Interviews:*

> It would be better for my particular poetry . . . not to over-complicate but to simplify down to an extremely individual kind of simplicity. I wanted to be simple without being thin. . . . I tried to see if I could make effective *statements* in poems, statements that would be arresting and yet syntactically clear and non-allusive, or at least as little allusive as possible, poetry which would be extremely lucid and would at the same time exemplify Alfred North Whitehead's great phrase, "presentational immediacy." I wanted immediacy, the effect of spontaneity, and reader involvement more than anything else. (*SI*, 47)

Yet for Dickey clarity and simplicity are not all. Contrasting his own artistic aims with those of another poet famous for a precise and lucid diction, he says: "Auden does not give you the feeling of experience—experiencing—that I want my poems to give" (*S*, 92). And, in one of his predictions for modern poetry, he indicates his wish that his language convey us in a specific direction: "I think that the new poetry will be a poetry of the dazzlingly simple statement, the statement that is clairvoyantly and stunningly simple . . . a stark warm simplicity of vision; the simplicity that opens out deeper into the world and carries us with it" (*S*, 204).

In spite of his wish for simplicity, there is throughout Dickey's poetic work a striking contrast between his disarmingly familiar language and the bizarre richness of the unfamiliar effects he produces. Because he wants to reveal primitive processes that are often hidden by the modern trappings of contemporary life, he gives us a vocabulary of ordinary, even deceptively domestic, terms. In short, Dickey's language serves his specific emotional ends by giving his subjects an initial, apparent simplicity—often, a casual quality—that is transformed, complicated, and deepened by his poetic action. At times language seems to give way to the magical movement of exchange that animates his ontology.

## METAPHOR

Dickey's selection and employment of terms center around a concern with metaphor as the primary particle out of which the poet makes his statements. Commenting on an aphorism of the French poet Pierre Reverdy, Dickey mentions two aspects about metaphor: first, that dealing with the relational distance between the two terms involved in metaphoric comparison; and second, that having to do with the "justness" or poetic aptness of the likeness being drawn (*S*, 175). Any man, says Dickey, can see the degree of dissimilarity between two terms, but not everyone will agree as to the justifiability of the comparison itself. This justifiability is a major concern for Dickey, who speaks of constructing his metaphors by choosing those that have "threads of continuity running through them, threads of consequence and meaning which may work out into a narrative or dramatic action" (*S*, 180). His interest is with the emotive charging of terms themselves and with their overall relation to the making of the form that is to emerge through them.

Given the simplicity, clarity, and immediacy of language from which Dickey wants his narrative or dramatic action to emerge, one can see why he seldom constructs metaphors that are puzzling or intellectually challenging. In his diction, there is rarely an extended conceit or figure built upon a series of subtle, inobvious likenesses. One of the reasons for the immediacy of Dickey's metaphors is that they usually involve the comparison of some object to an analogue with which the object shares a sensible quality; thus the interpretative effort needed to make the metaphor intelligible is minimized and the material element the poet wishes magically to adopt is maximized.

To facilitate magical contact, Dickey often constructs his metaphors in classical fashion through the transference or substitution of names. For the most part, the direction of such transference is toward specificity in accord with his continuous emphasis on the concrete and particular. However, when he wishes to widen the scope of comparison, especially to animate physical objects, the transference may be from one species to another in a generalizing direction. For instance, in "Inside the River," after likening the river to "a fleeing coat," Dickey parenthetically widens the clothing likeness by calling the river "A garment of motion" (*P*, 105). More characteristic of his metaphors is the direction of particularity in which specific terms are substituted for the more general. We find this in "The Fiend" where Dickey says of the psychopath's sexual arousal: "rigor mortis / Slithers into his pockets" (P, 230). When coupled with *slithers*, the term *rigor mortis* not only signals the homocidal danger the man presents but also suggests a predatory snakelike movement. The exchange of specific names is even more clearly found in the synecdochic relation of forms of rope in these lines from "In the Marble Quarry": "I feel the great pulley grind, / The thread I cling to lengthen" (P, 147). This comparison gives the speaker a delicate, unearthly hold on things. In "The Lifeguard," an interchange of one kind of storage for another occurs with the poet adding a distinctive term of arrangement that stands in contrast to the swirling blackness that has claimed the drowned child: "In a stable of boats, I lie hidden" (P, 51).

Most of Dickey's metaphors are based not simply on the general or specific transference of names but on the proportional relation of analogy, usually by virtue of a common sensible property shared between objects. The terms chosen in such metaphors are most often familiar, though in combination they can be quite vivid and refreshing, as is the case in the fusion of domestic and threatening traits in "The Poisoned Man" when Dickey refers to "the seam of the scar" (P, 146). Often the analogy may be entirely familiar but precisely fitted to the occasion. In naming the center of an automobile junkyard "the hub of the yard" (P, 135), the poet presents us with nothing macabre or upsetting but signals with considerable charm that the action is taking place in the center of things.

Even at the level of metaphor, many of Dickey's poetic principles are reflected in his selection and construction of terms. Because his settings, subjects, and speakers at first seem so familiar, he constructs metaphors from common words to give his diction a disarmingly conventional quality that he often converts into a vivid or startling one by revealing an unexpected likeness. This conversion often occurs in stock expressions that are revitalized through immediate grammatical modification or a calculated contextual location altering trite usage. For instance, the contextual method is found in "Falling," where an expression such as "the waters / Of life" (P, 295, 298) is emotionally recharged in two ways: first, by virtue of its placement in highly charged emotional context powerful enough to subsume trite expression; and second, by virtue of the ironic contrast with kinds of water into which the stewardess might possibly dive and thus be saved, though the narrator is fully aware that her fall means certain death. Similarly, in his poem about visiting the ruins of the ancient whorehouse in Pompeii, Dickey uses the trite "house of this flesh" (P, 84) to refer not only to the body but humorously to a different kind of house. An example of Dickey's metaphoric invention by grammatical modification occurs in "The Eye-Beaters," in which he converts the first term in a dull phrase into a refreshing correlative by referring to the sun as a "fist of a ball of fire" (TCM, 49). Another of his tactics for rejuvenating conventional associations is found in this line from "Fog Envelops the Animals": "Above my head, the trees exchange their arms" (P, 63). The likening of human arms to tree branches is scarcely novel, but the attribution of exchange gives the entire figure a new, if not surrealistic, quality.

One of Dickey's favorite techniques for making metaphors animate his world lies in his construction of compounds, usually with hyphens. In a poetry in which textual and scenic detail serve to convey the movement of natural things, Dickey uses this method to assign a single quality to an object or act. He also employs the use of something like an impasto technique, in which a series of sensible properties color the entire lyric process or moment. Using a single term, Dickey includes double attribution (of duration and quality) in this description of his son's attempt to play a wood whistle as a "scratch- / long sound" (TCM, 38). In "The Bee" there is multiple attribution of qualities in a single compound when Dickey listens for further direction from the spirits of dead football coaches: "some tobacco- / mumbling voice in the branches." The impasto, or accumulation, technique appears in compounds that convert the stewardess's descent in "Falling" into something graceful: "body-whistling," "dance-weight" (P, 293). Even larger grammatical units are compounded when the poet creates metaphor through participial phrases in the line "On the rain-weeping wires, the hearing-everything poles" (P, 226) in "Angina," as an ill woman gains mystical access to the lives of her children. In the poem "Pine" the impasto method is in full swing, reminiscent of Gerard Manley Hopkins, as Dickey tries to approximate the sequence of moments in a complex perception that magically carries him to his gerundive world of constant motion:

> Sound merely soft
> And loudly soft and just in time    then nothing and then
> Soft    soft and a little caring-for    sift-softening
> And soared to.      O ankle-wings lightening and fleeing
> (*TCM*, 40)

To weave his various mixtures together, Dickey distributes the parts of a metaphor throughout a poem, either continuously within several lines or at strategic points depending on emotional necessity. After calling the porch "a lamp of coarse wire" in "A Screened Porch in the Country," he claims at the end of the poem that the human inhabitants can "enter the place / Of small, blindly singing things" (*P*, 97), thus likening them to insects flying about a lamp at night. Usually, when Dickey's comparisons are continuous, they are presented in a simile in which analogizing takes place part for part. Thus, in "Facing Africa" the shape of the continent is likened to an hourglass:

> Like a lamp of sand held up,
> A top-heavy hourglass
> With its heaped eternal grains
> Falling, falling
>
> Into the lower green part    (*P*, 103)

Rather than a part-for-part correlation, antecedent contextual knowledge is required for the intelligibility of this expression from "Madness" in which a family dog runs mad after being bitten by a rabid fox: "Soap boiled / Between black lips" (*EB*, 49). By using *soap* instead of a medical term, Dickey produces a disturbing effect by describing physical decay in familiar terms.

Dickey employs the continuous and contextual metaphor by making an initial comparison and then later reusing one part of the original metaphor to produce different or more intense emotional effects. For example, in "The Firebombing," the bomber pilot's targets are metaphorically reduced to parts of gardens ("The death of children is ponds" [*P*, 185]), while the entire scene itself is likened to a domestic oriental garden even as the bombs strike in a loomlike pattern: "Fire shuttles from pond to pond" (*P*, 185). After the bombing run, the narrator continues comparison with the garden as the plane heads home, "Following the huge, moon-washed stepping stones / Of the Ryukus south" (*P*, 187). By calling the islands "stepping stones," Dickey ironically and tragically suggests a path of escape for his victims from the "ponds" that he as pilot has just turned into an inferno. The islands are "stepping stones" only from the pilot's secure perspective. Thus, the inadequacy of the analogy from the victims' standpoint powerfully understates the reality of the suffering of the Japanese and reflects the narrator's own inability to formulate accurately the true objects of his guilt. The poet's terms render the events quite beautiful in a sheerly visual way, thus constituting the grounds for the pilot's dilemma.

Dickey's metaphors fuse his obsessive mixtures by qualifying abstract words with concrete and tactile qualities. In "Falling," the woman's ritual death waits for her on the ground, where her victimage will awaken the regenerative power of the earth as "extinction slumbers in corn tassels / thickly" (*P*, 297). A similar qualification appears in "Springer Mountain" when the poet explains the impulse for his behavior in terms of color: "The green of excess is upon me" (*P*, 132). Dickey is not above punning with his metaphors, usually to emphasize two different senses of a term. In "A Folksinger of the Thirties," two senses of *bed* are suggested, one associated with the narrator's immediate security, the other with his past adventure of pain: "On a bed of gravel moving . . . / I lay / As in my apartment now" (*P*, 149). Or, describing the airline stewardess's fall, the poet refers pathetically and comically to "the long windsocks of her stockings" (*P*, 297).

Dickey energizes his metaphors through coined expressions in which a word qualifies a verb while implying a visual comparison: "Vertical banners of flame / Leap scrollingly from the sun and tatter / To nothing" (*P*, 254). Or, describing a bee, he says: "One dot / Grainily shifting" (*P*, 279). Humor is also present in his metaphors in "Cherrylog Road," in which a metaphor within a simile sets the tongue-in-cheek tone for the entire adventure: "As in a wild stock-car race / / In the parking lot of the dead" (*P*, 134). At times Dickey mixes different senses by personifying through a transference of functions. As the quarterback in the football poem "In the Pocket" fades back for a pass, he says: "my arm is looking" (*TCM*, 32).

IMAGERY

Even more than metaphor, Dickey's imagery makes his universe concrete, vivid, and convincing. Whereas metaphor involves a justifiable likeness, conceptual or sensible, between items, imagery does not necessitate the mental act of comparison but simply connects some sensory attribute to a subject. Imagery thus tends to exhibit objects and activities with a greater immediacy and particularity than metaphor. In Dickey's work, imagery serves two primary functions in presenting not merely an experience but the very "feeling of experience." First, through detail, no matter how fantastic, his settings seem realistic, so that his agents' acts seem possible, in light of their peculiar circumstances. Second, Dickey's imagery sometimes points less to some objective external state of affairs than to an internal disposition of an agent to see things in a certain way, whether that perspective be emotional or some state of extraordinary vision.

Dickey has a number of techniques for convincing the readers of the objective veracity of his scenes. In "The Shark's Parlor" he illustrates the power of the shark by showing not the cause but the effects of the primal fish running with the baited hook from the poled cottage to which the boys have anchored their chain leader and rope:

> the house coming subtly
> Apart    all around us    underfoot    boards beginning to sparkle
>       like sand
> With the glinting of the bright hidden parts of ten-year-old nails
> Pulling out.    (P, 205)

Another of his strategies is to construct a scene through the imagery of accumulated detail to suggest that an agent would have had to know about or be present in a specific situation to be aware of certain facts. For Dickey such catalogs often serve multiple ends. In "Slave Quarters" detailed images of the interior of an antebellum southern mansion convey an authentic cultural historical setting while simultaneously serving as signs of the probability of the narrator's imagined identity as a slave owner. To the domestic images, Dickey adds a single perception that gives the list another function, namely, that of "proof" that this is in fact the kind of situation about which the narrator's observation is likely to be true. Ultimately, the entire complex of imagery and perception is set in opposition to the sexual and emotional world of the slave quarters. Thus, of the mansion's world, the narrator says:

> Very far from the silent piano   the copy of Walter Scott
> Closed on its thin-papered battles
> Where his daughter practiced, decorum preventing the one
> Bead of sweat in all that lace   collected at her throat
> From breaking and humanly running
> Over Mozart's unmortal keys—   (*P*, 235)

Dickey's detailed imagery also functions objectively to approximate the motion of a certain kind of instrument. For instance, in "Victory," the snake design the speaker has drunkenly chosen resembles the very motion of the tattoo needle, thus converting an inanimate object into something very much alive:

> . . . he grew,
> Red scales sucking up color    blue
> White with my skin running out of the world
> Wide sun.   Frothing with pinpricks, filling with ink
> I lay and it lay   (*TCM*, 37)

In addition to descriptive accuracy, an image may derive its appropriateness from the fact that it is an object belonging to a certain kind of place. So Dickey likens his father's pitching motion to something that would be found in the carnival atmosphere of his poem "The Celebration": "the waning / Whip of his right arm" (*P*, 201). Historical and cultural traits also make this visual and textural image appropriate in this description of the English shoreline from "Dover: Believing in Kings": "here, to the ale of shallows" (*P*, 87).

In addition to vivid description, Dickey's imagery reinforces particular themes by degree of precision or by specific selection (or omission). In "Slave Quarters" the opposition of nature imagery to that of the antebellum South serves as evidence for the preference of one kind of sexuality over another. In "The Firebombing" the use of highly detailed imagery to describe the narrator's personal possessions stands in vivid contrast to his inability to describe with precision the homes of his victims in his bombing raids. Behind this imagery is the idea that from the pilot's perspective bombing victims and their possessions are imperceptible, unlike his own comparable domestic items. Of his things, he says:

> But in this half-paid-for pantry. . . .
> I still have charge—secret charge—
> Of the fire developed to cling
> To everything: to gold carts and fingernail
> Scissors as yet unborn   tennis shoes
> Grocery baskets   toy fire engines
> New Buicks stalled by the half-moon
> Shining at midnight on crossroads   green paint
> Of jolly garden tools   red Christmas ribbons   (P, 183–184)

The imagery of his victims' homes tends to be general and stereotypic, moving from the imagined inside of houses to the external distant view of the pilot:

> It consumes them in a hot
> Body-flash, old age or menopause
> Of children, clings and burns
>                                   eating through
> And when a reed mat catches fire
> From me, it explodes through field after field
> Bearing its sleeper   another
>
> Bomb finds a home
> And clings to it like a child.   (P, 187)

A similar tactic is found in "Reincarnation II" at that moment when the transmogrifying seabird office worker perceives not just the navigational details of the Southern Cross but its conversion into an office window, a reminder of his human past. Using imagery as a sign of the subject's transitional state, Dickey's art is precise and immediate: "The Cross is up.   Looking in through its four panes / He sees something   a clean desk-top" (P, 247). In "The Vegetable King" the distinction between realistic and fantastic imagery is more clearly drawn as the speaker leaves his house and family for the dreamy, Dionysian world of contagious victimage. In the early stages of the poem, the imagery points to external facts that are vivid but not extraordinary. From his sleeping bag the narrator beats "a cloud of sleeping moths," and looking outside he sees his house leave "Its window-light on the ground / In gold frames picturing grass" (P, 23).

As his ritual begins, however, the imagery points to a surrealistic world of regenerative violence that only his mythic death can control. As the house lights go off "The lights of the house of grass, also / Snap off, from underground," and a remarkable new kind of light is seen:

> slant, green, mummied light
> And wintry, bell-swung undergloom of waters
> Wherethrough my severed head has prophesied
> For the silent daffodil   (P, 24)

Scenic imagery in "Pursuit from Under" and "Fox Blood" also points internally to the poet's activity but in different ways. In "Pursuit from Under," the seal imagery has little to do with the real pasture through which Dickey is walking: "All over my father's land / The seal holes sigh like an organ" (P, 209). Instead of accurate external description, the organ sound converts the pasture into arctic wastes to which the speaker analogizes his existential situation as he recalls starving explorers who were followed by a killer whale under the surface of the ice. Dickey then universalizes this state by likening the pursuit of the whale to a universal image of death that follows him even into the apparent safety of his father's pasture, where the living and the dead meet once more:

> . . . not only in the snow
> But in the family field
>
> The small shadow moves,
> And under bare feet in the summer:
> That somewhere the turf will heave,
> And the outraged breath of the dead,
> So long held, will form
> Unbreathably around the living.   (P, 210)

In "Fox Blood" Dickey uses an accretion technique of hyphenated images, past tenses, and omitted articles to animate his narrative of a fantastic fox hunt. As the chase develops, all natural objects seem to become single, discrete images thickly accumulated like laid-on brush strokes in a Fauvist painting in which, typical of Dickey, everything in the landscape is in motion. Of the fox's running, the poet says:

> Sails spread, fox wings
> Lift him alive over gullies,
> Hair tips all over him lightly

> Touched with the moon's red silver,
> Back-hearing around
> The stream of his body the tongue of hounds
> Feather him.   (*P*, 212)

This is no real place but rather a "day-and-night sign" of a magical country in which Dickey can move between the human and animal world.

## SYNTAX

The clarity, simplicity, and immediacy of Dickey's word selection are not always characteristic of his syntax. Just as a world of complex movement and magic underlies the surface of events in his universe, so beneath his simple language are complex syntactic structures that approximate emotionally and rhythmically the kind of experience he wishes to convey. To effect animated exchange and to move us gracefully through violence and fantasy, Dickey uses a syntax that forces us through the appearance of natural surfaces to the unseen world of primal appetites and processes.

Dickey often develops a topic by amplifying a term, perception, or thought through continuous qualification. In "Buckdancer's Choice," using appositives, prepositional phrases, and adverbial clauses, he constructs a thirty-three line poem in only two sentences. Instead of breaking up the poem into a number of discrete sentence units, Dickey constantly qualifies in order to approximate the uninterrupted manner and rhythms of the "thousand variations of one song" whistled "all day" by his invalid mother. Using appositives and parallel prepositional phrases, he converts his mother's bedridden condition into a dance by likening it to the motion of a minstrel dancer. Although dying of "breathless angina," she

> . . . still found breath enough
> To whistle up in my head
> A sight like a one-man band,
>
> Freed black, with cymbals at heel,
> An ex-slave who thrivingly danced
> To the ring of his own clashing light

> Through the thousand variations of one song
> All day to my mother's prone music   (*P*, 189)

An even more complex example of Dickey's use of qualification is found in a remarkable four-stanza sentence from "Mangham," the poem honoring the courage of his high school geometry teacher who persisted in conducting class while suffering a stroke. After beginning the sixth stanza with the conditional imperative "It should be," the poet uses adverbial phrases and clauses to continue the description of Mangham's last day and to sketch briefly one of two imaginary scenes (a sort of Pythagorean desert) by which Dickey thinks it appropriate to remember such a day. In the seventh stanza, following a colon that also functions as a period, a series of phrases depict the second imaginary scene—a sort of cosmic dunce's corner—while leading to the primitive, cosmological imagery in the eighth stanza. In this section, a participial phrase beginning with "Proving" modifies the "dunce cap" last seen six lines earlier. Dickey uses this complex phrase, which directly precedes an even more complex subordinate clause, to assert that even though he has "no head / For figures" and that even though Mangham's mathematical teaching was less than effective, the kind of knowledge gained from the man is to be evaluated in human terms. The last stanza consists of several prepositional phrases, an adverbial clause, a past participial phrase, and two more qualifying subordinate clauses—one the object of the gerund "explaining" from the stanza's opening prepositional phrase, and the other in apposition to the immediately preceding clause. These final two clauses conclude the poem by announcing (then negatively qualifying) what the poet never "Could get to save my soul," that is, mathematical identities, with the meaning of *identity* clearly taking on a psychological sense. By using colons instead of periods and by using a continuous elaborate syntax, Dickey builds a resounding oratorical conclusion to his poem without stopping for breath. Here, with all its grammatical momentum in celebration of a heroic common figure, is the sentence:

> It should be in a tent in the desert
> That I remember Mangham's last day
> In that class, for his cracked voice was speaking
> Of perfection, sphere-music,

Through the stroke that blazed in his mind
As our hive toned down
And Pythagoras howled

For more ice; it should be in contemplative sand
Or in a corner that I ought to sit
On a high stool, Mangham's age now,
On my head a comical hat, a dunce cap
Covered with moons and stars and jagged bands
Of brain-lightning, the ceiling above me
White with the chalk motes

Of stars from my shoulders, the night blazoned
With the angles of galaxies forming
To a silent music's accords,
Proving once and for all that I have no head
For figures, but knowing that that did not stop
Mangham for one freezing minute
Of his death

From explaining for my own good, from the good
Side of his face, while the other
Mixed unfelt sweat and ice water, what I never
Could get to save my soul: those things that, once
Established, cannot be changed by angels,
Devils, lightning, ice or indifference:
Identities!   Identities!   (*P*, 225)

Dickey also qualifies words and word units by omitting punctuation marks and using instead what he calls "the 'split line' in which spaces between the word groups would take the place of punctuation" (*BB*, 290). Not only does Dickey use the split line for syntactic ends such as accumulation, qualification, and strategic appositional ambiguity, he charges his world with a fusion of qualities by cataloging objects serially in almost pointillist fashion. For instance, he omits commas while emphasizing the different shapes an undeveloped perception can take: "For hoeblade   buckle   bifocal / to reach you" (*P*, 258). At times, to accelerate action and to jam different kinds of movement together, semicolons are absent: "The screen door banged and tore off   he scrambled for his tail   slid / Curved   did a thing from another world" (*P*, 207).

Dickey omits all marks in a stream-of-consciousness technique in which punctuation marks would interfere with his subject's fluctuation between human consciousness and animal instinct in this passage from "Reincarnation II," while the split line paces the process of exchange in the manner of a soaring bird:

```
To rise above it      not knowing which way
Is up      no stars crying
Home      fire      windows      for God
Sake      beating down      up      up-down
No help      streaming      another
Death      vertigo      falling
Upward      mother      God      country      (P, 249)
```

Another aspect of the split line is Dickey's use of caesuras to approximate a manner of speech that someone in a certain mental state would be likely to use. For instance, in "Turning Away," a poem about marital disintegration, at first *this* and *that* seem to be pronouns, the objects of "Got in between" but they are really adjectives modifying *you* and *one other.* Dickey's intent here seems to be that of forcing a syntactic and rhythmic pause to emphasize the grammatical disjunction of the latter pair of terms and, more importantly, to call attention to the human separateness of the persons for whom these terms stand. In the third line of the poem, the split line caesuras reflect the halting uncertainty of the speaker's depressed state while simultaneously emphasizing the poignant immediacy of the moment: "Something for a long time has gone wrong, / Got in between this you and that one other / And now   here   you must turn away" (*TCM*, 53). The split line is also used to produce a more emphatic kind of apposition than that effected by commas. In "The Eye-Beaters" lineal separation serves as a form of double attribution as the poet assigns two senses of a hyphenated adjective to two different modifiers. "Sweet-faced" both in the sense of sweet corn and in the sense of physical attractiveness refer respectively to "corn" and "blind hunters" (the institutionalized children): "And now, blind hunters / Swaying in concert like corn   sweet-faced   tribe-swaying at the red-wall / Of the blind like a cooking fire" (*TCM*, 49–50).

Dickey employs the split line for a different kind of syntactic omission to produce suspense of subject in "Reincarnation II," in which he withholds the identity of his subject until the latter stages of the poem. Throughout the piece, we are given suggestions of human traits present in the bird. It is not until two extremely clear signs are given late in the poem, however, that the human origin of the subject is fully known. Before and after these lines, Dickey continually fluctuates between the pronouns *he* and *it* when referring to the man-bird and even carried this procedure to the concluding lines where we find that the twice-used *it* may refer to the man-bird, the cycle of change of which he is part, or the "stars and the void" which guide him instinctively. The conclusion underscores the poet's pantheism at the moment when the subject's human consciousness has been totally assimilated to animal instinct:

> Hovers for years on its wings
> With a time sense that cannot fail
> Waits to change
> Him again   circles   abides   no feather
> Falling   conceived by stars and the void
> Is born perpetually
> In midair   where it shall be
> Where it is.   (*P*, 251)

A different subject conversion takes place in "Slave Quarters" as the narrator's consciousness melds with the identity of the southern plantation owner he imagines himself to be. Again Dickey uses transitional pronouns to signal this change with the switch from the third person *he* or *his* (designating the narrator's dreamed identity). Syntactically, this transition is initially indicated by the poet's grammatical ploy of presenting what at first looks like a subordinate clause (beginning with "who") but which is really the subject of a new sentence that obscures momentarily the referent of the relative pronoun. At first, one takes the *who* to refer to the hypothetical slave owner, but actually, the *who* is generalized, referring to no one specifically. After this moment of equivocality, the narrator explicitly takes on the slave owner role:

> Who seeks the other color of his body,
> His lines giving off a frail light
> On the dark lively shipwreck of grass      sees
> Water live where
> The half-moon touches   (*P*, 235)

A final example of multiple reference is found in "Madness." By omitting quotation marks and subjects from verbs at the beginning of the

poem, Dickey at first confuses us as to who precisely the narrator is—
the mad dog himself who would have intimate knowledge of the
poem's minute actional detail or some unidentified, omniscient third
party. It is not until the hound is slain and the narrative continues in
the same voice that the issue is resolved.

In addition to continuous qualification, one of Dickey's most effective syntactic techniques involves the accumulation of epithets for
constructing scenes in which nature itself is reconstituted. Dickey
connects sexual and natural forces in "Falling" to reveal the stewardess's mythic increase in sexual power. Dickey uses verbs, infinitives,
and present participial and prepositional phrases in parallel sequences
to sustain—through a six-page poem—the pervasive, immediate ur-
gency of her plight. He builds a complete Midwestern landscape of a
sexually charged atmosphere with ascending terraces of rhythm,
while ironically understating her tragic situation by listing the alter-
natives she does not have:

<pre>
                    She goes toward    the blazing-bare lake
Her skirts neat    her hands and face warmed more and more by
    the air
Rising from pastures of beans    and under her    under chenille
    bedspreads
The farm girls are feeling the goddess in them struggle and rise
    brooding
On the scratch-shining post of the bed    dreaming of female signs
Of the moon    male blood like iron    of what is really said by the moan
Of airliners passing over them at dead of midwest midnight . . .
        for her the ground is closer    water is nearer    she passes
It    then banks    turns    her sleeves    fluttering differently as she rolls
Out to face the east, where the sun shall come up from wheatfields
    she must
Do something with water    fly to it    fall in it    drink it    rise
From it    (P, 296)
</pre>

Dickey also uses accumulations in catalogs like this one from "Reincarnation II," where the listing of constellations gives a sense of the
scenic scale, filling the sky with a celestial "heaven of animals":

<pre>
A string of lights    emblems    patterns of fire    all
Directions    myths    Hydras
Centaurs    Wolves    Virgins  (P, 246)
</pre>

Accumulations are used for ironic understatement in this series from "Adultery," in which Dickey analogizes the emotional dangers of an illicit affair to the hazards involved in completing the transcontinental railroad. The very banality of the objects on the cheap hotel's wallpaper from which his example is taken severely qualify the strength of his argument, an argument which in no way comforts his lover:

> for death is beaten
> By praying Indians   by   distant cows   historical
> Hammers   by hazardous meetings that bridge
> A continent   (P, 259)

Sometimes Dickey modifies syntactic conventions for certain ends. In "The Celebration" he converts an adverb into an adjective by inverting and hyphenating the normal construction of a conventional expression ("barely moving") into the country carnival's fire breather burning a stripper's gown "Above her moving-barely feet" (P, 201). Dickey also distorts conventional syntax for emphasis as in "The Firebombing" when he interrupts the natural subject-verb-object sequence to insert a prepositional phrase that vividly distinguishes the state of his doorway from that of his bombing victims:

> It is that I can imagine
> At the threshold nothing
> With its ears crackling off
> Like powdery leaves   (P, 188)

At times, he upsets conventional word order to effect a more emphatic form of apposition. In "Reincarnation II" the poet coins a compound and then places it at the end of a line to call attention not only to the unexplored vastness of unnamed constellations but also to the fact that the central subject of his poem is himself "as-yet-unnamed." The entire adjective explicitly modifies *stars*, but because of its linear placement, it could also refer to *he*, thus suggesting multiple reference in a world where objects and events magically share similar attributes: "Where he soars among the as-yet-unnamed / The billion unmentionable stars" (P, 244).

# V / "The Shark's Parlor":
# Testing the Hypotheses

Dickey's linguistic preoccupation with the tactile and the concrete narrows the scope of our study even more. Moving from principles that identified the major patterns of experience in Dickey's work as a whole to specific devices embodying those principles, we may now test the particular power of the four hypotheses on a single poem. Formal principles are useful only insofar as they illuminate poems, not insofar as they demonstrate their own circular validity, a fact still sadly often lost in the intoxicating, artificial scope of speculative analysis. For it is the particular and the light shed on it that have the final authority, not the general formula. Let us thus examine "The Shark's Parlor" in a manner resembling the shape of our inquiry thus far: first, a statement of the poet's central action and emotions as the overall components of structure; and second, a discussion of major secondary elements—speaker, narrative method, and diction—that provide further factual ground for the comprehensive, explanatory power of our principles while at the same time revealing more extensively the nature of those principles themselves. If the four hypotheses accurately fit this poem, we should have further proof that they satisfy both the general and particular demands set forth for them in the preface.

Memory: I can take my head and strike it on a wall    on Cumberland
    Island
Where the night tide came crawling under the stairs    came up the first
Two or three steps    and the cottage stood on poles all night
With the sea sprawled under it    as we dreamed of the great fin circling
Under the bedroom floor. In daylight there was my first brassy taste of       5
    beer
And Payton Ford and I came back from the Glynn County
    slaughterhouse
With a bucket of entrails and blood. We tied one end of a hawser

To a spindling porch pillar and rowed straight out of the house
Three hundred yards into the vast front yard of windless blue water
The rope outslithering its coil   the two-gallon jug stoppered and
    sealed                                                                                         10
With wax   and a ten-foot chain leader   a drop-forged shark hook
    nestling.
We cast out blood on the waters   the land blood easily passing
For sea blood   and we sat in it for a moment with the stain spreading
Out from the boat   sat in a new radiance   in the pond of blood in
    the sea
Waiting for fins   waiting to spill our guts also in the glowing water.        15
We dumped the bucket, and baited the hook with a run-over collie pup.
    The jug
Bobbed, trying to shake off the sun as a dog would shake off the sea.
We rowed to the house   feeling the same water lift the boat a new way,
All the time seeing where we lived rise and dip with the oars.
We tied up and sat down in rocking chairs, one eye or the other
    responding                                                                                  20
To the blue-eye wink of the jug. Payton got us a beer and we sat

All morning sat there with blood on our minds   the red mark out
In the harbor slowly failing us   then   the house groaned   the rope
Sprang out of the water   splinters flew   we leapt from our chairs
And grabbed the rope   hauled   did nothing   the house coming
    subtly                                                                                         25
Apart   all around us   underfoot   boards beginning to sparkle
    like sand
With the glinting of the bright hidden parts of ten-year-old nails

Pulling out   the tarred poles we slept propped-up on   leaning to sea
As in land wind   crabs scuttling from under the floor   as we took
    turns about
Two more porch pillars   and looked out and saw   something a
    fish-flash                                                                                    30
An almighty fin in trouble   a moiling of secret forces   a false start
Of water   a round wave growing: in the whole of Cumberland
    Sound the one ripple.
Payton took off without a word   I could not hold him either

But clung to the rope anyway: it was the whole house bending
Its nails that held whatever it was   coming in a little and like a fool       35
I took up the slack on my wrist. The rope drew gently   jerked   I lifted
Clean off the porch and hit the water   the same water it was in

I felt in blue blazing terror at the bottom of the stairs and scrambled
Back up looking desperately into the human house as deeply as I could
Stopping my gaze before it went out the wire screen of the back door          40
Stopped it on the thistled rattan    the rugs I lay on and read
On my mother's sewing basket and next winter's socks spilling from it
The flimsy vacation furniture    a bucktoothed picture of myself.
Payton came back with three men from a filling station    and glanced
     at me
Dripping water    inexplicable    then we all grabbed hold like a
     tug-of-war.                                                              45
We were gaining a little    from us a cry went up    from everywhere
People came running. Behind us the house filled with men and boys.
On the third step from the sea I took my place    looking down the rope
Going into the ocean, humming and shaking off drops. A houseful
Of people put their backs into it    going up the steps from me              50
Into the living room    through the kitchen    down the back stairs
Up and over a hill of sand    across a dust road    and onto a raised field
Of dunes    we were gaining    the rope in my hands began to be wet
With deeper water    all other haulers retreated through the house
But Payton and I on the stairs    drawing hand over hand on our blood         55
Drawing into existence by the nose    a huge body    becoming
A hammerhead    rolling in beery shallows    and I began to let up
But the rope still strained behind me    the town had gone
Pulling-mad in our house: far away in a field of sand they struggled

They had turned their backs on the sea    bent double    some on their
     knees                                                                    60
The rope over their shoulders like a bag of gold    they strove for the
     ideal
Esso station across the scorched meadow    with the distant fish
     coming up
The front stairs    the sagging boards    still coming in    up    taking
Another step    toward the empty house    where the rope stood
     straining
By itself through the rooms    in the middle of the air. "Pass the word,"    65
Payton said, and I screamed it: "Let up, good God, let up!"    to no one
     there.
The shark flopped on the porch, grating with salt-sand    driving
     back in
The nails he had pulled out    coughing chunks of his formless blood.
The screen door banged and tore off    he scrambled on his tail    slid
Curved    did a thing from another world    and was out of his
     element and in                                                          70

Our vacation paradise    cutting all four legs from under the dinner
   table
With one deep-water move    he unwove the rugs in a moment
   throwing pints
Of blood over everything we owned    knocked the buck teeth out of
   my picture
His odd head full of crushed jelly-glass splinters and radio tubes
   thrashing
Among the pages of fan magazines    all the movie stars drenched in
   sea-blood.                                                                                75
Each time we thought he was dead    he struggled back and smashed
One more thing    in all coming back to die    three or four more
   times after death.
At last we got him out    log-rolling him    greasing his sandpaper skin
With lard to slide him    pulling on his chained lips as the tide came
Tumbled him down the steps as the first night wave went under the
   floor.                                                                                      80
He drifted off    head back    belly white as the moon. What could I
   do but buy
That house    for the one black mark still there    against death    a
   forehead-

toucher in the room he circles beneath    and has been invited to
   wreck?
Blood hard as iron on the wall    black with time    still bloodlike
Can be touched whenever the brow is drunk enough:    all changes:
   Memory:                                                                                 85
Something like three-dimensional dancing in the limbs    with age
Feeling more in two worlds than one    in all worlds the growing
   encounters.    (P, 205–208)

In "The Shark's Parlor" Dickey presents a speaker who recollects an
experience from boyhood when he and a friend went shark-fishing
from his family's poled summer cottage in a body of water he calls
"Cumberland Sound." The reminiscent nature of the poem is initiated by the very first word and by the subjunctive assertion in the first
line: "Memory: I can take my head and strike it on a wall    on Cumberland Island." Although Dickey has admitted that the event "is
completely made up" (SI, 145), what follows is a highly detailed account of the boys' confrontation with the shark that is recalled in no
simple way but through a remarkable state of mind: "whenever the
brow is drunk enough."

To best describe this mode of memory and what it does for the speaker, we should look to the end of the poem. After the dead shark floats off belly-up in the night sea, the narration returns to the present with a rhetorical question that contains its own answer and is followed by a series of concluding sympathetic assertions. Not only does Dickey specify the meaning of this past event for the speaker but also how this meaning is possible. The narrator has bought the old family cottage "for the one black mark there    against death," that is, for an old blackened bloodstain left by the shark's head. Even though many years have passed, the blood is still "hard as iron" and constitutes a personal emblem that emotionally stands against the speaker's own mortality. Dickey's own commentary on the poem testifies to this reading:

> The necessity for kids, especially boys, to overmatch themselves, to take on more than they are qualified to handle, seems to me absolutely characteristic of male youth. . . . But the poem is not so much about the actual incident as it happened *then*, but as the man who took part in it remembers it—what it meant to him then and what it means to him now. The terrific energy of the primitive creature and its blood have sanctified the house for him, and he has bought the house and lives in it. As an older man he realizes that this is the reason he bought the house: for the symbolic charge of energy it has come to have for him. . . . Now that the man is growing older, he realizes in retrospect what significance this event has, for it has become full of implications that he would never have thought of as a boy. (*SI*, 164)

The central problem in reading the concluding section lies in Dickey's use of three consecutive colons following *enough, change,* and *Memory*. The poet uses these colons for two central reasons. First, while serving as especially emphatic interrupters between word groups that are already separated, the colons serve the conventional function of calling attention to what follows. Second, and more important, they reflect the poem's world of perpetual change by hurrying the reader's perception from one word group to another, thus proving that everything is in contiguous motion.

Because the first two colons appear to be substitutions for periods, "all changes" constitutes the central problem for the narrator who wishes to "touch" the blood and somehow take on its original power. One more variant of Dickey's cyclic world of mythic motion, this condition of flux requires a special act of entrance by which to arrest change and to establish the magical connection which will convert death into its life-giving opposite. Just as he reclaimed the "sailing leaves   in memory" from the "river always" in "Mary Sheffield" and just as the Eskimo shaman had to travel heroically to the center of creation to bring fate (in the form of the poor hunt) under control, so Dickey's drunken brow of memory constitutes the ecstatic trance that enables him to recuperate the primitive power of the past event from the cosmic circle of change.

Initiated by the sympathetic magic implicit in his claim that he can still strike his head against the cottage wall, the poet's ritual begins in comic imitation of his totemic animal whose head slammed time after time against the walls of the parlor. Although the setting at first seems tranquil, even the bait, "a run-over collie pup," portends the poem's bizarre mixture of primitive and domestic elements that later swirl in a comic trial-by-ordeal in which the two boys undergo a rite of passage by overcoming a natural force far superior to themselves. After the shark strikes, the effort to land it grows in importance and becomes communal (if not tribal) as the "house filled with men and boys," each group signaling one of the two poles of identity between which the narrator and his friend are traveling.

Whether it be Jonah and the whale, Melville's *Moby Dick*, or Hemingway's *Old Man and the Sea*, the idea of ritual combat with a fish is not new. To be sure, Dickey's modern heroes engage their opponent on a less grand scale. Yet there is a certain amount of danger in the boys' experience. Not only does the shark pose a serious threat but the boys themselves as participants in their rite constitute a focal point for violence. The shark is certainly a monster who initiates chaos and whose killing satisfies the basic requirements for scapegoating. Yet the vividness of Dickey's descriptions of the shark's power leads our attention away from the fact that the agents undergoing a rite of passage are also dangerous. As René Girard notes, "The individual who is 'in passage' is regarded in the same light as a criminal or as the victim of an epidemic: his mere physical presence increases the risk of violence."[1]

1. René Girard, *Violence and the Sacred* (Baltimore, 1977), 281.

To control the danger of their own transition, the boys imitate the ritual rite of victimage in which contagious violence is controlled by partially focusing evil upon the shark, though the boys themselves are responsible for the resultant chaos which infects cottage and community. Still, the boys are at the center of things. They themselves suffer like a scapegoat and pay a considerable price, what Girard calls "a foretaste of what lies in store for anyone rash enough to neglect or transgress prescribed religious rituals." In order "to change into certainty that awful uncertainty that accompanies contagious violence," the two young men suffer a hardship that speaks "louder than intellectual argument" and "makes the establishment of the socio-religious order appear an extraordinary blessing."[2]

Whatever its serious primitive roots, Dickey's initiatory rite clearly has its comic aspect. The boys' fellow hunters strive "for the ideal / Esso station across the scorched meadow," and when the shark is finally pulled into the cottage parlor, he unweaves "the rugs in a moment" and knocks "the buck teeth out of my picture" while "thrashing / Among the pages of the fan magazines." By introducing comic images implicit in the very title of the poem, not only does Dickey lighten the mood of the ordeal but also tells us that he himself does not take the entire process too seriously. That is, as a modern man thinking in modern images whose society is not fully primitive, he discounts his principles of magical connection yet simultaneously believes in them. He knows that the entire ordeal is a kind of unnecessary joke—as he says in *Self-Interviews*, the two boys make a mess of everything so that we can only laugh. Yet behind the surface of the event lie the mechanisms of ritual transition that still hold true for us emotionally. At the end of the poem, the speaker can still touch the blood on the wall, which not only revitalizes the energy from his initiatory crisis but also provides continuity in the dangerous transitions "in all worlds the growing encounters."

In light of the poem's central action, the narrator's recollection makes certain demands on Dickey's method of representation. For instance, one striking aspect of the piece is its length. To represent adequately the agonlike dimension of the encounter would be impossible

2. *Ibid.*, 285, 284, 285.

in a scale limited, say, to sixteen lines. For, underlying the selection, sequence, and scale of moments is Dickey's intention to force his agents *through* an extraordinarily detailed process, approximating along the way the emotional impact on them and on the narrator as he recounts the feat. In spite of its length, the poem's representation telescopes the actual event. Whereas the original process took a full day, the poem itself lasts only a few minutes with the emphasis falling on preparation, scenic detail, the struggle itself, and the narrator's reflection. Prominently represented are calculated accumulations of blood, sea, household, and swamp imagery, plus careful detail of instruments and preparation. By using extensive detail in such scale, Dickey implicitly provides representational warrant for his concluding analogy that memory is "like three-dimensional dancing in the limbs" in the sense that the depiction has rendered the account extremely lifelike or multidimensional. Not only does Dickey's method make the shark hunt thoroughly authentic, his interweaving of imagery and action so fuses qualities from the worlds of man and shark that there is an emotional interchange as well. Thus, the poet symbolically effects the psychic transference of primal force from the shark to the boys as they emotionally take on the power of their victim through conquest, one of the ritual ends indicated in the coda.

Even with the introductory announcement of the poem as memory, after the first several lines the depiction seems to have the manner of a documentary as Dickey sets forth his expository elements of time, place, agents, and instruments. As the narrative proceeds, however, the poet begins to produce effects not at all required by the simple conveying of information. For instance, his continuous use of detailed blood imagery gives the scene a ghoulish, slaughterhouse-like, sacrificial quality, reminiscent of the pervasive biblical emphasis on blood as both sacred sign and ablution. When mixed with seawater beneath the house, blood literally colors the whole "ground" from which the boys act. Also, the frenzy with which the whole town participates in the rope pulling suggests an intensity of purpose disproportionate to a simple sporting capture of a shark. Frenetic detail also serves to convey the contagious nature of the violent rite that infects all in its explosive wake. Like the middle part of "The Vegetable King," the middle of "The Shark's Parlor" is so explosive that it resembles a dream, a kind of comic nightmare, as a primitive animal intrudes upon the human world with a hybrid motion endangering both species. This frenzy is the middle of the ritual storm, the source of both primal renewal and possible catastrophe.

Because of its rich detail, the text needs little direct commentary by the narrator about the facts of the shark hunt. In the poem's reflexive conclusion, however, Dickey chooses to make a brief seven-line statement as to the meaning and mode of the narrator's account. Topics are merely sketched or hinted at rather than extensively developed. The central terms require attention by the reader as to implication only— partially, as noted, because of the poet's grammatical eccentricities. The primary artistic reasons for the brevity, dictional character, and location of the commentary appear to be two. First, a longer, more formal treatment of these topics would be emotionally inappropriate at this point because of the mood created by the extensive account. For almost three pages, the poet has set out his vision of a daylong agon between human and primal forces. For him to break suddenly from the emotion he has been carefully constructing into complex analysis would seem highly improbable. Dickey has emphasized the doing or performing of the capture. For the narrator to abandon his present sense of power over his own death produced by this memory for a less intense analytic act would be unlikely. Thus, interpretive terms such as the "one black mark still there against death" are simply and briefly inserted. The full implication of these signs is left for the reader to draw for himself.

Second, without the reflexive closing, the depiction of the shark hunt renders the event exciting and lifelike, but merely "instantial." That is, we know how and why the capture occurred but not that it possesses the enduring death-defying meaning it has for the narrator. In a sense, the prior representation anticipates the terms thematically and emotionally in that the shark incident is designed to serve as the factual ground and evidence for the narrator's evaluation of each point. Each term thus becomes a sign indicating specific technical requirements in the depiction. For instance, behind the word *growing* in the last line lies the narrator's indication of the formative power of the boys' ordeal as the sign of a completed stage in their maturation. In addition, *growing* serves a twofold classificatory function by naming the kind of experience the shark hunt and the poem itself now constitute for the narrator. Whereas the shark ordeal was an adolescent growing, the lyric recollection is a mature visionary growing or understanding.

Several other factors mark Dickey's method. Although the narrator's primary action is verbal, the original shark capture is not. Except for two utterances in lines sixty-five and sixty-six, the poet has chosen to emphasize the physical activity of the past, while his narrator talks about it in the present. Had the experience been literally depicted, there would certainly have been more conversation. The two quotations in the piece, "Pass the word" and "Let up, good God, let up!" really serve as further signs of the account's authenticity, suggesting that the speaker has remembered even these remarks in addition to the extensive detail. Also, the representation is cast in the poet's own voice. That is, we take the I-figure to be Dickey himself, though no real biographical evidence is required to augment or complete the poem. The first person narration simply makes the recollection more personal and authentic, as if the speaker had actually been there.

In this poem, as in most of his work, Dickey's word selection is simple and familiar. Given the poem's central action, the primary function of his language is to depict as clearly as possible the elaborate process of the narrator's reenvisioning. Appropriate to this end is the poet's selection of common domestic terms, which he animates vividly through the shark's intrusion into the usually quiet house. By making ordinary dull things function as signs of the shark's power—for example, the "ten-year-old nails / Pulling out" at the bait taking—Dickey consistently follows his procedure of producing bizarre and vivid effects from familiar elements. By making almost every object register the force of the encounter, the poet makes the whole poem dynamic in a way that echoes the narrator's thoughts about the pervasive, transcendent power of the shark, still effective years after the event.

In the first third of the poem, Dickey uses metaphor frequently to make the scene authentic by building a swampy atmosphere in which everything seems quietly alive. The night tide is "crawling" under the stairs and the sea is "sprawled" under the cottage. Similarly, the "two gallon jug" used as a bob has a "blue-eye wink" and shakes off the sun while bobbing in the water "as a dog would shake off the sea." Even the instruments for capturing the shark are assigned the traits of swamp animals with "the rope outslithering its coil" and "a drop-forged hook nestling." Dickey also uses metaphor to build and to change the mood when the shark first takes the bait as a triad of per-sonifications spark the moment: "the house groaned   the rope / Sprang out of the water   splinters flew." In these early lines, word selection is restricted to scenic elements within explicit comparison as parts of the house coming apart are likened to parts of the swamp: "boards beginning to sparkle like sand." Metaphor serves other ends in lines thirty and thirty-one when synecdoche plus analogies of a purposive and athletic sort obscure the identity of the hooked force taking the bait to make more mysterious and suspenseful the boys' adversary. Not until twenty lines later does the poet resolve this sus-pense of agent device to let us know that the thing at the end of the rope is "A hammerhead."

After the first thirty lines, Dickey tends to use metaphor more spar-ingly. From lines thirty-four through seventy-eight, the emphasis is on the process of landing the shark, and perhaps Dickey felt that de-scriptive detail of the house and actional terms would better depict the battle than saddling the account with continuous comparison. The remaining metaphors have two central functions. The first is to give the contest a gamelike quality with the haulers all grabbing the rope "like a tug-of-war" or "like a bag of gold." Second, the metaphors continue Dickey's procedure of weaving together the human and ani-mal, the modern and primitive. Thus, the shark has "sandpaper skin" that the boys grease with lard while pulling on "his chained lips" to ease him out of the parlor. Several lines earlier, when still thrashing about the house, the shark seemed to have an almost purposive aspect to his movement in that he did not simply tear up the rugs but "un-wove" them and then "knocked the buck teeth out of my picture."

In line eighty-one, one of the few similes in the piece describes the dead shark drifting off into the night sea with his "belly white as the moon," a novel comparison especially fitting at this particular point as the cyclic quality of the event is noted, the boys' vigil having started the night before. Two more similes are found in the coda as the narrator moves from physical action to the meditative. Explicit comparison seems appropriate here in that the speaker has finished his account. Finding himself distanced from the literal past, he now has a need for discovering analogies in the present for what has endured from the past. The language is still simple and commonplace: blood is "hard as iron on the wall" and memory is "Something like three-dimensional dancing in the limbs." Given Dickey's shamanistic disposition, the term *dancing* is especially apposite in the conclusion. Not only does *dancing* convey a celebratory feeling of the three-dimensional quality of the sight, sound, and tactility in Dickey's rich detail; the gerund is also another of the poet's terms of magical motion, in this instance suggesting the primitive technique of dancing used to produce shamanistic ecstasy and thus to provide entrance to the spirit world where blood consciousness can redeem and energize. Dickey's dance of memory recaptures the power of the past event with sympathetic contact and also operates contagiously, carrying the shark's power throughout the body of the ritual performer.

Of all his poetic elements, Dickey's imagery is perhaps the most powerful for making his experience feel three-dimensional. First, it plays a crucial role in providing the extraordinarily rich detail for rendering the account authentic and convincing. Second, it serves to register the shark's strength, thus providing evidence of the fitness of the boys' obstacle in their testing. Third, through accumulations of two strands, human and fish, Dickey skillfully interweaves the opposing forces, infusing the "civilized" with the spirit of the primitive. Fourth, much of the action's ritual quality is achieved through repetition of another imagistic line, namely, that of blood, suggesting primitive ablution, sacrifice, and victimage. Fifth, imagery even more than metaphor approximates the sensory impact of the entire process, producing responses in us similar to those experienced by the two boys. The revitalizing of feeling attached to the feat constitutes for the narrator the shark's animating power upon the old "black mark," now seen by him as transcending death itself. Imagery thus provides the primary emotive means for making memory not merely a cognitive recalling but a vivid and immediate rebirth of the original event.

Through repetition and strategic location, Dickey's imagery often works indirectly through accumulation to elicit effects that a single image could not possibly have. His use of blood, for instance, not only conveys the violent character of the rite, it provides a primal bond between hunter and hunted while also linking the narrator to a recuperable and immortal past power. Of blood imagery itself, there are four kinds or sources: first, that from the "bucket of entrails and blood" taken from "the Glynn County slaughterhouse"; second, that from the "run-over collie pup" used as bait on the hook; third, the human blood from the boys' hands caused by the rope's abrasion; and fourth, the shark's blood itself. In the twelfth line, blood receives a solemn quality that in turn is imparted to the boys' act because of its placement in an expression based on the famous introductory line from the eleventh chapter of *Ecclesiastes:* "Cast thy bread upon the waters." Dickey thus points to the solemn preparations of the boys by converting the line to "We cast out blood on the waters." In the same line, one of the first mingling of kinds of blood occurs as we find the narrator remarking on the bait's effectiveness: "the land blood easily passing / For sea blood." Forty-four lines later, as the boys try to land the shark, blood from their hands on the rope mixes with the "deeper water" from the sea where the shark had run with the bait. At this point, the boys seem to create their own sacred opponent as they are "Drawing into existence by the nose  a huge body becoming / A hammerhead rolling in beery shallows." Later, when the shark coughs up his blood with the baited collie pup inside him, the intermixture of all kinds of blood is even more thorough.

Blood is so completely diffused that it constitutes one of the central properties of the entire scene. Dickey carefully amplifies the importance of blood until it seems to be everywhere, inside and outside the house, in the mental and physical acts of the agents. Early in the poem, the boys so place the "bucket of entrails" in the water that it looks like "a pond of blood in the sea," with "the stain spreading / Out from the boat" in "a new radiance." Blood even dominates their consciousnesses as they "All morning sat there with blood on our minds." In addition, while waiting for the shark to strike, they think they have "to spill our guts also in the glowing water" if necessary to land their prey. Blood becomes all-pervasive as the scene narrows and the fish is pulled into the parlor where he throws "pints / Of blood over everything we owned." Like most sacrificial blood, this substance is both benign and malign. Not only does it contaminate the world it touches but also constitutes the sacred means of redemption. Like the well-designed scapegoat itself, blood is both inside the human community and outside it, in the parlor yet still part of the animal who draws violence to it and is soon to be expelled to the sea.

We may note once more that blood receives its mythic transformation in the conclusion when the narrator-priest codifies his violent past and transforms this event into a fruitful emotional condition. Even as the narrator speaks, the blood is still on the parlor wall but has naturally blackened with time. What was once the amorphous coughed up "formless blood" is now hard as iron, not just a red mark spreading out from the boat. In a world where "all changes," blood now has a specific shape, is fixed, unchanging. Not only does it have a physical durability, but more important, it has a kind of permanence that symbolically transcends physical decay. At the poem's end, blood is transcendent in at least four senses. First, it is a reminder of the past fact and meaning of the boys' formative victory as a stage toward maturation. Second, even though "black with time," it is "still bloodlike"; that is, the blood retains symbolically its original, animating power for the narrator in spite of universal flux. Third, distinguished from its original formless quality when it was coughed up, blood now has an assigned significance to it, making it a mark. By taking on a significant form or designation, blood thus transcends its initial, natural amorphousness just as the poem transcends the past particularity of the original experience by giving it a lyric shape it naturally would never assume. Finally, blood becomes an emblem of the enduring power of the shark capture within the narrator's vision whereupon blood symbolically and emotionally transcends the most powerful and inevitable of all forces, the narrator's own death.

Throughout "The Shark's Parlor," Dickey's syntax is exceedingly clear except for a few moments in the concluding lines. Even though the poet's style is complex with extended sentences often built of elaborate parallel constructions and serial modifiers, the poem's effectiveness demands that the shark hunt be narrated as clearly as possible. A convoluted or ambiguous syntax would ill suit Dickey's purpose of telling of an immediate, striking, and vivid agon of human and primitive forces. What syntactic complexity is present is found in the poet's use of his characteristic devices such as qualification, compound and parallel structures, eccentricities of punctuation, and numerous accumulations. From these elements, he builds extraordinary terraces of rhythm, different kinds of suspense, and powerful amplification.

Dickey's serial accumulations serve a number of ends. Series of adverbial phrases both qualify and amplify the spatial extension of the scene when the participants in the shark landing need more than the small cottage for their feat. In lines forty-nine to fifty-three, the poet uses over three full lines of adverbial phrases:

> A houseful
> Of people put their backs into it   going up the steps from me
> Into the living room   through the kitchen   down the back stairs
> Up over a hill of sand   across a dust road   and onto a raised field
> Of dunes

He also presents a series of short unpunctuated sentences built of compound verbs and parallel participial phrases to approximate the motion of the shark taking the bait with a violent jerk in lines twenty-three to twenty-eight:

> then   the house groaned   the rope
> Sprang out of the water   splinters flew   we leapt from our chairs
> And grabbed the rope   hauled   did nothing   the house coming
>   subtly
> Apart   all around us   underfoot   boards beginning to sparkle
>   like sand
> With the glinting of the bright hidden parts of ten-year-old nails
> Pulling out

In addition to the jerking rhythms, this syntactic complex presents its objects in discrete bursts of activity, emphasizing the series of immediate impressions that would occur in a fleeting and fragmentary manner to someone experiencing all of this. Even more important, Dickey's participles and compound verbs set his poem and its elements into motion so that his universe becomes the animalistic world in which miracles are possible. In the sequence on lines sixty-seven through seventy-one, the "Thing from another world" done by the shark is not only animalistic but mythic in the sense that the realms of man and animal combine into primitive realm not reducible to that of either species.

> The shark flopped on the porch, grating with salt-sand    driving
>     back in
> The nails he had pulled out    coughing chunks of his formless
>     blood.
> The screen door banged and tore off    he scrambled on his
>     tail    slid
> Curved    did a thing from another world    and was out of his ele-
>     ment and in
> Our vacation paradise    cutting all four legs from under the dinner
>     table

Dickey also animates his settings and conveys the shark's power through amplification. Adverbial phrases plus the sheer increase in the number of people needed to battle the shark heighten the drama of the event while simultaneously universalizing the scope of the comic ordeal: "We were gaining a little    from us a cry went up    from every-where / People came running. Behind us the house filled with men and boys." Dickey effects amplification at times by repeating the same term in parallel constructions and then changing the meaning of the term in its second appearance. Thus, the significance of the practical activity of drawing in the shark rope is widened into something else, as if the boys were creating, not merely contesting, the mysterious force at the end of the rope. By leaving the boys alone on the stairway, the poet focuses on them as the makers of their opponent, just as the narrator makes the shark a mythic entity from a mysterious region.

Characteristically, Dickey often qualifies through enjambment. For instance, he suggests two meanings for a single term without grammatical distortion by separating an adjective from its object through strategic lineation. With regard to the haulers' motivation, he indicates an impulse more intense than the practical physical act requires: "they strove for the ideal / Esso station across the scorched meadow." Enjambment plus the split line is used as a substitution for punctuation to isolate a phrase in this parenthetical qualification of *water:*

                                                              I lifted
Clean off the porch and hit the water    the same water it was in
I felt in blue blazing terror at the bottom of the stairs and
    scrambled
Back up

Enjambment also suspends completion of a correlative, holding for an instant the reader's interest until the full relation is drawn. This device serves to isolate and emphasize one part of the correlative to emphasize the congestion inside the cottage. Emphasis through enjambment is also accomplished by lineally separating subject from object, again with an effect of momentary suspense: "He drifted off   head back   belly white as the moon. What could I do but buy / That house." This kind of separation occurs with qualifying adverbial phrases when what we may call "delayed qualification" distinguishes different senses not only of single terms but of larger grammatical units. As is the case with so much of Dickey's enjambment, he continually forces the reader to reconsider what has just been read: "the town had gone / Pulling-mad in our house." Dickey employs suspense of grammatical function to disrupt prepositional phrases while delaying the completion of a compound constructed from contrary prepositions such as *out* and *in*. By delaying syntactic resolution, he draws greater attention to opposing realms of man and animal.

Another of Dickey's representative syntactic strategies is his replacement of punctuation with the split line. In the previous chapter, I noted the wide variety of marks this device supplants. In this poem he omits commas that usually separate sequential participial phrases (lines twenty-five through twenty-eight), compound verbs (line twenty-three), parts of a complex introductory adjectival phrase (line sixty-one), and an introductory clause (line seventy-six). Also omitted are periods, as is the case in the earlier example from lines twenty-one through twenty-four, and even a dash (lines twenty-one and twenty-two). When conventional notation is used, Dickey employs marks such as colons primarily to call attention to the following matter, as is the case in the poem's opening and closing lines. At lines thirty-two and fifty-nine, colons are also used to separate main clauses when the second clause explains or restates the idea in the first. And in line sixty-six, the colon conventionally and clearly precedes a quotation.

In order to jam images and events together to approximate the feeling of increasing frenzy, Dickey leaves out several grammatical marks in a single passage with no loss of semantic clarity or continuity of action in lines fifty-eight through sixty-two:

> the town had gone
> Pulling-mad in our house: far away in a field of sand they
>    struggled
> They had turned their backs on the sea  bent double  some on
>    their knees
> The rope over their shoulders like a bag of gold  they strove for
>    the ideal
> Esso station across the scorched meadow

In this example, a participial and two adjectival phrases constitute a series that may be read in apposition to *they* in line fifty-nine; or, presupposing a period omitted by Dickey after *sea* in the next line, the unit could be a series of introductory phrases modifying *they* in line sixty-one. Instead of separating the word units conventionally, Dickey refuses to indicate precisely the grammatical character of the words and lets the parallel verb structure signal what is modified. The *they's*, for example, all clearly refer to the crowd. Thus, without disturbing the narrative flow, the poet renders a sense of continuous activity while amplifying the incident's value and adding ornament, for example, the rope carried "like a bag of gold." For additional clarity, Dickey cleverly places two complete sentences beginning with *they* on either side of the series to avoid confusion. Just as the poet mixes primitive power with his modern setting, so his syntactic principles mix meaning and style in a rhetoric of interpenetrating grammatical relations that facilitates his semantic and emotional ends.

Of all his lineal strategies, the split line best dramatizes his universe of exchange. The split line is used in this poem to replace periods (lines fifty-three, fifty-eight, and sixty, after *dunes, gaining, me,* and *sea,* respectively), a possible semicolon (line fifty-seven, after *shallows*), and for a variety of comma functions. By using punctuation sparingly, Dickey can sustain his rhythm without the usual interrupters, while pacing the action in such a way that standard notation, when present, has an unusually emphatic force. Periods before and after many passages block off large sections of the incident in the narrative. For instance, having shown the force necessary to get the shark into the cottage, Dickey closes the capture with a period and then begins a new sentence in order to focus on the detailed effects of the beast upon the parlor and its contents.

# Conclusion

We have now come full circle: from inquiry into hypotheses about Dickey's thematic and structural principles, to classification and analysis of his central literary elements, and finally, to a close reading of a single poem that incorporates knowledge from the prior areas of investigation. The aim of this hermeneutic circle has been to explore these areas by using each to support conclusions about the others. My further aim has been to lay a foundation for addressing other issues about Dickey's poetry. The four hypotheses I set forth are *not* discrete, unrelated aspects of Dickey's poetic art; rather, we should use them *in conjunction*, depending on the particular demands of the poem we are reading.

I have been arguing throughout that James Dickey is a poet of thematic, emotional, and methodological opposites. At times, there appears to be no middle ground for this writer. Readers either love or hate Dickey's poetry, and his public prominence in recent years has made him an extremely visible target for academic broadsides, ranging from moral outrage at his use of violence to claims that his poetry is without principle or purpose. I hope that accurate statement of his poetic principles and solid analysis of his poems will stand as an effective counterargument to many of these negative judgments.

Each of the four hypotheses shows what Dickey has achieved in American lyric. Dickey's mysticism carries with it a gentle motion that emotionally unifies myriad opposites—life and death, permanence and change, man and nature—in a hypnotic, insightful method well established in the literatures of religion. His Neoplatonism reanimates the classical commonplace of motion and music in a method that gracefully recaptures lost love or unifies disparate cultures through song. Dickey's romanticism reintroduces the emotional topics of the great English nature poets while enhancing modern man's entrance into nature in both its tranquil and obsessive aspects. And his primitivism reveals once again the power and value of the ritual component in human experience, especially magical methods of controlling violence.

Equally important is Dickey's contribution to the advancement of narrative in lyric poetry. Critics who dislike Dickey never note his extraordinary achievements in storytelling, a central structural element in major American poets ranging from Robert Frost to A. R. Ammons. To ignore Dickey's exceptional strategies in lyric storytelling is to ignore the entire art of narrative technique itself.

Much negative criticism of Dickey seems unfair and impressionistic from the start. Although condemning a radically romantic and primitive poetry, few critics bother to use romantic or anthropological terms even as they excoriate Dickey. One must wonder how much of their dissatisfaction issues from sheer misstatement and misreading. Without selection of accurate critical terms, responsible literary analysis is doomed from the start. In Dickey's case, it is often crucial to note not what the critics say but what they *don't* say.

Many readers object to Dickey's use of violence without understanding the ritualistic structure he employs and without noting that such a method—especially with the use of the scapegoat mechanism—is one of the most powerful devices of all dramatic and narrative literature and of the ritual dramas of formal religions. The Stations of the Cross in Christian dramaturgy clearly makes use of the killing of the god, and there is more cathartic bloodshed in the concluding scene of *Hamlet* than in all of Dickey. Perhaps people assume that lyric poetry is the exclusive domain of the refined and delicate sensibility. If so, this view is not only prescriptive but totally blind to the history of the genre itself. Dickey's modern poetic companions include the electrifying imaginations of Theodore Roethke, Dylan Thomas, and Hart Crane, brawlers and behemoths all.

Personal taste is always a factor in reader response. Dickey is no darling of the neurotic, the timid, or the confessionally minded, nor of those who believe that serious poetry must be based on some grandiose philosophic principle or theory of art. If we follow the New Critical dicta that poems must be short, paradoxical, and ironic, Dickey is no artist at all. As noted in the section on romanticism,

Dickey is an outdoor poet, exceptionally *un*academic. He has plenty to say but does not do so in a library, museum, or on a psychoanalyst's couch. Dickey is the opposite of the intellectual, both in subject matter and emotion.

Nonetheless, Dickey has his problems, foremost of which is control. At times, his vision is so expansive that it eludes all consideration of method. Although I have tried to show that Dickey is often a disciplined and careful craftsman, he just as often leaves himself open to the charge of emotional diffusion because his themes, methods, and lyric speakers are undeveloped. Discursive argument is not important in his world; Dickey depends on dramatic means to structure his poems. Above all, he is a storyteller whose craft is often closer in method to that of novelists, playwrights, and screenwriters than to most lyric poets whose own inner mental and emotional lives constitute their subject matter. For Dickey's poetic principles to emerge in convincing emotional fashion through his language, his characters must do something concrete that is dramatic and often sequential: fall from a plane, recount a murder, protect one's family by sleeping overnight behind one's house, hunt for relics in a battlefield, or follow the course of a sex fiend.

Not only must some sort of serial narrative be present, Dickey must turn his story in interesting, surprising ways and close in a strong, satisfying manner. "Falling" begins with a common airline stewardess and ends with her fabulous, mythic deification. "May Day Sermon" begins as southern religious oratory and ends with the overwhelming, primitive sanctification of spring. "Hunting Civil War Relics at Nimblewill Creek" begins with a souvenir hunter and ends with the affectionate, charming communion of a modern man with his historic fathers. What we value in Dickey's poems is the same formal storytelling devices we value in dramatic action: changes of fortune, dynamic characters, overwhelming and challenging conflict, suspense, emotional catharsis of some kind, and a summarizing revelation that is the equivalent of a discovery scene in drama—in short, a dynamic sequence of events animated by a continuous threat (or problem) to someone we care about with a compelling resolution or revelation at the end.

Dickey's narrative structures need not be sequential in only a temporal way. When major stages in his poems are those of rituals that give direction and value to his action, his writing is smooth and powerful. When these stages are unclear or missing, his poems fall apart. For example, two poems that need rebuilding of their narratives are "The Eye-Beaters" and "The Zodiac." Read as a therapeutic ritual, "The Eye-Beaters" is overburdened with catalogs of imagery, and the shaman-poet does not change in any interesting, human way no matter how heroic his attempts to heal the blind. Perhaps the shaman could engage his blind patients in a series of different, graduated cures, performed on specifically characterized children, while the poet focuses on the overwhelming realistic problem of failure. For a temporal restructuring of "The Zodiac," perhaps the poet could more effectively connect his speaker, a dying, drunken sailor, to the universe through a series of flashbacks of the hero's adventurous life, port by port or person by person, recounting one anecdote in each of the poem's main sections. Instead of continuous cosmic assertion carried primarily through celestial imagery, the poet might guide the sailor through an extensive attempt to connect specifically detailed events or revelations from his past in a final, poetic summation of his life. As the poem now reads, with page after page of cosmic metaphor with no narrative progression, no turns, and no engaging surprises in the current fortunes of the speaker, the narrative grows boring quickly.

Another of Dickey's problems is that he is overpublished. Were he to edit more judiciously his selection of published poems, he would leave himself less open to criticism. The reader of Dickey's books of poetry must at times bypass several pages of lesser poems to get to the real gems, which are often never mentioned by critics, leaving the erroneous impression that Dickey is no good at all. Many readers dislike Dickey based on their reading of very few of his lyrics. They simply haven't read his better poems, and their opinions are based on his less successful pieces. For example, in one review, the reviewer mentioned ten poems. Eight were not successful, one was fair, and another—which the interviewer found minor fault with and misread—was, in my opinion, first rate. Most important, the reviewer mentioned *none* of Dickey's exceptional pieces. When readers are exposed to Dickey's most powerful work, they are soon converts to his cause. I for one would like to see Dickey publish a volume of selected poems with only his very best work included. I believe such a book would not only solidify beyond question his reputation as a major American poet but would be one of the truly distinguished volumes of American lyric writing.

Dickey's excesses are part of what he is as an artist. Like his own lyric speakers, Dickey courts danger; he is the great experimenter, risk taker, and poetic gambler, inventing and courting a dangerous world, with much to lose and even more to gain. He aims high—at times, at nothing less than the cosmos itself—and thus has farther to fall. Yet even his falls are more interesting than the less ambitious successes of many of his timid contemporaries.

If Dickey is anything in modern American poetry, he is a home run hitter. He may strike out more than one wishes, but when he makes contact, the results are spectacular. In similarity of vision and especially in poetic achievement, Dickey ranks with Hart Crane, Robert Penn Warren, and his own beloved Theodore Roethke. Here are ten poems that compare in quality with anything written by these men: "Falling," "May Day Sermon," "The Fiend," "The Shark's Parlor," "Hunting Civil War Relics at Nimblewill Creek," "False Youth: Autumn: Clothes of the Age," "The Rain Guitar," "The Firebombing," "Root-Light, or the Lawyer's Daughter," and "The Dusk of Horses." These lyrics alone constitute a basis for placing Dickey among our major poets, not to mention the extraordinary advances he has made in the mode of romantic primitivism. Long may James Dickey be the slugger of creative daring and commitment to poetry so that we may continue our circle and sing, even as we conclude, with Roethke in "Bring The Day":

> . . . Hardly any old angels are around any more.
> The air's quiet under the small leaves.
> The dust, the long dust, stays.
> The spiders sail into summer.
> It's time to begin!
> To begin![1]

---

1. Theodore Roethke, *The Collected Poems of Theodore Roethke* (New York, 1966), 78.

# Index